Times of Sorrow Times of Grace

Writing by Women of the Great Plains / High Plains

Marjorie Saiser • Lisa Sandlin • Greg Kosmicki
Editors

Cover Photograph by Randy Barger

Typesetting • Book Design and Layout
Judith Brodnicki

i

Published by: The Backwaters Press
                 3502 North 52nd Street
                 Omaha, Nebraska 68104-3506
                 gkosm62735@aol.com
                 (402) 451-4052
                 www.thebackwaterspress.homestead.com

ISBN: 0-9677149-8-2

Printed in the United States by:
Morris Publishing
3212 East Highway 30
Kearney, NE 68847

⤳ From the publisher...

Any collection of this size and scope involves the hard work of numerous people. Many thanks go to the two co-editors of the collection, Marjorie Saiser and Lisa Sandlin, who were responsible for selecting nearly all the works which have been included, and for shaping the manuscript into a coherent whole. An extra helping of thanks goes to Marjorie, who went several extra miles. This anthology absolutely would not have come together were it not for her efforts.

Special thanks to Judith Brodnicki who volunteered to typeset the book as well as to design the cover.

Thanks also to Nicole LeClerc, Rita Shelly, and Karen Gettert Shoemaker who have helped with preparation of the manuscript. Thanks to Randy Barger for allowing the press to use his sunflowers photograph for the cover, and to Janna Harsch for the wildflowers inside.

Thanks especially to all the poets and writers who submitted their work to the anthology. We received many wonderful pieces of writing and regret that we could not publish them all. *Times of Sorrow/Times of Grace* is a showcase for the talents that grow like wildflowers among the writers of the Great Plains/High Plains who happen to be women.

Greg Kosmicki
Editor and Publisher
September 2002

ᕲ Contents

Section 1: Golden Aster

Section 2: Turk's Cap Lily

Section 3: Plains Wild Indigo

Section 4: Scarlet Globe Mallow

Section 5: Wild Columbine

⇒ Golden Aster ⇐

Golden Aster, also called prairie aster. Dry sandy soils in full sun. Main taproot, extending to a depth of 13 feet, makes it well adapted to survive and prosper in dry hot environments. Several varieties have been identified.

Wonderful Words of Life

PAMELA CARTER JOERN

Mrs. Rosser Speaks to Alice at Church

After the last notes of the organ postlude and the pastor's *Amen*, Mrs. Rosser stops Alice in the church vestibule. She waits until the other worshippers have filed outside. Mrs. Rosser clutches her tattered coat around her. There's no one else she can ask. She sees that Alice's husband doesn't come to church with her. He waits outside in their truck, a big quiet man. Something's wrong there, and that gives Mrs. Rosser courage.

Alice stands holding her new baby. A girl, Mrs. Rosser has heard. Must be, she's wrapped in a pink quilt, appliquéd angels and *Now I Lay Me Down to Sleep* embroidered in a fine hand.

"What is it?" Alice smiles. She's known to be friendly which is why Mrs. Rosser has chosen her.

Mrs. Rosser wrings her hands. "I was wondering. I need to ask somebody a favor." She can't keep her eyes still. She knows they're roaming around the room. She tries to settle them on Alice's face. "Next Friday. Could you watch my children? There's something I need to do."

She watches Alice's jaw go slack. Mrs. Rosser knows it's too much to ask. Three of them, two boys and her own baby girl. "I can bring them to you."

"Mrs. Rosser. We live seven miles out of town."

"I know where you live."

That was a mistake. Mrs. Rosser realizes as soon as the words are out of her mouth. How would she know where Alice Preston lives? She can't tell Alice that her man knows where everybody lives. That he makes it his business to know. That he follows people and sneaks behind bushes and peers into windows. She forces herself to look at Alice while she lies.

"I know it's that road west of town. Out by Degraw School, isn't it? That's what people say."

Alice hesitates and bites her lip. Mrs. Rosser doesn't help her. She doesn't say oh, that's all right, the way she knows she is supposed to. Instead, she holds her breath and waits.

When Alice agrees, Mrs. Rosser steadies herself with a hand against the wall. She watches while Alice walks down the stairs and out the door. She believes her prayers have been answered.

Mrs. Rosser Gets Through the Week

She lives in an abandoned storefront in a ghost town across the North Platte River from Watertown. Her days are full. She wakes the children, carries wood for the stove, hauls water from the pump across the road, heats oatmeal, warms the baby's bottle, sweeps the dirt floor, stuffs rags in the cracks of the walls, slices thin pieces of bread for the boys' lunch, walks them across the highway to school, rocks the baby, hauls more water, washes the baby's diapers, simmers a pot of turnips, walks to Parker's Store, lets down the sleeves of the boys' coats, mends the torn knees of their pants, waits for a check in the mail. At night she lights candles, recites remembered snatches of poems, prays on her knees, comforts the boys when they wake from nightmares, walks the floors with the baby.

Some things she doesn't do. She doesn't bathe often. She doesn't find time to rest. She doesn't eat three square meals a day. She doesn't give up hoping that he will come home.

Alice Hears Gossip about Mrs. Rosser

In Parker's Store, on the way home from church, Mabel McNealy stops Alice. "You be careful with that Mrs. Rosser. I hear she's some relation to Mrs. Justis, over at the Assembly of God church, and you know how those Justises are."

Eleanor Wood leans over the produce bins. "Her husband is no good. If he is her husband. I hear he's a traveling man."

Mrs. Parker bumps Alice's arm when Alice holds it out for Frank's nickel ice cream cone. The old woman puts her hand up to shield her mouth and hisses, "I suppose she does the best she can, but have you noticed how dirty those children are? I heard all three have different fathers."

Alice hands Frank his vanilla cone and takes his free hand in hers. She tugs him out the door. "Jake's waiting," she says over her shoulder.

Mrs. Rosser Shows Up on Friday

Mrs. Rosser taps on Alice's porch door and waits. She's holding the baby who keeps reaching to be put down. A man and the boys are in the car. It's a dilapidated Ford, old one, about 1940. Alice comes to the door and looks surprised. Mrs. Rosser has a moment of panic.

"You didn't forget?"

"No, oh no." She's relieved to see that Alice laughs. "I didn't expect you this early is all."

Mrs. Rosser has been awake for hours. She's had the children dressed and waiting since dawn. Soon as he showed up with the car, she piled the kids in.

She waves her hand, and the car door opens. The boys creep out. They're in no hurry. When they reach her, they hide behind her back. She stretches around with one arm and drags them forward.

"This is Martin. He's seven. This is Robert, just turned five. And this is Elizabeth. She's about nine months. Still taking a bottle." She hands the baby to Alice. Elizabeth starts to cry. Alice has to hold her hard with both hands to keep her from jumping out of her arms. "Just milk'll do."

Mrs. Rosser drops to face the boys and gives each of them a quick hug. She pulls a handkerchief out from the sleeve of her coat, spits on it, wipes at Robert's face. He screws up his eyes and twists away from her. She straightens, her breathing shallow and fast. "Well, you boys mind Mrs. Preston, now."

Alice Listens to Queen for a Day

Women are telling sad stories on the radio to whoops and hollers of a studio audience. Alice turns the radio up loud while she inspects the Rosser children. Martin and Robert wear faded corduroys with patches on the knees and the butt. The stitches are big and loose, allowing the patches to curl away from the pants. Their shirts are not tucked in. No coats. Robert's sweater has holes in it, probably because Martin wore it first. Shoes scuffed, holes in their socks. Robert has a cold, his nose red and crusty. The baby is bald as a cue ball. She's wrapped in a couple layers of outing flannel. Underneath she wears a threadbare nightdress with the drawstring missing from the bottom. No booties.

On the radio, the audience gets ready to vote for their favorite story. Soon, everyone will know who wins a new washing machine. Alice hopes it's the woman from Tuskaloosa whose husband died trying to save the neighbor's drowning dog.

Alice Makes Do

When Mrs. Rosser doesn't show up by supper time, Alice starts to get worried. Jake's tired. Home from a day's work at the munitions plant. He hates that job and blames Alice for talking him out of farming. Never should have had that sale, he'll say, like he's forgotten all about seven years of hail and being chased off one lease after another. They've only been on this place a year, but it's not likely anybody's going to buy an old beet shack out from under them.

They get through supper, and then Alice doesn't know what to do.

"Let's wait a while," Jake says.

At 10:00, Alice decides Mrs. Rosser is not coming back tonight. She empties her underwear out of a dresser drawer and makes a bed for Molly in the drawer. She rocks Elizabeth until she's sound asleep and lays her in the crib. She finds old pajamas of Frank's for Martin and Robert. She lets them sleep in Frank's bed. She makes a bed for Frank on the couch.

"Just one night," she tells Frank.

"Just one night," she promises Jake.

When everyone else is asleep, Alice sits in the dying glow of the oil stove. Her feet are pulled up off the cold linoleum. In the dim light, she works on Martin's and Robert's corduroys. She removes Mrs. Rosser's loopy stitches and resews the patches with her own even buttonhole stitch. She hums softly while she works. When she's done, the patches lie flat. The way they're supposed to.

Alice Gets Nothing from Jake

Saturday is harder. Jake goes to town in the morning to get groceries. Especially milk for Elizabeth. Alice looks forward to these weekly trips to town, but she has to stay home with the Rosser kids. In case their mother shows up.

Martin refuses to eat pancakes for breakfast. "Where's Mommy?" He looks accusingly at Alice, as if she's hidden his mother somewhere. Robert manages to get syrup in his hair. Elizabeth won't sit in the high chair by herself. She throws anything Alice hands her. Alice tries to nurse Molly, but the commotion is too distracting.

Later, Alice hauls water from the pump outside and fills a tin washtub. She heats water to boiling in a teakettle and pours it into the tub. She rigs up an old blanket to curtain off one corner of the living room. Starting with the babies, she wrestles all five kids through a bath. The boys wriggle under her hands while she cleans their ears, pours water over their heads. So much water splashes out of the tub that afterward she has to mop the floor.

She makes cheese sandwiches for lunch. For supper, she boils eggs, fries potatoes, and opens a can of peaches. She hauls more water, heats it on the stove, washes and rinses dishes in two washpans lined up on the kitchen table.

By night, Mrs. Rosser has not come.

"You just let her dump those kids on us." Jake hisses this to Alice in bed. They have to keep their voices down so they don't wake Elizabeth in the crib or Molly in the dresser drawer.

"Not now, Jake."

"What if she never shows up?"

"What was I supposed to do?"

"Did you get an address?"

"No. We've been over this."

"How could you let her leave like that, without telling you anything?"

"I thought she'd be back that same day. She didn't bring a single thing for the kids. Not even an extra diaper for Elizabeth. How could I know?"

Jake turns his back to Alice and pulls the corner of the blanket hard. "Next time somebody asks you to keep their kids, do me a favor. Tell them to shoot me instead."

Mrs. Rosser Loses Time

She's in a fog. Things have not gone as expected. She wakes now and then. The first time, he was there. The next time, only that nice woman. Mrs.

Rosser floats in and out, hears voices in her dreams, feels a knife twisting in her gut. She's warm and liquid between the legs.

"You got to get on out of here." This is that other voice. That other man's voice. Someone is propping her up, helping her stand, but she's so tired.

"Where's—where's?" Her lips have trouble forming words.

"The guy who brought her in." It's the nice woman again. "She wants to know where he is."

"Yeah? Tell her he's AWOL, like all the other guys."

"Sh-h-h." The nice woman's voice fades. "She'll hear you."

Alice Reaches the End of her Rope

Sunday morning Alice gets all five children ready for church. She dresses the Rosser kids in their own clothes that she washed out the day before. She's sure Mrs. Rosser will meet her in the church vestibule, and Alice intends to give her a piece of her mind. Imagine leaving those kids without a word. What kind of mother does that?

Martin has taken to jerking his mouth around, a nervous habit. Robert wet the bed last night. It's the last straw when Jake and Frank gang up on her.

"Let him stay home," Jake says. "You got your hands full with them others."

"He's not staying home. Get your coat on, Frank."

Frank gets his coat, but he stands in the kitchen with it tight against his chest. He won't put it on. "I want to stay with Daddy," Frank wails.

"See." Alice turns on Jake. "This is what you're teaching him. This is your example."

She turns her attention to Frank. "Daddy's coming with us."

"Like Hell I am." Jake sets his coffee cup down on the red enameled table.

Alice thrusts Frank's arms in his coat sleeves. "Daddy's got to drive. I can't manage all these kids by myself."

"Then I'm waiting outside with Daddy."

"We'll see about that." Alice's voice shakes. "We'll just see about that."

Mrs. Rosser Wakes Up

"He's gone? You mean—gone?"

"Sh-h-h. Hush now. You'll make yourself sick again." The nice woman pushes Mrs. Rosser back down on the cot. "Don't give him no mind."

"Did he pay?"

The woman wrings a washcloth out in a pan. "Yes. He paid, and then he left."

Mrs. Rosser closes her eyes and lets the woman bathe her face. She feels the warm water over her eyelids, her lips, down her throat. She pretends for just a moment that this stranger is someone who loves her.

"Why do they do that?" Mrs. Rosser whispers. Her eyes are still closed.

She hears the woman get up from the cot. She feels her move away from the bed. "He said he had to get over to Casper to catch a freight to his next job. Said you'd know what he meant."

"I do." Mrs. Rosser cannot open her eyes. "I know what he meant."

The woman has such a low voice. "Said to tell you he left you the car."

Mrs. Rosser whimpers. Her eyes won't open. She feels the woman's presence in the room. She knows the woman will leave soon. She must have some place to go. She smells of Ivory soap. Her hands are smooth.

"Do you—do you know any hymns?" Mrs. Rosser asks.

"A few."

Mrs. Rosser opens her eyes. "Do you know that one —*Wonderful Words of Life*?"

"Yeah. I know that one."

Mrs. Rosser looks at her now. She knows her eyes are full of tears. She can't help it. "My mama used to sing that one to me."

The woman stands and turns toward the window. She folds back the edge of a dark curtain and looks out to the parking lot. In her low, smooth voice she starts the tune. "*Sing them over again to me* —" Mrs. Rosser cries, and the woman who is a stranger sings her mother's song.

Alice Flies Out the Door on a Broom

Sunday afternoon Jake puts on his hunting jacket. "Where you off to?" Alice asks.

"Going to walk the fields a bit. Thought I might find a pheasant or two."

"Now?"

Jake faces Alice. "What do you want from me?"

He slams the door when he leaves. Alice watches him cross the yard. She hates the overalls he wears, despises his boots. If she sees his hat hanging on a nail, she will tear it to shreds. The thought of him makes her sick. She sees herself out the door, up the road, swinging her arms. A melody rises in her throat. She breaks into a run, and she doesn't stop, not for him, not for fences, not for ditches, not for miles. She flies out the door like a wild woman, a witch on a broom, her rage rolling her like a tumbleweed. She rises on the crescent moon, she splits into a glowing sun just before she sits down to tie Robert's shoe and read all three boys a story.

Mrs. Rosser Apologizes to Alice

Mrs. Rosser drives into the yard on Monday afternoon. Alice watches from the window as she gets out of the car.

There's no man with her this time. Mrs. Rosser moves slowly. Alice sees the way her arms cradle her middle, the hand she throws out to the fender to steady herself.

"Boys," Alice says to the room behind her. "Your mother's here."

Robert runs out the door and throws his arms around Mrs. Rosser's legs. Martin stands on the front step and bursts into tears. Only then, Alice realizes how scared Martin has been, thinking his mother might never come back. Alice places her hand on Martin's back. "Go on, now." She gives him a gentle nudge. "It's all right."

Frank's at school, so he can't say good-bye. Alice settles Mrs. Rosser in the living room while she fetches Elizabeth from the crib. She grabs the paper sack with the Rosser kids' clothes folded neatly inside. She stops to turn the boys' corduroys so the neatly sewn patches don't show. She doesn't want Mrs. Rosser to see. Not just now.

"Mrs. Rosser, would you like a cup of coffee?"

"Oh, no." Mrs. Rosser's eyes are glassy, the sockets dark and shadowed. "You've done too much already."

"The clothes they're wearing," Alice waves her hand, trying to suggest this is nothing. "You can keep them. They're just some old hand-me-downs of Frank's."

"Boys, will you take this on out to the car?" Mrs. Rosser hands Martin the sack. He hesitates for a moment, but when she smiles and nods, his face lights up. "C'mon, Robbie." He takes his brother by the hand.

Alice races through her mind for the proper thing to say, but she can't find it. Instead, she sits down by Mrs. Rosser and knots her hands in her lap.

"Your baby sleeping?" Mrs. Rosser asks.

Alice nods.

"Sweet," Mrs. Rosser says. Alice shrinks, but says nothing. She doesn't want Mrs. Rosser to keep on talking. She doesn't want to know any more about her.

"I'm sorry." Mrs. Rosser's voice breaks. Her breath comes out in staccato bursts.

Alice nods. A bit later, Alice walks Mrs. Rosser to her car. Martin takes Elizabeth on his lap. Robert waves as they drive away.

Alice takes a turn around her yard. She scuffs rocks with her toes. She rubs blue-petaled morning glories between her thumb and fingers. She pulls a few weeds out of the four o'clocks. She comes round to the drive and looks down the dirt road where Mrs. Rosser's car has disappeared. "Damn it all," she says. "Damn it all to Hell," louder still, and then she turns away.

Charley and Evelyn's Party

KAREN GETTERT SHOEMAKER

The pink roses in the pattern of her dress are as big as a man's fist. The purse she carries is a small oval box banded in gold with a large gold clasp that snaps discretely when it closes. It looks like a child's purse and makes her look even more vulnerable than the way she smiles. She came with the Flaherty's, Pat and Marie, and they keep her a part of things, making sure she is introduced to everyone at least once. Marie calls her Ruth, but Pat forgets several times and calls her simply, Joe's widow.

You could tell just by looking at her that she had rushed to get ready, had held that purse in her hands and watched the empty driveway for 20 minutes before the Flahertys had arrived. You know too that the empty driveway made her doubt her decision to go to this party. Maybe she noticed the seashell button on her dress looked loose, the one between her breasts. Last time she wore it Joe had pulled it, pretending he could hear the sea. Maybe she thought to fix it but the Flaherty's came and time to go took all thoughts but hurry from her head.

The party: a surprise for Charley and Evelyn's 40th wedding anniversary. But Charley is in the hospital with kidney stones. He fell ill too late to cancel the party. Fifty-some people invited to a potluck dinner. The family, together for the first time since Christmas two years ago, held an emergency conference and decided to substitute a video camera for their father. The camera is traded from shoulder to shoulder of Charley's sons and daughters for most of the night. They introduce the camera as Charley and guests talk to it. Some say how bad they feel that he couldn't be here, hope he's feeling better. Others treat the camera as if it were Charley, making jokes about how much better he looks, how much weight he has lost, maybe even grown some hair back.

Charley and Evelyn's son, Thomas, from San Francisco, is here with his gay lover. Simon is the only black man at this party but he doesn't seem to notice. When it is Thomas' turn to carry the camera he starts at the buffet table and pans the selection of food. I made your favorite, Dad, he says to the camera. Simon tilts a crockpot filled with barbecue ribs toward the camera. That's my favorite, too, Simon says. My mom used to make them like that. Thomas sticks his hand out in front of the camera and points his thumb down. I'll turn you both into vegetarians before I'm through with you. Simon laughs and says, no way. I'm with you Charley, give me steak or give me death.

Charley and Evelyn's oldest daughter, Linda, appears beside her brother's lover and takes his elbow lightly. Dad's not even here and you two are ganging up on my poor baby brother, she says to Simon. She steers them away from the food table. Be sure to get a picture of my handiwork, she says, and points toward the back of the patio where a figure is propped up beside the light post.

A cardboard figure wearing a golf shirt and Bermuda shorts sits in a folding chair, a can of beer duct-taped to its cardboard hand. The face, drawn with magic marker, bears a striking resemblance to Charley. Evelyn poses beside the caricature of her husband while cameras flash. When Thomas arrives with the video Evelyn turns toward him and speaks to the camera, I don't know Charley, this guy's a better listener. You better hurry back before I decide to keep this new version. You have to look closely to see there are tears in her eyes. It is late by now so it's no surprise when someone, one of Charley's golfing buddies, calls out a joke about the new version being better in the sack too. Evelyn laughs in mock horror and puts her hand over the lens of the video camera. I've got grandkids who'll be watching this, she says. You be good.

Pat Flaherty steps up then and takes the camera from Thomas. Let's get those grandkids in here, he says. Let's get Charley and Evelyn's family together for a group shot. He starts calling for kids and grandkids and waves them over as if he is directing this show. The camera, still on, dangles at his side, filming grass and feet. When the video is watched later you will be able to catch a glimpse Joe's widow. She has slipped off her shoes and is rubbing a corn on her right foot.

From out of nowhere it seems kids come running. Pat pulls the camera up just in time to catch the oldest grandchild, a lanky boy of 10, swing down from a tree limb and land beside his grandmother. Evelyn screams first then hugs him. She pulls a chair up beside the cardboard figure of her husband and reaches up for the baby, her newest pride. Linda sits at her feet and pats the ground for her husband to join her. Thomas steps in behind his mother, pulling Simon with him. He doesn't want to come, but to refuse would make a bigger scene. James, the oldest son, stands back for a moment too long, watching Simon. Pat handles the camera loosely. He never quite gets everyone into one shot, but at that moment, no one knows that.

The sky is dark now. But in the city like this you can only make out a few of the brightest constellations. Cassiopeia and the Big Dipper hang just above the pine trees in the back yard. A shooting star marks its short-lived trail just under the North Star. Ruth twists the seashell button on her dress and it comes off in her hand.

Galvanism

A.B. EMRYS

The month Jessie leaves for college lightning strikes family property four times, starting with the drooping weathervane on the barn, then the great hickory where the rotted rope of Jessie's tire swing still hung, the steel-toed work boot her dad had jammed onto a fence post, and going on to annihilate the cabinet radio he had listened to since before she was born. In her dorm the computer plugs into a surge protector just in case. Her gleaming room in the residence hall might be a cabin on a space cruiser. She might be light years away and moving, no one she knows left alive by the time she gets back.

Jessie's mother's body has started to sink downward as though it wants to rest. Her hair, jowls, breasts, and the flesh of her forearms all sag towards the floor under her old armchair that itself sags too. But her mom holds up as though rising through water with clinging sea creatures trying to pull her down. Jessie has her dad's boom and bust energy. They drift like jellyfish. Jessie's grandmother had stayed up in her house for two days with a broken hip. Her mom will go down bucking like a wild horse. Her first dorm night the smoke alarm outside her room in the hallway goes off twice, shrieking its distressed-metal note until the woman across the way who's on a basketball scholarship takes it out with a hair dryer and a slam dunk. At orientation on Saturday, in another shiny new spaceship, the fire alarm goes off. Jessie's group leader throws up her hands. They file outside and mill around. Students begin to drift away, as if the alarm woke them up to other needs. Jessie drifts too. She sits on her twin bed and reads her schedule again and again. Sunday night when the repaired smoke alarm goes off again, Jessie lies in bed and cries. The alarm screams through her tears. After a while she takes a chair and removes the battery. She will give it to the RA in the morning without a word, and they will both jump from the static charge between their fingers.

In her composition class on Monday, Jessie freewrites about mass media legends. She lists some: Robin Hood, Star Wars and the Force, Frankenstein. She writes about Frankenstein, about a high school play she'd seen where the monster stands alone down stage. She writes about how he looked so lonely and defeated even though he was still going to strangle Frankenstein's bride in the second act. Jessie used to sit on the porch after dark and imagine the monster hiding out there somewhere. She still feels sorry for him, his inert body lying around like crops waiting for rain.

Early in the mornings, drinking creamy coffee in the union, Jessie thinks of her absence. She packed her brains the day she graduated high school and lived through the summer as hired hands that weed and scrub.

Now there's nobody but her mom to can the tomatoes and beans and dry the corn. There's nobody but her dad and whoever he can hire to bring in the corn, which they're not getting shit for despite the droughts in the east. One of Jessie's brothers, the one they brag on, is a prison guard. Steady work. Like being in jail yourself, Jessie thinks but doesn't say. Her sis is married, another life sentence. Sis's husband is a county agent, and Jessie's parents view him with the envious contempt they might have for a wartime collaborator. Once in a while he attempts to give Jessie's dad advice. Her other brother is still in the Army. Jessie herself might have been married by now but she couldn't hold onto to Eddie Tarken long enough to get pregnant, that's what Sis said to her mother while they were cleaning up after dinner.

On Friday of the first week Jessie's history professor asks how many are first-generation college students. Jessie raises her hand. One of her scholarships is based on this. She wants to raise both her hands and stand up. The professor talks about the G.I. Bill and its economic effects. He talks about today's enablement programs. You're a revolution, the professor says, in your own lives, every one of you. Jessie sees her dad in class hearing this, his stained overalls invisible, the mud and grass odor of him undetectable. She sees him frown and scratch his chin, and finally back away, as he does from problems. Frown, scratch, back away. The lights in the classroom blink once, twice, pulse again. Everyone looks up and laughs.

Jessie knows she has been Luke Skywalker, yearning to leave the farm planet, but the closest she had to Obi-Wan was the one high school counselor and geography teacher, overweight, reputed to drink, who helped her apply for every possible scholarship, grant, and loan in the known universe. Not teaching, he said, not anymore. Pharmacy. Or criminal justice, a coming field.

Ten hours a week she shelves library books. Other times she studies there, leaving a trail of them like crumbs (she's still thinking of legends) that some other student cleans up. Another five hours she sorts knives and forks and spoons and rinses trays in the cafeteria. Her behind-the-scenes jobs provide books and pocket money. She hasn't spent a dime on entertainment yet. She watches people for fun. Just before her comp class the same guy stands outside the building smoking. His skin is permanently like Jessie's summer tan, his eyes and brows soft, bitter chocolate. She steals this in glances. She thinks he's from India because his English, what she's overheard, is British-accented. In her math class there's a pretty woman from Brazil. Jessie collects foreign students like stamps. She tingles with their voices, with the spice odor of the cigarettes.

Her scholarship pays tuition. Room and board she's borrowed like a farmer. That's the only part her dad really understands. If you want to go, go. But don't go in debt. The future's a sucker bet. He's said that as long as she can remember, just as long as her mother's said, we're a farm family.

When the second weekend comes, it's a long one, with Monday off for Labor Day. Her roommate goes home, and expects Jessie will too. "You're not going this weekend?" And not the next. "Not till Christmas, maybe," Jessie says. "Not even Thanksgiving?" Jessie looks embarrassed, and maybe the roommate thinks Jessie doesn't have the money it takes to travel the light years. Finally she says, "I work on weekends," which is true. Friday night Jessie walks around the deserted campus. She can picture so easily her family's house just now, smell the chicken dinner her mother's cleaning up, hear the shower running, her dad washing off the day's soil and cussing because the hot water goes out every time her mother rinses pots. She can so easily hear her mother saying, Your brother-in-law's willing to pick you up some weekends. Pause. If you're willing to lend a hand from time to time. Jessie stands long enough in the quad that the lights come on suddenly all around her. She walks slowly among them to the union, which smells like nobody's kitchen, fills a tray, and sees across the room the cigarette-smoker at a table alone. Later that night, Jessie watches this scene like a movie. She watches how she walks right over, asks if she could join him, and how he nods, surprised. She listens to how easily she asks where he's from, and hears how he laughs when in return she says, "I'm a space—pilot rebel from a farm family." She sees again the eyes of this student from Nepal, his amusement with Americans. He has finished eating but he sits and talks to her, fidgeting as though he wants a cigarette. "It doesn't matter if you get along with them," he says. His voice has the tone of one who knows. "You are entitled to them, and they to you. If I could go to my family this weekend," he says, "I would be there now."

Jessie has been drowsing with just one lamp on and it goes off. The sudden dark is like a hush. Jessie lies in it, thinking up reasons. She can't go home because there's plague. She might carry plague, or catch it. She can't go home because she's too famous, the one who got away. Because she's not at all famous, just one more student. Because home's not there any more, only Oz. Home blows up in a fireball and she runs away from it towards the camera, her hair crackling like flame.

She can't go home because it costs too much to leave.

She can't go home in case she doesn't have what it takes to disengage a second time.

The most exotic alien she has met is homesick too. Jessie stands up and opens the door to the hall, also dark. She goes back to her window, and duh, the grounds lights are out, that's why it's so pitch. How would you go home to Nepal, and then leave again? She has looked in the library at India on the other side of the world. The distance she's come is too small to pinch between her fingers, yet it seems to expand further every day, and she wants it to. Already she loves this space ship world. Already she's clinging to it the way her mother has clung to the farm. As though it's heaven or her hope of heaven, that's what Sis's husband said out on the porch as they were getting ready to drive off. Clinging stops you, fixes you and everyone who attaches to you like sea creatures. Better to be first generation monster, and know it. She lies down again in the dark and dreams at last of Robin, sneaking out of Sherwood to get one glimpse by night of home.

News from the Volcano

GLADYS SWAN

Rising up from land flat as sheet metal, the rock, sheer and huge, unprecedented, is a ship moving across the desert, its dark shape bearing straightaway, wherever it is headed, not to be put off course. Aeons ago it rose towering above the land, lava overflowing from the molten core. Now the core is all that remains, the rest worn away by all that time can do. Only the core, a relic of ancient catastrophes, before any were present to know what they might mean. Hardened now and silent.

But now and then the moon rises blue in the dust of ancient memory. A haze of particles hanging suspended in the air, as though from that time when the volcano erupted. Who knows how they've gathered or where they came from? They gather above the rock, above the desert, above the occasions of earth below, as though reminded by the original disturbances of the air. So I see it now, as the moon rises three-quarters full. And with a light that comes somehow from beyond it.

The moon sends its bluish haze over a huddle of adobe houses, from which the small lights float in the surrounding indigo, and the smells of chili and beans and fry meat mingle with the evening chill. The light touches on the headlights of the trucks parked alongside, as though they were closed lids, gives a sheen to their metal casings, and leaves the land beyond a dark sea. Prickly pear and yucca, ocotillo and scrub cedar raise dark silhouettes from darker pools. Along the road cars are moving, and among them is a stranger moving this way. He moves the way a shark moves toward a school of fish, a dark rush in the direction of the unwary.

Up the road a neon sign sets its glare against the landscape: a gas station-grocery-café, still open. Many times I have gone past, watched the customers enter and leave. Sometimes I've taken my loaf of bread and left change on the counter. Lupe I know from hearsay, for she does not speak much, at least to me. Perhaps she feels my gaze upon her and draws away, not wanting anyone to know too much. But I cannot get enough of certain faces, wanting to know what has shaped them. I only know I must not look too long. There is something frightening in too close a scrutiny. I keep close to myself and see things as they come.

Tonight Lupe sits inside as she usually does, on a stool behind the counter, waiting for Lorenzo to return to help her close up. He'd left her alone all that afternoon, away on some errand. He may have driven all the way to Gallup — he does that sometimes. She had already cleaned the grill and wiped the counter, totaled up the day's receipts. Whatever came in now belonged to tomorrow — it is good to begin the day with something.

A truck pulled in, three boys in front, two more sprawled out in the bed.

Lupe knew the truck — Manuel's. They were headed to the dance in Farmington. She could hear them outside. "No, man, you're drunk already." "Look with your eyes, man." "It's the Russians — they've set something off." "Why them? — maybe it's us." "You're crazy, man. We'd have heard it." "It's from outer space. A spaceship — a huge one." "Not that big — don't you know any science?" "I know the moon when I see it — only that's different." "I want another beer."

It was a game, of course. But there was a difference in the cast of things. They could tell as they stood in front of the truck, looking at the sky. They broke their pose just as Lupe reached them. "See, look how strange it is," they showed her. And she stood with them, her arms hugging her shoulders over her thin blouse. She'd never seen the moon like that. Just now a plume of cloud fanned its surface, trailing across like a scarf. Splotches of light and shadow lay over the dark vegetation.

A different moon. Where had it come from and what did it mark? Perhaps it was a sign if she only knew what it meant. That is always the way — it could be this or that. Her grandmother had been one to know. She could read the world like a map of secret journeys — there are some who can do that, who seem to be born knowing. She could enter certain moments like a doorway and see what pulsed beneath, even if she could not tell the exact shape of what was coming. She could tell people where sickness came from, the violence in the flesh, and if an ill wind was blowing. It was something. Though perhaps not enough — perhaps it is never enough. One keeps looking for news; perhaps that's why I stare so at the things around me, waiting for them to speak.

Lupe's grandmother was dead now. Lupe had seen her lying at the threshold of her hut, left behind by the soldiers who carried off her chickens. They laughed as they caught the squawking birds. And the one who struck her down, who can tell? Or the others they left, scattered in the postures in which they had closed with death, set upon with the marks of whatever impulse or intention had overtaken them. Rumor caught these things and breathed them on the wind. But the soldiers had disappeared as they had come.

Lupe turned to go inside, and Manuel followed her in to pay for gas. It was his truck, he'd bought it used and took jobs hauling. He had a sister and a mother to support. Though he wanted to go off on his own, down to Albuquerque to look for work and perhaps for a certain freedom, he didn't stray, not even for better wages. Lupe liked him — he was older than his friends, held something in his face she could trust.

"You going to the dance?" he asked her.

She gave a shrug. She didn't know, Lorenzo was so late in coming.

"We could wait," he said. "You could ride with us — in front."

She'd have liked to go with them. But she didn't like to leave when

Lorenzo wasn't there. "I'd better stay," she said.

"I could come back," he said. He wanted her to go. "Unless," he said. "You have someone else."

"No, there's no one else."

Very likely it was Willie he meant. Willie was always asking her to go with him. He had a motorcycle and liked to roar down the highway with a girl at his back holding on with her arms around his waist. I've seen him many times, getting in his brags, you might say. There'd been a number of girls eager for the thrill, but Lupe was the one he wanted. It was easy to tell by the way he looked at her, as though he were trying to take her with his eyes. But she'd never sent a glance in his direction, was never lured by his roaring down the road.

Willie was trying to make a special link between them: they knew more than the others. They were above doing what the spoilers had done. He had found Indian somewhere in his blood, past the blue eyes and white skin that had corrupted the original purity, and he'd come West to find it. He brought his camera with him, and his power lay in that. He took pictures of road kill — that's what the hunter's skill had come to. Having left the buffalo to die by thousands, this was what civilization had brought — dead creatures in the road, and the effete beef steak. He took pictures of junked cars and litter and dumps and faces from which every dream had fled. Warnings and reminders.

There is always laughter in his eyes, when he turns his glance on Lupe, though when I've passed him I've caught something cold and sharp that goes right through and doesn't disappear. And he turns away as though he's already revealed too much. I too draw back. I have no wish to meddle. There is always something back of his expression when he's flirting with the girls, taking in their measure, taking the square root, storing things away for the next time — something quite beyond them that perhaps he doesn't see himself. But his attraction works like a scent drawing to him all that might speak to his contempt.

Perhaps Manuel was relieved to know he didn't have a rival, for Willie was always asking her to go. "Maybe you'll come later," he said, taking up his beer and the change. "Save a dance for me." And he gave her a smile that she held on to after he had gone.

The truck started up, moved out onto the highway, and was gone. It was quiet now but for the refrigerator making cold, and the buzzing of the fluorescent lights inside taking the beer cans into their glare. She doubted she would go to the dance: Lorenzo would be too tired.

Once or twice a month he took her: she knew it was for her sake. He'd come through the door around closing time and say, "Let's go have some fun," and they'd climb into his pickup and go to join the crowd. Lorenzo didn't dance himself, but stood on the edge among the spectators, drinking a beer and talking intently to whoever might be standing next to him, man or woman — he knew everybody. But he always kept an eye out for what was happening on the dance floor. If things started to get rowdy, Lupe had only to look for his nod, and they would leave. There were always those who hung around the edge, usually outside passing around a bottle, sometimes hooting and laughing, hoping for a fight. It was a question of whether they'd get bored and go off to further adventure or start something there. More than once the sirens came shrieking down the road, and someone got carted off to the hospital. Lorenzo kept a sharp eye in his head.

Lorenzo had had a wife once, but she'd run off to Denver with another man. Her lover had disappeared long since, and others had followed. But somehow she'd remained in Lorenzo's life, even though she never came back. If he went to see her, he never said. She called him at least once a month and told him her latest round of troubles and asked for his advice, and sometimes money. For a time he'd given her both, but the money blew away like scraps the wind had brought and would, as far as she was concerned, bring again. Now he gave neither, but listened to her stories. From time to time, he was with a woman. Now he had no one, though there were women who'd have been glad to have him. He was a generous man, who liked people around him, but who kept back a certain melancholy he never imposed on anyone. People liked him.

A restless mood came over Lupe. The night was growing too long, and the lights were not strong enough to keep certain shapes from invading from the darkness outside, nor the cans of beer and the packages of snacks and loaves of bread solid enough to keep her solidly among them. She got these moods. And you could watch her struggle against them. I can remember when her look spoke only of this.

When they had first arrived, she and her mother, it felt strange to her to stop moving. She felt the moving still in her body, and a danger of falling over if she stopped. It was strange not to see one landscape shifting into another, whether they were on foot or in the waddling buses. She could not believe that if she closed her eyes the same objects would be standing in front of her when she opened them again or that she would wake in the same bed in the same room, the mountains beyond the window still solidly standing, and Lorenzo's place down the road.

She refused to go to school — they had to bring her home. She wouldn't be separated from her mother, though in many ways she was no longer a child. When the two of them came into the store, Lorenzo gave her sweets. When her mother sank into the drunken stupor that lay at the end of her pursuit of safety and could no longer take care of her, Lorenzo gave her credit. And when her mother went off with the man who took her by the hand and led her to his car, Lorenzo took her in and taught her to make change and add figures and how to brew the coffee and cook hamburgers. She had finished growing up there.

The other girls envied her. Like one chosen, she had been given a place where she could earn her own money and put it in the bank. She had a future. She could go where she pleased, though she seldom left her place behind the grill or the cash register. She could lead her own life and didn't need a man if she didn't want one. She sensed their eye on her, their gaze as sharp as desire. But what was there to envy? The dark rush of her dreams? Sometimes she dreamed of animals devouring one another that lived like a menace just under the surface. She'd crossed boundaries where she'd had no wish to go, and who would care to follow? For she'd had experience, and no one could wipe it away. And what was there to be done with it?

She heard a car door slam and hoped it wasn't Willie come to lean over the counter to try to lure her in his direction. She had no idea why he continued to pursue her. Lorenzo never spoke to him. She was always pressed back by the tightness of a face that seemed to close behind some secret scorn, while his eye let nothing escape his notice. Then, unexpectedly, his face would break into a grin and he would tell her a joke, a bit of gossip he'd been saving up: who Manuel was sleeping with and which of the boys liked Lupe. He had something to tease everyone with, those he wanted to get the better of. He tried to tease her about Manuel, but she never blinked an eye.

He never had enough to do, it seemed. He was always around. Sometimes he showed off the photographs he took of mountains and desert plants to sell to tourists. Compliments made him smirk. There were times she saw Willie every day. He'd come in and pull down a loaf of bread, a can of soup, a jar of peanut butter, as if eating were a matter of indifference to him, slap some bills down on the counter, and leave without a word, sometimes without his change. Or he might come in for beer and disappear for days on end. He'd be off in his room, chain-smoking, his music turned up loud so he wouldn't have to listen to the noise of cars. Sometimes he slept all day and went prowling out at night. Sometimes he stayed drunk until he felt like being sober.

But it wasn't Willie come to pass the time. It was a stranger. He stood with his back to her as he filled his gas tank, then replaced the hose and came inside: a tall man with a ponytail pulled back from a narrow, bearded, hawk-nosed face. He closed the door and surveyed his surroundings as though to take a reckoning. She caught the restless glitter of his eyes, a film of weariness over something leaden and driven.

He did not offer to pay but placed himself on a stool at the counter. The lights were off in the kitchen; it was too late for food, but Lupe did not tell him so.

"What do you have to eat?" he wanted to know.

"Omelette," she said, "or a sandwich. Ham or cheese."

He considered the choices as though they were the only things he'd ever be tempted to eat.

"Till tomorrow morning," she explained.

"I could be lying half-starved on the slope of Pike's Peak by then."

She didn't deny it. One could be anywhere, without so much as a piece of bread. He wanted an omelette with ham and cheese and coffee — lots of coffee. She put on a pot on the Silex in front and went back into the kitchen to beat up the eggs, take out the cartons with the ham and cheese. She watched him while she worked. He drummed impatiently on the counter, glanced in her direction when any noise came from the kitchen. He took out a cigarette, lit it, took a long, deep drag, and let the smoke out slowly. He set it in the ashtray and left it. She saw him reach toward his belt, draw a hunting knife from its sheath, and lay it on the counter. She hadn't seen it under his jacket. It had what looked to be a bone handle with dark streaks, perhaps a design carved into it.

He gazed at it for a moment, then took it up, ran his thumb across the blade in a way that suggested that he wanted her to take notice. He glanced up in her direction, but she'd felt his attention coming and had ducked away in time. This was something she had no business with, she knew it under her skin, but it would be hard to keep away from it. He turned the knife over in his hand, familiarly, as though he'd gotten it as a bargain and he could take pride in whatever the knife might bring him. A certain energy pulsed out of his weariness as he turned the knife back and forth cutting the light into metallic slices.

She didn't want to look at it, the way it cut the light, the restlessness of it in his hand, as though straining in the direction of what it had been shaped to do. It knew killing. Lupe saw at once. The knife had killed someone. It had leapt into the place where killing was and caught the secret scent. Who knew how it had happened? But it was glutted now with what it knew, even if it had blundered into that space, been caught blindly or risen up and driven forward in a flash. The man was hectic with the consequences, but he could not get rid of the knife. It was joined to him now like his flesh.

He set the knife down, then pushed it to one side when she brought him his food. This gesture was for her benefit, she was no fool — to show her it was subject to him. She asked him if he wanted ketchup, then came with his coffee. She wondered why he hadn't threatened her before, hadn't robbed the store of what he wanted and gone on his way. There was food enough to cram into his maw. The threat itself was enough to get him whatever he wanted.

But maybe he wanted to be reminded of something, the smell of cooking in the air, the aroma of coffee. She filled his cup. His hand trembled as he took the mug, raised it to his lips. A bit spilled over the edge. It was the knife — it had him in its power and wouldn't leave him alone. The knife had no interest but itself.

Every now and then he paused, his fork poised as though he were listening, perhaps for something that pursued him or something that had momentarily stopped, as though a buzz had been set ringing in his ears that wouldn't shut off. Till he was weary of it, sick to death of it. She could see how he was trying to push it away, rid himself of it as he tried to eat, as he tried to chew his food back into savor and to warm himself with coffee. He craved the ordinary and was working to get food to his stomach before it gagged him and turned to sawdust.

She breathed sharply. The knife was greedy too, as it strained against its moorings. It would spare nothing. In the fullness of its impulse it was trying to get her to form the image of her death, make it coalesce before her eyes. It wanted her to reach toward a source of terror, where its power lay. If she tried to run away, it threatened to pursue her. Not because of anything she would do, but because she was there and had seen it. It wanted her power-lessness. If Lorenzo wandered in, heedlessly, it could rise up against him. He could walk right into it. She saw that and stepped into uncertainty.

She put herself back into what she knew, those nights when the coun-tryside had turned into the shadows of fleeing forms. They were all joined together in the shadows, pursued and pursuer, having shed everything but the one impulse that bound them. It lay at the bottom of the world. Out of it she could imagine her death. The absence of herself standing there — that was her death. It formed a space of stillness. The part of herself she was most familiar with would die. And whatever it was that lay behind it — that would leave her too. But she let go of that. She would not give it to him. It did not belong to him. Though she was looking at him, she seemed not to see him at all.

When he'd stopped eating and made a swipe with his napkin across the last of his food, he stood up and took his knife. "I'm finished now," he announced. "You can open up that drawer and give me what's in it."

"I'll give you nothing," she said. "You'll have to pay."

He looked at her like a snake risen in his path.

She did not let go. Neither did she pretend to innocence. She had passed beyond that long ago. She looked directly into his eyes with the knowledge of what he had done. "You have to pay," she insisted. "You've eaten, you've filled your car with gas. Now you have to pay."

She had no pity and asked for none. The knife had no pity. It was look-ing to make an excuse of her weakness, to bury itself in that. But she had let go of her life — it did not matter.

"I have no money," he said, as though it were a joke. "When you have this, you don't need money."

She stood there like a wall: he could kill her if he wanted.

He didn't move. Perhaps he caught a sense of what she knew and how the space between them joined them now. She was no accomplice. Or per-haps it was her voice that struck him, twisted inside him. It had found him out, gone to the bone. That can happen — I have seen it. It made him want to let go of all he knew, as if there were a moment in which both of them might rise above their images to something else. Everything wavered in that effort, that possibility. Then in a sudden movement he flung down the knife, reeled as though it had taken all his effort, and threw himself out the door. He stumbled and nearly fell before he reached the car.

Lupe did not move. For a long moment she seemed to stand outside her body. The knife had put her there, and now it was lying on the floor. She would not look at it. Dizzily she sat down, trying to regain herself. She tried to call to mind whom she'd seen that day, who had come for gas, for food.

She did not notice when the door opened again. And when Willie came up behind her, he startled her.

"You falling asleep?" he said with a teasing laugh. "Who's the guy who left — friend of yours?"

"I never saw him before."

Nothing to make a difference. "I thought you'd be closed up by now. Why hang around. Let's go to the dance."

"No," she said. "Not tonight." She wanted to pull the grin off his face like a mask.

"You always dance with me. Just to tease, I bet."

"I dance with everybody."

"You don't trust me."

She shrugged. "Lorenzo would take me, but he's not back. I won't go till he comes."

"He's not your father — he doesn't own you," he said meanly. "What's he saving you for — himself? The big man." His foot struck against the knife. He bent down for it.

"Don't pick it up," she warned him.

"Why not?" He stood up with it.

"It isn't yours," she said.

He turned it in his hand, watching her as he fingered the blade. "It's a good knife," he said. "You don't find one lying around like that every day. Finders, keepers."

"Fool," she said, turning away, as he toyed with it.

"I've always wanted a knife like this."

She tried to ignore him.

"Look. Go with me," he insisted.

And if she went with him . . .

"Or you'll be sorry." Willie turned away, as though the threat would hold force without him, and strode out the door.

Now he had the knife. He would go where it took him. She would be sorry, he'd promised her that, when he turned again in her direction. He was asking her again to reach into the fear that filled the space the knife was ready to make. To live in that darkness. If she looked into the space, would she see only the blank tearing of flesh, the deep wounding that asks for revenge, the endless chain? What was to be saved, and what would save her? She stood for a moment as though waiting for news, for something else beyond her to come to speech, if it were there to speak. That was the question, the one that takes us to the depths, nailed by the moment, as though to listen for our lives. She could hear, she could almost see a great struggle roaring in the dark on the verge of some upheaval. She expected it to appear in front of her, but when she ran outside, into a brisk wind that was raising up the dust, the road was empty. The moon was still rising.

Nowhere All at Once

And content, for the moment, to be
so far above it all, the Rorschach
of midwestern landscape far below
repeating *square, square, square.*

The world looks different
when you are forced to face it
from such heights and before dawn,
in hours when you're accustomed to be
lost in dreams — that other world
you create to help make sense of,
to recover from, this world

you now look down on, moving
between destinations — each a place
you have called *home* — meaning something
different each time, you realize, just as
you realize this nowhere place you are now,
this up in the air, is where you always are.

GRACE BAUER

Geography Lessons

What's Nebraska? asks Adam,
who is eight and curious
about why I have left the familiar
state we both lived in since
the year he was born. Too wide-eyed
for irony, he studies my face
for an answer, a definition of this
marvelous word I now abide in
but can't yet explain. So I mumble
It's flat and far away, trying
to sum up the difference between
now and the four hours of Blue Ridge
we once drove across to visit.

If I had a map, I'd point
almost dead-center, as if abstractions
like that would satisfy a child,
even one who understands directions
a damn sight better than I do,
with my endless circling
of back roads and main streets
trying to find my way back
to places I've just recently been.

He knows distance, I'm sure,
and something of longing—
one of the first lessons anyone learns.
But how do I describe the absence here,
that so many fall in love with?
Which words will allow him to picture
the predominance of sky? I take his *what*
at face value, an honest inquiry
into more than location, and struggle
with the wide space in the language
I am still trying to imagine into place.

GRACE BAUER

Spring: The Second Night

To the west
in a cloud-free sky,
early night,
the quarter moon
on its back high and dry
in a line directly above
Venus and Jupiter

hurtled now, I'm part of
some cosmic pinball game,
my body weightless as a ballbearing
rolling around the heavens,
tripping wires that ding and flash,
bouncing, flipping up and up
until the scoreboard reads so high
it'll no longer register

and Oh! if I could choose,
I'd die on a night such as this,
full south wind through my scalp,
going out
like energy from the stars,
my light burning bright
for a billion years.

TWYLA HANSEN

Mother of a Wind

Gusts out of the south in March
56 miles per hour after hour.
East west traffic, take note:
High profile vehicles at risk
On bridges and overpasses.

Kansas wind bears away the trash
and wraps the packaging around posts.
Plastic bag ghosts fly across the prairie
and tangle themselves into tumbleweeds.
She eddies across asphalt roads
and licks clean the plains,
bows saplings and mocks
the windbreaks that square our farms.

This wind carries Oklahoma red dirt
sifted fine to fill the corners of steps and porches
and blast away the sharpness there —
smoothing, rounding, bending,
teaching us the circle.

MARY YADON

Buffalo Stones

To help digestion, the buffalo swallows small stones
that sit in one of its two stomachs. We can imagine
these tumbling like pennies in a dryer, only hidden.
When the stones are found, they're round and polished.
But first the buffalo must go down, be picked clean.
Then only through bones will the stones show through.
Imagine millions of them winking in grass and sod
during the late carnage. So many there couldn't be
enough kids in dungarees with pockets to pick them up
for good luck. So many they'd become commonplace
as shells on sand after a high and violent tide.
And as we all know, the commonplace doesn't astonish.

LAUREL SPEER

Where Are the Poems

Where are the poems
of mothers, deep
in the night, noises
not subsiding.
The robe going on,
yellow circle of lamplight,
infant taken, murmured to,
face next to face.
Show me a poem about
grogginess become resignation,
becoming the hand in the night,
become the woman settled
into the overstuffed rocker,
the single-minded little one
in the corner of her arm,
woman smiling—
furrowed eyebrows,
searching mouth.
Where is the poem
of eyes locked,
bodies going soft,
working, working,
belly-hurt fading,
mother tired yet savoring,
knowing how brief is
this opossum time,
infant crawling from
womb to pouch,
born but not yet separate,
sweet sweet grace flowing
from one worn body
on into this tender
new one.

PAM HERBERT BARGER

Yellow Gold

We are happily lost,
the effect of unmarked mountain roads that imply
If you don't know where you are,
you've got no business being here.
We women have a job —
taking supplies and grub to trail hands
for the payoff of a summer day in the mountains.
But finding the moving herd is no easy trick.
At the ranch they gave us directions,
perfunctory ones, as if heritage must have provided
knowledge of all mountain roads
in the same recessive gene that produced red hair
and freckles, as if our very being here
had supplied us with a "compass for a brain"
like my navigator father used for aerial mapping.
Let's see. Fourth day out, they ought to be
about to bear-trap meadows.
Two buttes past where the creek flows into that draw.
You know, the first road to your right
off the main stock trail.

We did not know, but no one confessed it.
Vigilant in our calculations,
we're not sure what we're looking for, really —
a road that's an eroded truck-tire rut,
or just a place where this spring's grass
has been trampled and driven over?

Pulled like a compass needle toward what we will encounter,
we take a chance, turn off, and struggle open the old fence gate
on what must once have been a road,
but one that has known no hooves this season.

As we approach the crest of the hill, an unseen meadow
bursts, for our eyes, into a yellow confetti chorus
as if a lifetime of old friends shouted, *Surprise!*
As far as we can see is a gently swaying prairie of daisies,
balsam root, snow thistle, little sunflowers, all yellow
as a brood of chicks scurrying in a blur of sunlight.

This spread of butter has been churned by a wet spring
and might not coalesce like this again in our lifetime.
The sun hid here a stash of yellow
by which it might replenish in October.
It is as if the sacred trove of an Inca empire
had not been plundered, but sprinkled secretly
over this hillside to await our (being lost) discovery.

We get out of the pickup and sit down in the storehouse,
chest deep in deposited sunshine, smelling of pollen.
We are rich.
Silently we fill our vision to the brim,
stuff recollections with gold,
gather all the treasure our nostrils will hold,
and climb back into the truck
to look for the turnoff we must have missed.

MAUREEN TOLMAN FLANNERY

Snow Geese Over Lincoln, Nebraska

All evening, they pass and keep on passing overhead,
a delirium of voices calling. Over this town
pressed into prairie, over snow
dingy in mounds along curbs and sidewalks,
their chatter goes on and on on the wind.
I've come from further East, not from this flyway,
the ground I've left is still wedded to winter.
I'm headed West into rain. I'm not prepared
for this stirring, this language of longing,
these invisible wings beating north to the tundra.

After dinner, my friend and I walk her neighborhood:
curved streets, landscaped yards, little ranch houses.
We see through picture windows to empty front rooms
— lamps lit at sofa ends, but no one sitting there —
and we wonder: is all of America asleep?
Perhaps the earth has stopped, perhaps she and I are suspended,
alone on this street, and only the wind and the voices are moving.
There's a half moon, stars cluster the sky.
It's cold, a blizzard blew through here a week ago.
We're wearing coats and gloves, scarves at our throats,
and the wind takes our breath when we speak.

Yet even through earmuffs we hear them,
insistent, demanding, calling back and forth in a frenzy.
At the corner, we peer above chimneys and treetops.
They circle our heads, but the night's without end
and we're tied to this earth—left gawking, looking up.
At last they light the sky and they're fireflies flickering.
No—they're snowflakes swirling. No—ghosts trailing shrouds.
They're buffetted this way and that.
They swirl white. They vanish. We find them again.
They're angels sending messages. They're a galaxy,
a milky way spinning off. They're singing hymns to the earth.
They're drifting away. They're leaving us behind. Their song is
Desire. Desire. Desire.

JUDITH MINTY

Deer at the Door

What drew them up the hill, away
from sheltering pines, overgrown sumac, everything
in leaf now that summer's nearly here?
Was it light inside this little house,
our soft conversation, our attention
to the roast, the salad, before us?
What is it they saw, standing by the window,
their gentle heads raised, then browsing
again in the grass? Was it our shadows
bent over our plates, our acceptance
of what we have, what we are,
as the slow weight of day began to leave?
—I remember the beginning of a moment:
the sparrow's throat opening, the dog
rising from her place on the rug, me standing, you
looking up, the song starting, the dog and I
crossing the room, my hand on the door,
the smiles on our faces, the song on its last notes,
everything in harmony for a few beats of the heart.
Then the door opened
and their heads lifted, the air turned still.
I heard the rustle of grass, saw their white tails flash
as they darted awkwardly down the hill,
and dusk came on like the closing of an eye.

JUDITH MINTY

Hawk

Dead hawk outside my bedroom window,
even the cats won't touch it.
I laid low for three days,
didn't leave the house,
and wrote my Cherokee friend.
He hasn't answered, the hawk's
been waiting. Today I took

the tail feathers and feet.
I feel worst about the feet,
hanging from the backporch beam—
fists clenched, claws like my own hand
holding the knife. I knew
when the other one flew over, keening,
he wouldn't recognize her like that.

JUDITH MINTY

Recognizing

On M 46, just west of Cedar Springs,
after the Chrysler in front swerved and sped on, I had to brake
for the mallard. Eleven ducklings followed,
so close she looked to be dragging broken feathers.
After they'd crossed and disappeared in tall grass
through a cut in the barbed-wire fence, I smiled at the east-
bound pickup, also stopped. Blond man with a beard:
he grinned and waved. Both of us were shining.

JUDITH MINTY

Another Chance

Staccato rain hammers on our yellow slickers
and splatters mud on our Wellingtons. The beam
of the flash light wavers through the turbulent
trees searching for the sound.

Greta's loud bawling, as we locked
the sheep shed, made us count heads;
then head back to the woods to find
her missing lamb.

The tinny maa-a, like a flickering beacon,
pulls us to the edge of the thirty foot drop
down to the creek bed bottom.
How could that narrow ledge have caught him?
Is this a Disney movie plot?
Three feet below us, battered by bullets
of rain, he answers our lantern with loud bleats.

Belly in the mud, ankles anchored by my mate's
grip, I swing arcs in the dark below.

Why, why do I do this? Only to save
him for a future sacrifice?

My hand catches a spindly leg. Groping
across the kinky ridges of budding new
wool, I secure his chest. Pulling myself
up to the level ground, I cup in my arms,
like a sheltering womb, this trembling life.
Incense of musky lanolin smokes my eyes.

JEAN MILLER

This Road I Walk from Defiance in Late-January Thaw

for dad

A lone steer lifts its muzzle, cuts across
the moon. I plod down rigid hills
where Mosquito Creek drags its ditch
under ice as thin as silver coins.

Along highway 191, a boy in a pickup
offers beer and a ride to Panama.
I should remember his father's name,
but like smoke or the scent of cologne exhausted
on the arctic air, it has vanished.

Instead I see in his rearview mirror an image
of the half-shaven face of an old man
in olive green shirtsleeves and Osh-Kosh overalls
with threadbare knees. I say,

No thanks, I know this road: It begins
in a small-town tavern where farmers pitch
nickels and dimes for beer and cigarettes,
and it runs out in a gravel bed where stones
mark the years hills were carved up,
divided among the eldest sons.

The boy and his Chevy move off in a huff
of blue smoke. Taillights burn the sky,
ice breaks on the river like thunder
and stars shake loose from their branches.

In the morning, my mother will shovel ashes
from the fireplace, toss them on the snow.
She'll take the moon from my window, hang it
in the closet with my coat, and for breakfast
bring me sleep.

JUDITH BRODNICKI

The First Bite of an Apple

The neighbor's winesap straddles
the backyard fence. A low branch hangs
in the garden, offers a fair harvest
for those of us too impatient for sap to slow,
for fruit to fall with the leaves, ripe
and red in the grass. Plucking one
from the tree, I catch my sleeve,
bring down three more. The one in my hand
I rub on my jeans until its skin
is smooth and dark.

The first bite is like the first boy
I ever kissed. In a shed behind a neighbor's shop,
wedged between tractor hulls and tire rims,
he pressed his sticky lips
hard on my mouth, the saliva slick
on our chins and cheeks. The smell of axle grease
mixed with his wintergreen breath
forced me out, clutching my gut and praying
to the Virgin between gasps for mercy.

Now, rolling under the bridal wreath,
I find another apple and polish it
above my breast. I take the taut flesh
between my teeth and suck the dark skin;
wipe my chin on my sleeve.

JUDITH BRODNICKI

City Life

at dawn
when Mercury
still hangs
in the west
and the scattered
night clouds
are beginning to
turn pink
around the edges

and the street lights
down across the valley
sparkle
bright
through the rising
river mist

and a row
of crows
lifts off
out of the cottonwoods
along the river
to become black
silhouettes
over the new sun

city life doesn't seem so bad

SHERYL L. NELMS

How Do I Tell You About
the September Day

how the sky was the blue
of a child's crayon drawing
the clouds spider dreams
how the Huajatolla Peaks
were a fifth grade diorama of
mountains in Central America
the scrub oak was 1970's shag
carpeting in orange, red and brown
how the Camaro took La Veta Pass
like a needle threading lace
how the red shoes of the
Flamenco dancer shimmered
outside Doc Martin's
how the dress's white fringe
glistened on her skin

KYLE LAWS

Chasing Fireflies

You have to have heat.
The kind of heat that shimmers
in dusty opulence above
July's fields, engulfing small
towns, refusing to leave the
bricks of houses. Heat that can
warm the deepest lake and snake
through the thickest oak.

You have to have jars.
Not just any jars but
Mason jars; thick-walled,
green-tinged real glass with
metal lids...and oh, an ice pick
to make holes...
Without air, well...
you have to have air.

And then you have to have dark.
Real dark, no moon, but stars,
...lots and lots of stars,
and children,
you have to have
children, children with
scabby bare legs
and quick young hands.

Only then, when the porch
light goes out; only then
when night is so
black you are
wrapped up in it
and the stars
are moving and blinking,
only then
can you go
chasing fireflies.

PEGGY KIRWAN-DINKEL

Shoreline

Cumulus clusters ebb and flow
in the sea over Kansas.
The depths hide turbulent crosscurrents
and perhaps the debris of all those tornadoes:
birth certificates and
oven warranties floating aloft,
cancelled checks and school notes —
Do you like me? Yes____ No ____
Messages without bottles
pitching above the clouds
for weeks until
they wash up on the hollow branches
of an Iowa hedge.

The Astles never found their Chevy pickup
after the storm of '92.
Perhaps pieces of it
still hover in the stratosphere,
hubcaps waiting for just the right time
to return to Detroit.

The celestial tides lap and pull
where the stubble field strikes horizon.
Rolling waves of wind
crest over the cottonwoods
And the sun sets dripping
out of the deep blue air.

MARY YADON

Alone in the Middle of Somewhere

Halley has slipped like a wish
through my hands, and I'm left
holding the limp leash—
knowing my one-armed, hook-handed
neighbor will shoot her
hot on the trail of his cold
lard cattle. She does her work
well, her teeth like table forks
testing the delicate tendons
above their hooves—
even before she was born,
she knew her job. Shot
or not, she'll do for a coyote's
lunch: I've seen them flirt with her,
Come be our love. Halley smiles

when they howl at night, believes
they are singing her love songs while she
paces the cabin walls. My husband
sang such songs to me under the beady stars,
and now my voice frays but she will
not come. Instead she braids
invisible trails in the tall alfalfa—
bunched, the cattle bore her now—
squeezes back home through the taut
barbed wire, ricochets straight
for the falling-down barn where
golden marmots sun blonde limbs
for the coyotes. She will not hear
my voice—the grass is loud
with the musky talk of elk,
skunk, raccoon and porcupine—
and she will not believe that there is
no safe side to any fence that holds us.

KATHY MCKEOWN ROUSH

Eavesdropping, Celia Hears the Roof Cave in with Stars

Celia's children, grown and gone,
worry over her with words
from distant cities: *You can't
be safe alone in that rickety*

*farmhouse—and frankly, Mom,
you just don't seem quite
right. Why are you dead-set
against that nice rest home*

we picked? But telephone voices,
foreign and remote as cast-off
satellites, rarely interrupt
her fertile silence.

Alone, she's learned to listen
in. Celia hears the wayside
gossip of busy creeks, the sly
nuance of breezes scouting

the aspen grove. Morning voices
cheer her now that everyone else
has left. Breakfast-table
conversation used to congeal

like bacon grease, but now
she hears all the raucous news
that squalls of blue jays bring—
and the bright, familial bickering

of chickadees at the feeder.
Apples wait on the windowsill
to speak in their crisp tongues.
The old refrigerator purrs

a cat's contentment by the stove.
She's thrown away the radio.
What's the fuss, she wonders,
over paperboys and headlines?

Loose talk eats up a perfectly
good morning—almost as much
as some stray nights devour,
when breezes sniff and worry

deer in the pines where coyotes
wait, and the solitary
cries of shooting stars
fall through her dreams, dying.

KATHY MCKEOWN ROUSH

Working Late

The bat did not really seek the attic
but through a miscalculation found himself
in the empty space. Dignified in his terror,
he glided gracefully in search of nothing,
no walls, no attic rafters, no boxes, cradles,
steamer trunks, floor lamps, no rocking horses,
and at last detected a void, fitted himself
easily through, and found himself in my office,
where I burn a 40 watt light bulb for sight,
and the computer screen hisses its piercing
electronic song. He aimed his radarscope,
swooped close and sailed above my head.
What did he think life would be like? Endless
knots of easy insects waiting to be taken.

DENISE BANKER

Her Poker Eyes

See her as I imagine her:
Looking out umber wood-
mullioned window, slate sky,
old snow, weak winter after-
noon light. Minnesota, 1941.

Barely twenty-one, keeping
books in her father's construction
camp. Smoking thin feminine
cigars, her dad tucking
and patting his own blend
into onion skin papers.

Green wood hissing
in a bellied stove.
The odor of cut, stacked
timbers. #4 pencil tucked
through black hair.

Hand cupped, thumb cradling jaw,
forefinger crooked around red lips.
Learning to hide behind poker eyes,
arch of eyebrow, tilt of head.
They played cards; the men and

my mom, dealing Spades, Pitch,
Hearts. Something about that Paradise
holding her there, distant, as we play
cards, my dad's death only months
old. Mother keeping score.

The game didn't matter.
She usually won. Stingy,
even on the nights we drank
too much. Holding back her best hands.
She'd like to talk to her father again.

He'd help her live without her husband.
I keep books in my mom's
flower shop. She's training me
for her old job. Partners. Each day
a gamble. In waning light, coaxing

numbers to ordered columns,
the room richly incensed
by damp greens and flower stems.
Gray concrete under cold feet.
We drink and smoke. Paradise.

Now, years later, living without
my husband, I see her
in her chair, back-lit in east
light cutting dust fingers
across her shoulders, crown

of head, face, whispering prayers.
Notice the way she guards
her holy cards. Drawn close
to her chest, still holding back,
her poker eyes still brilliant.

DENISE BANKER

Company for Breakfast

The sound of water running
brings a row of birds
to perch reproachfully
on my porch railing.
I leave off preparations
for my own breakfast
to carry out seed and water.
Amid the sounds of
perking coffee and chirping
birds, I set the table,
happy that I don't
have to eat
another meal alone.

PAT PIKE

Monster Truck

At the gas station, they all look monstrous
from down here inside my little blue car,
and in the cold, they snort out enough exhaust
to seem living, fire-breathing, predatory.

Like horses corralled in winter, they pace,
nuzzle and sniff one another, pulling
grandiose horsey K-turns
dangerously close to the pumps.

Where's a cowboy when you need one?
Someone to direct traffic, round up the dogies.
He could take breaks at the little campfire
in the grass by the drive-up pay phone.

He could drink manly-bad gas station coffee
and sing lonesome monster truck cowpoke ballads:
Home at the Pump; My Darlin' Valvoline.
And I guess I'm saying I need a cowboy —

Because this monster truck next to me —
the driver can't see me as I back out
and try to make my way around him
in my tame little Toyota.

He's doing that *rev-rev* thing, like the truck
isn't loud enough just idling, and he guns it,
and it roars, and I think, this could be it —
taken down by a monster truck at the Gas 'n' Shop.

He can't see me, I can't see him — it's snowing,
and I clutch the wheel, and flash my lights, and I whisper
a prairie prayer, and I turn, and I turn, and he just misses me,
and hi-ho silver I'm alive, and I ride my pony home.

LIZ AHL

Latter Day Saints

They introduce themselves as *elders*,
these three fresh-faced boys whose knock
has roused me from my bed, but now
they're blushing bright red as I say *Grace*,
and extend my hand as if I were the one
who had come to witness or solicit
for the Lord. It is, no doubt, the devil
in me who revels in their obvious discomfort
and keeps me babbling on about Buddha,
the Goddess, my brand-new deck of Tarot cards.
But hell, it may do them a world of good
to see temptation in a black robe
and sweat socks, sleep still sticky
in the corners of her eyes. I may save them
from a fate worse than the fire and brimstone
they came to warn me about—or at least
from the doberman chained like Cerberus
to the rickety wrought-iron next door.
Once I took heaven literally myself
and practiced what I'd say to the angel
at the gates when I arrived. I forget now
what words I settled on — something clever
and direct, as I recall, that would not sound
like mere excuses for the failures I knew,
even as a child, I would accumulate before
the final trumpet blast when we would rise
from our graves like bad actors in B movies
to shuffle toward the clouds where God,
looking like Charleton Heston before
he sold his soul to the NRA, would sit on his
ethereal throne — scary — but nice enough to let me in.
I want to tell these speechless preachers
I am not beyond belief. Far from it. I refuse to be
agnostic about anything except the events
I see unfold before my eyes day to day.
Whether they'd call that sin or salvation,
I don't know, and they're far too anxious now
to escape from my tirade to explain.
They back off, just slow enough to stay
within the bounds of politeness, inching away
from my sermon till I am alone in my pulpit,

mumbling to the welcome mat. As I kneel
to retrieve my *Journal Star,* this morning sun
looks as gold as a halo. And I claim it as my own.

GRACE BAUER

Girl Friend

When I was between the devil and the deep blue sea
And had to spend an hour in the rain
And caught a cold
And ruined my blue suede shoes
You said, "Come on to my house, Baby."

When the sky fell
And took the skin off my nose
And broke my heart
And chipped a bone in my elbow
You said, "Hey, I'll buy you a cuppa coffee."

When I hung on the horns of a dilemma
And had a terrible headache
And a terrible tummy ache
And a terrible leg ache
You said, "Sweetie, let's you and me talk."

When I was between a rock and a hard place
And a bumble bee stung me on the ear
And I sprained my wrist
And twisted my ankle
You said, "Honest, little buddy, things have got to get better."

When I was in a pretty pickle
And broke my glasses
And burned my thumb
And lost my way
You said, "Look, I want you to know I think you are somebody."

When the devil danced in my pocket
And I had to go to the dentist
And my phone was out of order
And I took the wrong road
You said, "Hey, what are friends for?"

When I was at 6's and 7's
And almost lost my faith
And had a heart burn,
And got a DEAR JOAN letter
You said, "You know something...nothing can be that bad!"

JOAN HOFFMAN

The Picassos

From the cool, dry sub-basement of the American Art Museum on a green
Midwestern campus at the edge of the Great Plains, the Picassos are borne up
— like gold from the tombs of Pharaohs, like apples from the root cellar,
like treasure from beneath an "X." None of us would have suspected this
wealth — a modest deposit of precious ore shooting through the common black
dirt, under fields of corn and soybeans and milo. For a special exhibit,
they're plucked from darkness — even though Picasso's no American — and
walking among them I feel dumb and sucker-punched — I didn't see these
Picassos coming. Who could have? In the Midwest, even museum curators play
it poker-faced and stoic. I wander through the gallery, already
anticipating the exhibition's end: the return to dark crates and corners of
Two Nudes, *Le Repos du Sculpteur IV*; the man and woman of *347 Gravures*
— a pair for the ages who live, with all the others, in the basement. We
all live in Nebraska: me, bumbling along the earth's surface, the Picassos
deep beneath, sleeping like missiles tucked into one roomy silo, waiting for
the word, for the call, for the order that opens doors in this unlikely
place, where art and missiles hide in the earth, the fertile American
prairie earth, the last place anyone would look.

LIZ AHL

Speed Demon

"Do you know how fast you were going?"

The trooper leans in, filling the window
with his shoulders, shiny sunglasses, badge.
This is, of course, a purely rhetorical question.
Like: "How many times do I have to tell you,
put your damn clothes in the damn hamper?"
Like: "Were you raised in a barn?"
Like: "Who do you think you are?"

I've been snagged somewhere on the Pennsylvania Turnpike.
It's the oldest highway in America.
They have signs that announce this, proudly.
But I've felt the potholes kick my Toyota hard in the guts,
and I'm wondering if they should be so proud
about the age of the Dwight Eisenhower Highway System.
I'd like to know what they're doing with the $4.40
I shell out to get from Pittsburgh to Breezewood.
In another life, I ask the trooper his opinion on tolls and potholes.
But in this existence, I answer his question with a contrite, "No."
I am waiting graciously and patiently
to be tagged and released, like some stunned bear
who'll wake up hours later with a headache
and a flashy new earring. But he has another question:

"Does everyone drive that fast in Nebraska?"
In another lifetime, I actually answer him:

"Yes, officer, everyone
drives this fast in Nebraska. You see,
Nebraska is flatter than your forehead,
and there's basically one main road,
and all these other little roads, and they go
in straight lines forever and ever, and you can see
for miles and miles, and most places you don't see much —

    fields of corn
    fields of soybeans
    grain silos that are somehow always in the distance

cows that are somehow always near the silos

— and of course you see the road,
stretching out like purgatory
not a curve or a rise in sight
one or two scraggly trees trying their best
and you drive it straight
and on some stretches you can go an hour
at unspeakable speeds and not see another soul
so you might understand, officer,
why we drive how we drive in Nebraska,
if you don't mind me answering
what you may have intended
as another purely rhetorical question."

But in this lifetime, I shrug, surrender my license,
say something that might as well be nothing,
which is what he wants, and at this point
I want what he wants, if it means I get to leave,
which is what I really want.

Well, what I really want is to park the car somewhere —

in a field of corn
in a field of soybeans
maybe next to some cows who could use the company

and move back to Boston,
where parking costs more than rent does in Nebraska,
where everyone who drives is a certified jackass,
where I get to ride the subway.

LIZ AHL

Camp Clarke Days Celebration

I want Chuck Berry singing
"coffee colored Cadillac,"
but too many pointed boots for this band
to keep a rock and roll promise.
Lucky likes them, but staggers home, calls
Josephine before the other regulars.
Jeff is in a Three Stooges move on the floor
and Leo tells the baby bartender
about his green and yellow Harley
he tried to enter in the tractor pull.
Disinterested, she
cuddles her money and pushes through the bar
where little communities stroke each other
'till the whiskey gets thick
and some strokes become punches
and tomorrow at the Bull Riders Contest talk
will be of the fight and which Larsen brother
fought, the frizzy-haired one or the good-looking
one that practices on his wife,
talk until Rocky from Wyoming
gets a hoof from a Brahma,
X-ray machines down,
thirty miles to the next town,
sheriff's posse waves the rescue past
horse trailers and the Camp-n-Dancer's RVs,
Sunday
crowds home
watching Eastwood on their satellite dish,
sitting in church, or practicing their golf swing,
resting up,
Demolition Derby,
Rubber Check Race, tonight.

MARY JACKSON KRAUTER

After *Seit und Sein:*
Marilyn Monroe in Omaha

How Marilyn got to Omaha, I'm not certain,
but there she was standing in the kitchen,
wearing Grandma's WPA apron, frying bacon.

"Hey," I said. She looked up from her work
at the stove and said, "Hey. Over easy?"
"You bet," I said, and she served them up,

bacon, eggs the way I like, hash browns,
toast with butter. And lots of hot coffee,
which she drank, too, sitting at the kitchen table
in early fall, late on a Sunday afternoon.

"What you doing here," I asked. "In the kitchen?"
"Why Omaha? You're here.
How else am I to see you?"
"Making bacon and eggs," I said, marveling.
"Because your mother died and her mother.
I'm a woman. I had a mother. I'm dead,"

she said by way of explanation. She was right:
it was soothing having her here.
I would have never guessed it, Marilyn
pouring coffee into my cup here in Omaha.

I got to thinking, people don't know Marilyn,
just hang their own clothes on her. "I played
my part in it," she said smiling, and I noticed

as her lips met the coffee cup that they were
regular lips. "When men saw them,"
she said, suddenly, "they thought of their cocks."

I was shocked. "You're pretending,"
she said, and I had to agree. "But what
does this have to do with my mother?" I asked,

and she shrugged that shrug of hers, only now

I saw it was an I-don't-know shrug not
a breast-hiking shrug so men would notice,
though it might be that, too.

"We're both dead," she offered. "*Dasein.*
Heimat. Dwelling," she continued, recalling Heidegger,
"We learn from the dead," paraphrasing Hölderlin.

So we do, I thought, *andenken,* my mother's cascade
of words, rain over the falls, generation
after generation into the ultimate silence.

Marilyn came around the table to hug me.
It was not like hugging a star. It was not
hugging a sex goddess. She was no bimbo.
Her dress stayed down; breasts have many uses.
"*Heimat,*" I repeated and I felt her head nod.

We were two women, in embrace,
the dead giving life to the living,
along the *auseinandersetzen.*

MARY K. STILLWELL

Arthur County Sunday

a sestina

The biggest thing in Arthur County, Nebraska, is the sky.
Lope north at one o'clock on a tawny August afternoon
Out of Ogallala. The sun strides across the flat sand
So boldly that soon it crumples into lumpy hills
Of baked yellow grass. Only the shadow of one bird
Drifting breaks the long pale stretch of quiet.

Feed your eye mile after mile, words spare in the quiet
Heat. Fix your hopes on one small cloud in that sky.
It lays a finger of shadow light as a bird's
Wing on a brown ranch that nests this Sunday afternoon
In cottonwood green, hidden from the mystery of hills,
A sweetwater refuge from naked sky and indifferent sand.

Time between passing cars trickles slow like windrifted sand,
One grain then another, listening for voices in the quiet.
One thirty, a truck—two o'clock, two cars—pass among the hills,
Ribboning up, down, and around under the great sky,
A sparse and silent flock of wingless birds.

Arthur, Nebraska, is the only town, a lone and lonely bird
Squatting serenely at dead center of the sandy
Square of county map. On this soft cicada afternoon
Population 128 has vanished in thirsty, dappled quiet.
Front porches are empty, one black dog blinks at the sky
That perches lordly on the shoulder of the hill.

Your footfall echoes down Main Street, folds into the hills.
Stroll along the Arthur Rodeo fence, where like still birds
Seventy sunbaked boots on posts point their soles to the sky.
Brown, black, dusty red, they draw seventy stories in the sand
In shadows. Victory, defeat, maybe death are written quietly
here in the melancholy of the aging afternoon.

At six o'clock, look back on your Arthur Sunday afternoon.
The sage casts its mounded shadow among the hills
And spurts of golden grass stand tall in the quiet,

Contented. Stop. Listen for the call of a single bird.
It is song enough for the simple landscape of sand,
Grass, hills and a world of sky.

Hear a quiet trickle of longing sift like sand
Below the evening sky, soft as the breath of a bird.
Try to remember who you were before this afternoon of hills.

KATHLEEN DAVIS

Laying the Snakes to Rest

PART 1: NEBRASKA
Our first winter in Nebraska
melts into spring. Dandelions
vigorous amidst leeched browns,
dirty snow. Grass blades, like
whiskers, grow sparse out a mole.
On the sidewalk a garter snake.

Late spring that same year,
on the lawn, in tepid sun,
two garter snakes. Stepped
on one. I remember a hissing
peck-thud against my booted calf,
remember a slate-gray stick flinch.
The snake lowers and with severed
undulation rolls away. The smooth
symmetry of its dance cracked. My
emotions are padded, quilted. I
remember sadness at the break
in the flow.

Later, at the playground near
the stream that gurgles between
breaking ice floes, I hear hissing,
caution my children, yet feel contempt
for these wimpish cousins of the snakes
I'd grown up with, feared in South Africa.

PART 2: SOUTH AFRICA THEN
I watch from behind a willow tree.
Selimo pours milk into a saucer, steps
back, whistles softly. Two black heads,
beady black, wave like dogs in the back
of car windows. Split tongues flick, dart
as they drink milk.

The day before, when laborers thrash alfalfa,
they find, coiled, a rinkals. Speared to a pitchfork,
it's paraded on the dirt road past our homestead,
granary, mill, cattle dip, then unhooked onto the barbed
wire fence. A full grown male rinkals. Cautious rustle
of voices—tomorrow, the day after, sure as

the dung beetle rolls dung, its mate will look for it.

Is its mate the one grandfather slams the kitchen door
on, as bobbing inches off the floor, it slitters through?
Grandfather hit the hissing bullet head with his cane
til weak from dodging, it lowers. Breath raking,
Grandfather grabs a copper vase, splits the snake's
head. Blue blood trickles on green polished cement.
The housemaid, in starched apron and cap,
kneels, washes the floor.

The maids; ironing girl with peppercorn hair,
tallow skin, baby pepaded on her back; cook,
teats hanging like shriveled watermelons;
house girl, bony, tall; all eat lunch under
the juniper. A Nagadder, a stumpy
six inches of nightmare, drops out the juniper
into the three-footed pot of putupap, then, like
a fish jumping out of water, catapults into the
maroho. Juices splatter, maids scream, scatter
like a tower of marbles shot by a gunny dropped
from a child's hand.

That same year, I follow father into the garage
where the Dodge, Landrover, and tractor are kept,
I feel the oily dryness of a rinkal against my heeel.
My skin jumps back. Father rides the garage door
as it swings outward, waits til the cobra hood deflates,
the snake lowers, slithers into farmland.

PART 3: HOMECOMING
When first we came to Nebraska I felt confined, constricted
by the evenness of the landscape. I called it bland, blanched,
thought the people lived diluted lives leached of emotion, opinion.

Now, I find the undulation of land reassuring, the prairie cropped
close to the ground tranquil, the plowed earth untussled by the wind
like a freshly swept Japanese meditation garden. Farmhouses, barns,
corn silos, huddle close, look tidy, lived in. I find comfort in the
Missouri River's broad, full waters as they snake around Omaha.

MIRIAM BEN-YAACOV

Driving My Glass House

Prairie was, this highway six lanes wide,
where we bubble people, rubber-tired, speed.
Wild geese glean the edges that remain,
their black necks hooped, bills rooting in grass.
Prairie dogs claim the median for a town,
upright, on guard, beside their burrows.

On this open book of land, mile after mile,
we write our testament of disregard
for what the prairie was. Its life is
marginalia scrawled page after page: here
flocks of question marks; there, makeshift towns
of exclamation points, some smudged in red.

Inside glass bubbles, we precious jewels
travel river bottom, as they say, reclaimed.
At edge of mind, it seems I hear in tires
ringing on the road, the river's song, and
see again a Great Blue Heron fishing there.

When we, who carry in us what is lost, are
erased, who'll speak for what the prairie was?
From my glass house, these words I cast return,
cracking my windshield, lodging in my throat.

KAYE BACHE-SNYDER

The Spheres

A train rolled through my town —
    Aurora.
I remember seeing a president
    (Was it Truman?)
standing beside a birthday cake,
waving from the caboose
    as it bounced along into sunset.
Summer trailing with its locust encrusted
    noisy nights.
Sweating in our running games,
    chasing after lightning bugs, each other.
Catching ourselves,
    touching in the darkening yards.
Mothers' voices,
a hovering of familiar insects
    at the edge of the lawn.
Smoke from fathers' manly cigarettes,
    potent as winter bread baking.
Not wanting the night to end.
The wildness, running free
    in the lively dark world.
Twirling, whirling, dizzily landing hard
    against ground so firm everywhere.
Cheeks down in clean grass,
    earth's musky fur.
Trusting in a kindness we could touch.
Rolling over
to face the sky bowl of floating star lights,
    this earth ball's home.
Everything moving—
    myself, the train, my town, the world.

ANNE WHITNEY

Life Lessons from My Part of the World

Follow the lead of the wheat
and the prairie grass.
Bend with the wind or you're sure to break.
There's usually a wind from some direction.

Flatness and sky seem to go on forever.
There may appear a lookout spot:
a creaking windmill,
a lonely tree to climb.
Pause;
look back at where you have been,
plan the next step of your journey.

Ominous clouds take shape,
thunder, lightning, rain,
even hail.
Eventually,
there's at least a glimmer of sunshine,
maybe a rainbow,
but rarely a pot of gold.
Look carefully though.
There may be a few bright coins.

There are long hot summers,
icy cold winters.
Be patient.
In between, albeit they may be brief,
there are fresh springs with promises,
colorful autumns with harvests.

See that funnel coming in from the west?
Lie flat;
hang on to something,
preferably someone.
Pray.
You'll probably survive,
pick up the pieces,
and go on.

MARY ANDERSEN

Catch and Release

The ground shifts still
thinking of ice
when the tires slid but
my luck held

struck the rail then rolled twice
landed upright
walked away with a scratch and a broken camera
roof crushed mirrors snapped tires flat

After the first blow a silent underwater roar
flying glass sparkling in the late sun
It was like being at the center of a kaleidoscope
a circling blur

I didn't let go the wheel
Other cars pulled over
drivers ran to my window
someone loosened my hands

What I remember best is the long diagonal slide
like being pulled
It seemed I'd known in advance
I thought *So this is it*

and I think I went limp
my body ragdolled against the straps
caught
and thrown back

MARTHA ELIZABETH

On the Occasion of My Ninth Year's Thanksgiving, I Invite the Town Handyman

I tiptoe down the stairs
lean against the banister, listen
as Dad says, *But he's a. . . ragpicker!*
He slumps forward, elbows on mahogany,
stares at my mother rattling dishes
and silverware in the kitchen. I hear her say
She's already asked him
water flowing full force, steaming
over dirty pans.

Their friend Goldie, with dyed black hair,
pinched face, squawk-voice like the chickens
on her husband's farm, will not
share a table with *that man, that bum
missing half his teeth, work boots flapping
against ruined feet, head wound with tattered scarves.*
We'll miss you, Mom offers, gently closing the door.

Harry, right on time, touches the bell,
grey pinstripe shiny, pressed,
stiff-starched collar rivaling the snow,
thin hair fragrant with oil.
He corrects a dark-striped tie
slowly crosses the tiled hallway; he's wearing spats.
At the door of the dining room, he pauses
at silver-edged blue and cream china,
crystal goblets, damask linen, lighted candles.

Our forks raise pumpkin pie, fresh-whipped cream;
Dad's laugh is warm and full: Harry takes us back
fifty years, with this small town's monarchs—rascal boys,
brassy girls. Torn-down buildings stand, mud streets
fill with horses, rigs, Saturday night commerce.
Harry's fifteen then, gone from school six years,
widowed family desperate for his pay.

Later, Mom arranges turkey, potatoes,
French beans, cranberry sauce in a foil pan, seals it

with waxed paper and a rubber band.
The two men up front in the '54 Dodge,
I ride in back, balancing a dish of pie.
Dad drives up a steep hill near the edge of town
to a windowless shack smaller than my room.

For years after, on birthdays, holidays,
greeting cards arrive, *Your secret pall*
misspelled in laborious, shaky script.
I smile, surprised he knows the truth.

PAT HEMPHILL EMILE

Men Working

It's Sunday, Father's Day,
driving east on 275, along the Union Pacific line near Valley,
slowing for white buses that idle alongside the highway, empty and
    waiting for the men.

Men, who at this moment lay tracks and drive large
orange machinery, the heavy kind,
like out of a science fiction movie: monsters of pistons, belts, cranks, wheels,
    claws, long arms
churning, reaching, pushing large metal objects —
called Kershaw, Jackson 6700, Hyundai, Cat.
Men, standing, bending, digging on one side of the track or the other,
some waiting and leaning.
Connecting us. Building the *infrastructure,* holding all this, all this
    together.

Driving on, I think of these men and I love them all right now,
in their tallness, shortness, men brawny, loud, gentle or rough,
how they smell from working,
Coming in dark with dust, pungent with sweat and grease.
I fancy myself a feminist, subscription to *Ms.* magazine, and there are a few
    women out
there in hardhats, fluorescent vests with reflector strips,
but, god help me, Betty and Gloria, mostly, wonderfully, it's
these men.

SHELLY CLARK

Dad

Me and my Dad generally have
no conflicts.
He fixes my '91 Grand Prix
when it stalls too much.
He comes over about once a week
to chat with me. We order supreme pizza.
He eats most of it. We listen
to oldies on the radio. He sings.

We talk about how he used to leave
boxes and boxes of Twinkies
on our large wooden table.
A cream filled breakfast to go,
with early Saturday mornings, cartoons.
Tokens of the life he's spent
working for Wonderbread,
working since 18 for four
of us.

He would always leave the blue uniform
heaped next to the washer.
Not in it, so that we were never
rid of the smell of fresh bread
and driving too much.
Like a Folgers commercial
he gets up every day at four
o'clock to start over, again.

MELISSA BEERY

Litany for a Rancher
for Frank Tolman, December 28, 1998

Bless this man who lies abed
with so much riding on the way he dies,
bless his riding the range, his bronc riding,
his riding it out, letting it ride,
riding herd on, riding rough-shod over,
and his sometimes riding the fence.
Bless his fence building, fence fixing,
his offense, defense, nonsense and his sensitivity.
Bless his camp tending, crop tending, pretending,
his tenderness tending sick lambs at night,
his tending to park at the Ten Sleep bar,
his being wrong and his being right.
Bless his bull breeding, bull-shitting, bull-dogging,
his shooting the bull and his humble going home.
Bless his fishing, hunting, dogging the timber,
sheep dog training, curses blaring, pups birthing,
nursing into dog days of his doggedly caring for sheep.
Bless his lambing, docking, shearing,
his mouthing out, his dressing out,
and his being out of time.
Bless all that husbanding and the wife
a lifetime at his side. Bless their siring of a dynasty.
Bless their dancing at the Wagon Wheel,
his sheep wagon, covered wagon leading the train,
his being on the wagon and
the wagging tails of his well-trained dogs.
Bless his logging and cabin building,
the cab of his pickup truck,
his wethers, ewes, his bucks,
his cussing and his cussedness,
his luck and his being down on it.
After tending his land and tending to land on his feet,
bless his recent forgetting, falling, recalling,
calling out in the night,
his victories, feats, defeats.
Bless his branding cattle, branding sheep,
rounding and rounding up,
rough riding, rodeo riding, riding high,
riding west into the sunset.
Bless him.

MAUREEN TOLMAN FLANNERY

No Sweat

It's no sweat, driving
this patrol car, I've got it now,
I'm clear, signal 88, just me and the car
and all those switches, those darn
switches, which one lights which light?
Oh, yes, I remember now,
so why is that man in that car
beside me laughing? uh oh,
light was green, wasn't it?
And I was just sitting there studying
those switches, he'd have honked
if I'd been in my car,
but it's no sweat, it's just new,
driving this cop car, I've got it now,
I'm clear, signal 88.
Hard to see when you get in at night,
no overhead so no target, the Sergeant
explained it all carefully,
but it's hard to see when you
get out at night, too,
so it's really no surprise
I left the keys inside, I just couldn't see them
hanging there in the ignition
it's so dark you know
and anyway the woman Sergeant
who came to my assistance
assured me that the men do it all
the time, no sweat, she said
while another officer broke in
with a long screw driver,
I was impressed, I don't mind admitting it,
such a young officer to be so skilled
they're all so pleasant,
even the guy in the tow truck
who came in the morning to jump start
my dead battery, no, I don't know why,
and, yes, I'm **sure** I turned the radio off
this time, although earlier I did forget
once or twice, but really it's no sweat
driving the patrol car, now that I've
finally caught on.

Clear.

SARAH VOSS

≈ Turk's Cap Lily ≈

Turk's Cap Lily, also known as wild yellow lily.
Roadsides, thickets, river valleys. Nodding
flowers on long stalks at top of stem. Often each
plant may bear only one flower. Becoming
increasingly rare.

Children in the Earth

Lavender irises grow oddly wild
in the pioneer cemetery
south of Wayne.
My friends exhume the antique bulbs
for reburial in their own garden plots.

I don't dig . . .

. . . fearing the madmothers of the plains
forced to leave their babies and hearts
in this land with few flowers,
who wait through seasons of hot wind
and brittle leaves
and the crystal stillness of winter
for April
when their children spring from the good earth,
briefly and colorfully alive,
blooming playfully by their chalky stones

KAREN LIST WINGETT

The Sending

How many children crowd the heart,
and what do we owe our sister?

I. Ann, Who Was Sent

In Germany in the forties
a woman with too many children
and a guilt-ridden faith
was asked by her sister
"send me a daughter;
you have so many
and I have none."

Ann, a pretty six, was chosen,
we'll not know why,
traveled to her aunt's house
in America, a tiny immigrant,
an orphan sent by her mother.

Dark-eyed untethered girl,
opening gifts from overseas
each year, stranded in the
terrifying push from the shore
of Mother's unsteady affection
to the arms of an aunt
too empty to ever fill.

Wretched world anyway,
no wonder no one again
met her expectations.
The ribbons that lace us
one to another
were knotted in her,
the fabric greyed and
grieving.

II. Maria, Who Stayed

"My mother sent my sister away
to live with an aunt we've never seen
in America. My mother says

my aunt was lonely, needed a child,
and that Ann would fare well there
in the lap of her sister's prosperity.

I have a scrap of Ann's dress
that I cut away from the inseam
before she left. I hide it in my
bedclothes and finger it at night,
remembering. I am afraid I will
forget her small face, I am afraid
I will forget her dark eyes, I am afraid
that another aunt will need a child.

I watch mother closely now,
never again sure of my place
in this fickle woman's household.
I hold Ann as my secret sister,
my missing one, the smallest lamb."

KELLY MADIGAN ERLANDSON

Fists of Honey

The woman said, "The parents
don't like her, maybe
because she is dark."
She sleeps completely,
her fists of honey
and amber knees
curled into the woman's shoulder.
The weight of her makes
one small melon.
She blooms like a tulip,
whose plum
salmon or lemon petals
enclose
the same fragile imperative.

JAZMYN MCDONALD

Gone Boy

Danny was just a mite,
squalling and squirming as Edith and Daniel
planted posts,
corralling their bit of the range in 1902.

The sun bit like a rattler
and work stretched as far as the prairie.
Edith lugged posts with Daniel. How
could she lug Danny too?

They tucked him into a post hole.
He nested in the damp soil,
worm boy, root boy,
vein of gold boy.

In the gloaming they returned. Who knew
it would be so long? Picture
Edith's frantic glances, Daniel on his knees
at each gap in the prairie's smile.

Has Danny burrowed away? Was he eaten
by coyotes? Even if he is alive
his brain will be boiled. When he is grown
he will dig you a grave
and never look back.

O foolish fencers
who sacrificed their baby
to the sod.

Who would have guessed? is what
Aunt Edith says. *Who could have guessed?*

AMBER DAHLIN

Miserable Marty

If you let her sit upon your front stoop,
she will call the cement company
and they will pour fresh sidewalk
just to write her name.
She is the boss of the neighborhood,
boss of the Super Bowl,
boss of the Oscar Awards
and boss of the trash can.
I want to stuff her in,
close the lid,
and play bongo drums with a fork
until the neighbors call "midnight!"
Then the rats climb in,
as I escape.

DEBORAH T. MCGINN

Backward Child

Broken,
tiny glasses mend
like magic as the baseball
flies away from her face. Blood
flows back into her nose, tears
dry. Classmates' taunting grins grow
indifferent. Terror hides
in her false smile.

Father's hand
backs away from her bare
bottom, wet fingers poised
in midair. She stands at the door
where she has been waiting since   .
Mother yelled: You just
wait until your father comes home.
He'll give you a spanking
you won't forget. Hands cup
her ears, she runs.

Gagging stops
as Grandfather's huge limb
leaves her mouth and shrivels
into a withered branch. Her scream
reenters her mouth, dying
as she swallows it. Ogre backs
out of her bedroom into darkness.
Her mouth feels baby clean.

She feels
herself growing smaller
her mind shrinking. Soon
she's aware only of food
and sleep. Her fingers and toes
fascinate her. One day noises
flashing lights and pain dissolve.
Unborn, all she knows now
is the sweet silence
of unknowing.

ANN BARDENS

Craft

Our grandmother used to sew her own thumbs.
Stitching those dresses for hours, she'd become

automated to its motions, its mechanical song
that pulls fabric through the foot-feed and along

the digit's middle before nerves awoke, numb
from the Singer's steady lullaby and hum.

The drops slid along the threads like crimson
wash on a line, till they dashed themselves upon

the fabric as she fumbled with a ripper. We used to run
our fingers over the smooth white divots, the ruin

of the nail's grain, dividing the coral-pink half moon—
imagined threads, ropes strung through a harpoon,

that plunged at her hands, that cracked through her touch.
We imagined it held her, a merciless tether's clutch.

The needle exited the thin loops in her finger-prints,
anchoring her flesh to the weave. It pulsed with hints

of a heartbeat, the thumb's artery, as its eyed end
retraced the fresh wound.
                              Know this, we faced her legend

repeated, almost chanted, more than any Grimms' tale
or happy ending—how our aunts still wore the whale-

boned corsets with her flesh basted into the linings,
stains ironed into seams. How they celebrated the tying

down, beheld their mother's blood in its folds.

SAM LINES

Who Would Know

No one would know
to look at you,
the sweet blue-haired lady
necked with pearls
in a rose print dress,
that your husband,
ravaged by heart disease,
blew his head off
in a closet.

No one would know
to look at you
as you tended newborns in the hospital nursery,
like you once tended me,
that your baby brother
disappeared at age twenty
and no one knows
if he's alive or dead.

No one would know
to look at you
that you raised four children
on bread and gravy
to survive the depression
on a desolate farm
in the middle of Nebraska.

No one would know
to look at you
kneeling in church, intent on your prayers,
that you were orphaned at an early age
and were raised
by a maiden aunt and uncle,
who forced you
to scrub floors on hands and knees,
their voices echoing,
"it's good treatment for the curse."

DEB WALZ

Strong Onion Lullaby

It's past my bedtime she says, pulls
over my chin the layers of patchwork
quilts she pieces each winter — the ground
too frozen to work the garden — tucks
them tightly between mattress and springs, locks
me safely in for the night, smooths
covers with her hands, a pair of crumpled
napkins from days washing
dishes in the cafe by the railroad track where
the Quaker Oats men come to eat plate
lunches — meat two vegetables homemade
roll 49 cents, ice tea free. She dusts
my forehead dryly with lips sealed like the crack
in biscuits, pats the pillow like punching
dough, turns out the fat spider of a bulb dangling
over me, cracks the door to let dingy light from
the cafe crawl in. In front of the hazy mirror,
sitting on the twig stool some hobo traded for
lunch, she takes out hair pins — fingers flying, keys
on a cash register. Stringy gray hair streams
down in a widow's grief below her waist, and
she slaps at it with the brush, like the snap
of wet sheets before she hangs them on
the line. *Bubbe*, I murmur from the bed, knowing
she expects me to be asleep — *Bubbe, can I brush your
hair sometime*. Her worn eyes appraise
me in the mirror, she puts the brush back, worries
the stuck drawer shut, and, as she lies down beside
me, her fierce body making no dent, she warns,
*Close your eyes now, it will be morning before
you know it*, and the snug smell of strong
onions, grease, oats steaming curls
around me and lulls me
to sleep.

BARBARA SANDERS

Depression

I had a fine
fine herd of Shorthorns
back in the '30s

till Uncle Sam come in

paid me
to shoot them all

buried them in a gully
right south of Oketo
along with hundreds
of other herds

worst thing I ever saw

felt like
they'd prodded me
down

into that pit

and blowed me
away too

never could
get over
that

never did

SHERYL L. NELMS

Carol's Hand

Short nails,
liver-spotted,
you can carry irrigation pipes,
scoop ice cream for 12 hours,
hitch a load to the pick-up,
hoist the tent,
cradle
a cigarette.
If I could take you where
I wanted, you wouldn't be
so hard,
you could weep
instead of sweat.

ELIZABETH CLARK

Photo of Women Plowing
(circa 1899)

The driver's face has no features,
a dark day-moon
above eight women harnessed to the plow.
They do not look up or talk
of beauty wrapped in cotton.
They hide their eyes
in bonnets, nothing certain
but the driver, slow
and heavy-booted.
They know they are better than horses.
They have eaten silence
with chapped lips at table,
more bitter before son
or husband than this boss man.
His face blackens from too few words.

Under billowed skirts, soft
forms blur the ugliest field. Wind
melds with grain dust, and moths
fly up suddenly at night
when the women wash their legs
lifting them softly in the half
light behind the shed.

CAROLANN RUSSELL

Grandmother

I've seen her pull an onion
from the garden, dust it on her skirt,
and eat the whole thing raw.

She's the one who told me
what to do if a boy tried
to hold me down on the ground —
kick him where it hurts and run.

Last summer, when she heard me swear,
she marched me to the pump,
washed my mouth out with a bar of soap.

Now Grandmother says,
Kiss his hand.
You must, she insists, *or he won't rest.*
And so I bend.

The smell alone warns me I have no business here,
but Grandmother's fingers
grip my shoulder.

When my lips touch my father's phony
skin, I know I'll pay.

SONDRA UPHAM

Advice

When she saw him at *St. Petka Sabor* he wore pigskin shoes,
torn trousers covered with mud, dried-up grass,
"This is my fiance," she had to tell her friends,
a little embarrassed about his untucked shirt, as well.

But Dad's parents were poor farmers. He had to plough fields
with a tractor, make money in the spring and fall.
After the War his family had nothing to eat but
Truman's white and yellow powdered milk and eggs.

The American Red Cross sent old clothes, too,
and only the poorest of the poor wore them.
American fashion was different, easily spotted,
everyone laughed at Dad's checked flannel coat.

But he had nothing better to wear in the cold
having to walk ten miles to school, over the Morava River,
to the city of Aleksinac, while Allies dropped bombs,
exploding just far enough from him to spare his life.

At the Kiwanis dinner in Nebraska I sit with ten old men;
one tells me he dropped bombs over my country during the War.
I thank him for the muzzleflash red in the coat.

BILJANA D. OBRADOVIC

How My Doll Stopped
Speaking to Me

I can still see him.
He strides away from the house
over knotweed and gravel
in sweaty denims without looking
back. He shakes his seed cap, disappears
into the barn's non-judgmental mouth.

From the kitchen sink,
my mother watches him
through the window, muttering
his name into humid air.
The supper plates are stacked, waiting.
An acrid taste of change on the tongue.

With one hand she wipes a soapy rag
over and over the same spot, the other
pushes hair off her damp forehead.
This time the bank has refused,
and she didn't want to hear it, it's no use,
there's nothing, nothing more to say.

TWYLA HANSEN

The Red Barn

"See the pegs there," I said, and the insurance inspector
— I can't remember what he said.
The wide side door of the barn had been rolled open
and I could see two pegs holding a beam in place.
The red barn color is a particular red.
My stepfather worked steadily every day
of his life there keeping up the buildings,
the barn and corn crib, the milk and cob houses,
the cattle shed and the chicken coops, the lean-to.
Later he poured concrete where the manger had been,
where I milked Roanie and later Chocolate before school,
because he thought there was money in hogs.
I hear cows stomp for flies, pigs squeal,
and this intense silence. "If you want to insure the barn,"
he says, "you'll have to nail over with sheets of corrugated tin."
I look up, past the loft tight with bales,
with the warm sweet smell of living things all around
and the kitten the house cat finally had, the one that survived,
and the feeding bin full of oats where the chute
was worn smooth by the time I moved here,
to where the owl sat every night like a stone column
his head cocked for field mice.
And that's where we ran the hogs and put the heifers
for shelter and the roof lets in odd angles of a gray steel sky.
The two plots of land side by side have passed
to my brother and me and we each live our own 100 miles away
and rarely see each other. It's the land
that keeps us in touch, and, if we don't sell,
that we will pass to our four children
who will remember their grandmother as an old woman.
They will half remember the stories we force on them
and only then after we are dead and they have buried us.
There is not corrugated tin enough to protect anything
from weathering. There is no insurance with life benefits.
A series of windows look to the east
to let in light for the pigs when they lay farrowing.
It is only now that I see that the windows overlook the road
that took me elsewhere, that takes us all away
and back home again.

MARY K. STILLWELL

Gathering Morning Fire

Thinking this may be the last time
sets my mind drumming
on what I had always meant to do.

So humor me and go in darkness
to the Colorado prairie
to watch this April day come in.

We'll sit cross-legged on the sandhills,
lean back against the rolling wind,
and fill our lungs with aromatic sage.

We'll watch dawn's wild fire spread on the horizon,
the silhouettes of pronghorn flowing down the ridge,
and hear from bowls of darkness the dance of grouse begin.

I'll cradle the memory on another morning,
when a nurse comes to shave my thighs and stomach,
then rolls me pinioned on a cart towards the knife.

So go with me to gather fire from this dawning,
as it ignites the eastern sky, and pray
that as surely as sun rises, so again may I.

KAYE BACHE-SNYDER

Closet Cleaning

Ghosts of the grandmothers prod me
to the back of my closet. Another box
unlabeled, left over from the last move.
So there's the old house keys, sunglasses,
doll house furniture, silk scarves, my old eyes
that first saw you in a doorway in Milwaukee,

my throat that drank your health 'til bar close
at Axel's on the frozen blue corner of Oakland
and State, and these curling letters tied with string.
Shovel it all away labeled 1982. Far back
and taped against its splitting sides. I can't
even spell whispers hurled at me as the vacuum
roars dust from matted corners: "*Yoi yee stonem*!
So much dirt it flies out the ass of this machine."

"*Gott en himmel*, if tears could settle dust,
you could breathe in here." Be still. Here are
the shiny red shoes I wore that New Year's
I took you by the hand and didn't we dance,
even after the little ankle straps rubbed me raw.
And here's the twist-tied plastic bag of junk
jewelry I'm saving for Caitlin. And this black
velvet remnant bought for half nothing
at the Second Chance will make her hat
for sporting the huge rhinestone star. Just
seven and her face outshines the generations—
even Great Aunt Louise in her photo as a girl.
"*Cana horah*," echoing grandmothers rock
behind my head, "give the child a chance."

These are the leather jeans that used to fit, empty
chocolate box too pretty to toss. That sneaking
cat has slept grey hair all over my bulky sweater,
clotting the green deep as the pine barrens
along Lake Michigan that set off my eyes
to make you hold me your fuzzy sweetheart.

But where are my silk wedding pumps,
clean and burning like lamp light
on a release of wings?
I have lost them.
They were never here.

DRU WALL

On the Path to the Dry Pond

I felt her there, or tried to

tried to believe
she *was* there,
paying attention
and talking again.
She said she loved me

in the wind, I heard
with my skin

in the wind and the way
of sun and wind together
on an October morning

and the way time and weather
can join as a gift.

What she said
(if she was there,
if she could say)
was that she loved me

missed me at least as much
as music and flying,
babies, bargains, dinner out,
and any occasion for gathering, any at all

and this old earth
she fought so hard to keep

which ought to be enough,
and isn't.

MAUREEN TOBIN

two small sundaes, extra topping please
for aunt nellie

in the early kansas evening
i remember going for ice cream for us
down to the soft serve dairy queen
the air hot and moist, sun rays long
golden as childhood
ordering our sundaes at the screened window
with the sweet and cool breeze

returning up the slight hill fast as i could
watching out for uneven cracks
in the sandstone slab walk
panting against the inevitable
melting in my hands
first the cream curls would soften
blend into the topping

you liked yours swimming in strawberries

no matter how much melted
when we sat down in the metal rockers by the roses
your blue eyes danced in your old skin
when you took your first bite
you closed your eyes and sighed
as if this ice cream in a waxed cup
was all you'd asked for in life
and here it was again

JOSEPHINE JONES

out on the farm

blown sideways by wind
my daughter and i walk over harvested fields
then through land struggling to return to prairie
pry open the doors of the dead
homestead empty for a generation.
mice have made sense of the overalls left hanging
the day grandfather fell
never to completely rise again
a part of him gone from his eyes
his smile wandered from his face.

the pantry smelled of grandmother cooking
ten years after she moved in town
but the year she died the roof fell in,
aromas of cookies and cakes escaped
over the barn into the endless blue.

we're looking for the letters grandmother and grandfather
wrote each other before they married that my mother says
grandmother says she burned after a fight.
my daughter finds the baby book grandmother kept
of her long-dead son, my uncle,
cigar smoking interloper on protestant ground.
i find his high school portrait, his easy smile somehow ruthless
and the commencement notice of my 65-year old aunt
jumbled with milk bottles, endless farm magazines
egg cartons to re-use for customers
a chalk slate of powdery homework, quilt squares
cut, never joined for warmth
half-finished embroidered tea towels
and one perfect table
with one drawer
with one pair of scissors.

my daughter asks for a pack of cards to pass the night
and i remember they were forbidden.
we look through photographs instead.
she finds photos of her mother and father
together with her, happy in love
watches my face tighten and his darken
until he doesn't figure in the group portraits anymore.

we go through stack after stack
see everyone i remember and more
except one person. my father.

we find a passport picture of my mother
shaded with the fear of leaving home
find the same sneer on her mother's face.
see two generations of sisters always looking
away from each other, light and dark
blue eyed and brown, we trace through tightening
jaws how love leaks out, generation after generation.
wonder where it started
see where we fit in this chain.
feel the dead flutter around us
finding a way to break into our hearts.
we watch the calm confidence
of my brother's son talking of his father
how at age four, he thinks he knows him.

the wind blows here as it has always done
fierce and mean.
if the prairie grass is high enough to reach a low sun
it glitters
like a sea of promise, it waves
as if to greet us here
strangers
come home.

JOSEPHINE JONES

Her Old Songs

I
Grandma's eyes dance
as I show off
on my new harmonica,
reminding me
that she played
for parties at my age.
Begging for the old songs,
I hand her my Hohner
and wince to see
her crippled fingers
flop over the sides,
futile as fish.
Though her hands
shake with pain,
she trusts the harp
to the grip of her palms,
plays waltzes
and hoe-downs,
a perfect
Auld Lange Syne.

II
Today I pick up
my Hohner again
and cannot stop
playing; then the phone
rings: Grandma's heart
has forgotten its rhythm,
her lungs are failing.
Unable to sleep,
I sit on the back steps
breathing prayers
through my harp,
her old songs:
Amazing Grace,
Wayfaring Stranger,
Oh, Give Me a Home.

SARAH FAIRCHILD

Weathering / boundaries / what is good

—after Hilda Raz

                                    First light
frost on railing, tingle as my fingers melt dark ovals
in the layer of white. Translucent katydid shell,
amber clinging to weathered decking. Pine resin,
lemon mint, honeysuckle breeze. Miniature moths
pulsing on sedum. Maple seeds cascading wings,
oriole trill, surprise call!—my daughter back—
good trip; her car humming into the driveway.
Last crop of roses on the table—rose bush
rescued before the plow undid its roots—
bloomed and bloomed all summer.
Water burbling from the faucet, girls running
down the street, body sweat, salt in the shaker,
basil in the cupboard, fresh apple bread
melting cream cheese. Socks without holes,
holes in the vegetable steamer. Carrot crunch,
ozone of cucumber silk dark peel, green
tomatoes snapped from the vine,
the neighbor is up and working in his yard.
Pampas grass plumes,
               a friend asks how I am and wants to know.

Rasp of teeth filing fingernails,
               tiny particles, magnets
        pulling toward gravity;
nail clippings left in the coaster,
                       slivers sticking to wet glass.

      My friend tells about an Indian
man who cut off his braids and was freed from illness
and the weight of his grief. I contemplate shaving my head,
instead cut off split ends.

      Here is a clip of my hair
that you tuck in a leather bag. Here is my bag, my
body that gathers and presses
        lilies in waxed paper.

And when wind blows,
body aches, rose wilt blackening the edge.
The barren cricket chafes and chafes
its bleak monotone whittling away—you run your fingers
through my hair,
the shiver of brittle leaves.

ROSEMARY ZUMPFE

Transplanting

All day I had been working
at the work I love:
transplanting columbines and ferns
kneeling beside beds of astilbe and chrysanthemums,
tucking them in tight.
I planted impatiens in pots, violet vincas with silver lace—
making combinations.
When it was dark and I could no longer see,
I went in.
I had not thought about my sister dying all day
except to wonder about
the Black-eyed Susans on her bare clay hill.
In the evening walking, what a delight the scent
of honeysuckle, lilac, delicate hint of bridal veil,
maple seeds helicoptering around me,
their lime-green rotors gently clicking.

That night I dreamed we were back on the farm
sun and blue sky,
standing at the backyard clothesline.
Our nightgowns hung by their slender shoulders,
the breeze filling the skirts, the sleeves,
puffing out the bodices—
lifting them gently
white against the green grass below.
Linda's was cotton and lace,
filled with fresh air.
I unpinned it
and placed it in her arms.

LUCY ADKINS

Lamentation

And my life draweth nigh unto the grave.
Psalm 88

My hands hold Flash, old cat, tenderly—she's dying.
Delicate in her Chanel suit of grey satin, snowy neckband
shapes her throat, outlines her jaw. I want to give
her evening dusk, the cave beneath the maple tree.
She'd sit quietly by the musk-rose, forepaws two
white blossoms neatly posed on dark brick.
She's taken weeks to die, grey pills on a pink
protesting tongue. Enduring unfamiliar hands that
seek useless marvels. X-ray outline of black evil
distorting silver jewelry of her fragile ribs.
Eyes, cloudy with unearned pain, ask me for help.
Helpless, I once again recall my mother's end.
Alone she died. If I could have read her favorite Psalms,
held her thin hand in the night! Instead, I hold Flash, dying.

ELIZABETH CALLAWAY

Renting Empty Space
for Grandfather 'Chuff'

The house
will be rented soon,
pine, some brick.
She meditates these walls and

the dry dirt,
falling high into
the white pines left
to grow tall.

She remembers her grandfather on a stump,
shotgun across his legs,
waiting for the bats to surface
in the little light left.

She feels his "Hell" and "Damn"
fixing the door knobs and
the curtains long to the floor,
all a promise like
the gun to his shoulder.

TAMMY TRUCKS

The Picture

You may think
I am sitting here at the kitchen table
looking out the window
but I am really standing
in my Grandma Rose's window
where geraniums in tin cans
are blooming all around me.
I am five years old and
my tow-colored hair is wild
around my face. Surrounded
by red geraniums I am looking
through the window
squinting into the sun.

Uncle David is outside the window
aiming his studio camera.
Across the years he motions
for me to look up.

IRENE ROSE GRAY

The Oak Desk
for Adeline Woodward Baker

Her elbow rested here
a century ago.
This is the field

she looked upon,
a mad rush of wheat
anchored to the barn.

What her thoughts were,
the words she penned
are driven into the grain,

its deep tide crossing
under my hand. She breathes
through the knothole.

Outside, the wind
pushes the farm
down an alley of stars.

WYATT TOWNLEY

Heaven as a Church Fellowship Dinner

I'm slipping off my choir robe, ready
to streak out before somebody says, *hey,
why not stay? There's plenty.*
When in walks my husband,
which is miracle enough,
but behind him is my father who,
when alive, swore he wouldn't
be caught dead in a church.

I luxuriate in ordinary worries
like where's our contribution
to the table, hoping Mom's behind them
with a chocolate cake or jello salad.
But it's just me and my men,
and I pray no one cares that none
of us carries a dish to pass.

I ladle giant scoops of au gratin
potatoes, baked beans, and pasta salad
on their plates, can't wait to get
something solid down them.
Dad mentions the cribbage tournament
he's headed for right after dinner
way off in another state.
What a guy, I think, to make
such a journey with his heart.
We smile and wish him luck.

Waking up, I recall the hospice chaplain
asking what denomination Dad was,
his answering as though the words were
almost more than he could chew: *cribbage player.*
Good, she'd said, *God needs
more cribbage players.*

JUDITH SORNBERGER

The Whiskers on His Face

Heinrich Frank loved onions and mustard.
I can still smell his breath, feel the whiskers
he scraped against my brother's face and mine.
I loved the scraping, his breath,
his game of clamping his arms round our necks
till we laughed, stuck in his lap.
That's all I remember of him.

My mother gave me his sweater
after he died. It was amber like wheat,
the wool rough as his whiskers.
I wore it a year. Yellow buttons
the color of his breath, his bones
the size of mine at thirteen. I could trace
the sea in the seams, follow the listing ship
that carried him across the Atlantic at two.
The sweater gave me his passage,
the reason his bones remained
small as the handbag he slept in
those months beyond land.

The sweater grew a hole in the elbow.
I gave it up. My aunts tell me
the ship sank in the harbor.
I want to sink to my grandpa in his grave,
to his dust, what's left of his bones,
the odor of tubers stained on his teeth.
He freezes each winter in the North Dakota plains,
but when the soil warms in May,
he grows restless, his fingers
wiggle like worms:
it's time to make hay.

CONNIE WASEM

Green

Everything green,
the trees, the grass, even myself, green to the ways
of this city. No cows bawling to be milked this morning,
no windmills creaking. Here in this rooming house
all is square-cornered and shiny, no farm dust invading
these wax-worn halls. I rise early, put on my pinchy
white shoes and my green dress, the one that goes best
with my hair,
I watch the time so I won't be late on this very first day
of my very first job, trying to walk tall like honest-to-goodness
secretaries I have seen, their hair rolled just so, heels smart
and clacking, fingernails pink and perfect playing the keys
of Royals and Underwoods, but I am green and I know it,
just as small and green as a worm crawled out of an ear
of Boone County corn.

MARILYN DORF

And So —
October 2000 — Breast Cancer Month in America

It is after surgery and 13 days into chemo. There is a certain give and take between expectation and happening. The unknown is the fear: the waiting for what does come, does not come, might come; the stiffening against any pain, nausea, discomfort, disfigurement, grotesqueries; the mind steeped against anticipation of cell migration, and an amazement that one's own body may continue to allow these things to happen within itself.

And So—

I have put on the dress of waiting.
Its sleeves hang loose and long.
The bodice needs tucks.
The hem at my ankles is frayed and
stretching to reach the floor.
When I walk in the rain its colors change.
Its fabric shrinks to shape my form.
My body pulls in and back—
resists the garment—
is eager to know, to do, to act, to be.

My hair falls out and down upon my shoulders.
It drops, settling to cover my arms, back, breast, and thighs.
I watch peacefully as it disconnects from its rooting
like sheep's wool in the shearing,
merges into my dress's weaving like fiber,
threads into threads, garment into garment,
leaving my head bare, and shiny, and smiling
under the cleansing water from the sky,
regenerated, refreshed.
My dress hangs heavy with the rain.

A sliver of moon lights the southwest sky
as would fit around the curve of my breast like a Moroccan sword.
Blood-filled clouds are drinking in the red setting sun's lowering.
My breast, healing, throbs with identity.
I tell it it is okay.
The sun, weaving its rays down and around the world in a wrapping hug,
will soon hide in the dark night.
The moon alone will stay, curved into its side smile, a parenthesis
standing aside with me, keeping the watch.
My dress slides gently from my body into a heap at my feet.

MEL KRUTZ

For My Students

I know that you don't know me,
don't know anything about me or care
about what I care about,
but will pretend to the end for that
She's gotta give me an A she likes me so much a-ha
moment as you remove the yoke of this class
and hand in your very last draft
of your very last paper
with that I wrote this at 4 a.m. glaze in your eye

don't lie to me,
I know what your other teachers
made English mean to you, I remember
the regulation and strangulation of my own
high school English courses,
the dull eyes of my classmates when even
their cries were stifled with rules and manuals,
the love of reading and writing
pressed out under year after year,
class after class, and word after word,
slowly enough they strangled the soul-speak
from me and made words into enemies
I couldn't handle, they
grammared the faith, pentametered the rhyme
and corrected my stammering yammering voice
into silence.

I know how language gets stuck behind swollen tongues
and writing gets deformed in the strict form of our instructors,
and now, as your instructor,
what do I want for you?

In my own life our recovery looked other places, our faces brightened
in the pleasure of words. My friends found tattered copies of Emerson
and Thoreau, stuck Vonnegut in their guts to simmer
and began to spill over running over talking over writing over
everything they had encountered. Myself, I tripped and fell
into the happy chasm of Walt Whitman who made me
realize once more the job of tongue on teeth as air slides through,

but for you, for you —
I want something more.

For you I want word magic to weave itself back into your lives,
I want you to thrive in desolate deserts of language,
to desert the hard-edged worlds of the words you learned
and build an oasis of sound round your young body,
I want to show you that Webster's doesn't always provide
the most appropriate word, can't spell *mmmmmm* or define it as
noun: a fine looking young man or an adjective denoting beauty,
I want you to learn to love the way you cook up noun and verb combina-
    tions,
to stop quaking at the thought of comma or semicolon locations,
to allocate the phonemes and tonal variations of your own dialects,
and use them. I want you to see the beauty of this tool wielded by
and no longer upon you, to recapture the shimmer and glimmer
of words, hold them close and never let anyone red-ink correct
them out of you again. I want to see and hear you in everything
that you do, find your fingerprints in every piece of writing and finally,
finally, I want you to hand in your last draft of your very last paper
and leave this class, wear that yoke as a blessing,
your dressing denoting your own struggles with tongue and pen,
your quest to break out of corrected and dejected mute stupor
and take flight once again with your own recaptured soul-speak.

MONICA KERSHNER

The Man at the DMV

He looks at me as if I've just shaved my head,
barked like a dog, or spoken to him in inspired tongues,
his sidelong glance says *You are annoying me*
as he rips up my driver's license renewal form
and explains that, under race, I can mark only one.

So I try to explain that I am two in one
and you'd think I had belched in his face
the way he frowned at me and stiff-fingered the form
just over the directions: mark one.
Choose, he says. *Only one.*

So I try to explain again that I am two in one,
choosing my words more carefully now,
and he looks as if I've just insulted his mother's chastity,
Then mark 'other' he spits.

Other. I laugh.
You don't have to tell me that twice, I say
and the woman next to me chuckles,
her dark curls bouncing around a darker face,
shoulders rising in comaraderie,

and I know he thinks I should avoid this battle,
should mark one to make his life and my life easier,
thinks that I'm light enough to escape it all
because now his eyes only ask why.

MONICA KERSHNER

Among

Among notebooks, I am the bent spiral one with thoughts scattered
between lists and lyrics

Among crayolas, I am the spilled out blues—midnight, navy, cerulean
azure, sea, slate, turquoise

Among doors, I am the weatherbeaten side door to the cellar
and the trapdoor inside

Among jeans, I am the ones you slip into as soon as you can
at the end of the day. I fit you soft as skin and my waistband
embraces all

Among fruit jars, I am the one preserving cinnamon flavored pears
pink, spicy smooth with a small stream of sticky juice
awaiting a wipe

Among slantedness, I am the one gauging just how far it is to the next flat
surface, putting it all down to more physical therapy

Among larks, I am the western meadowlark at home among milkweed,
goldenrod, milo, side-oats grama

Among stories, I am the O. Henry one
with the quick twist.

LINDA STRINGHAM

A Pantheist Comes Upon a Church
Five Miles from Manhattan, Kansas

1
Its window glass has been removed
to grace the barn across the road.
An upturned pew collects stray dust
of cropless years. The bell finds no one
to call out to. Walls are shedding
white mantles of the town's last meeting.

2
I should be moving forward, also.
There are cows nosing weeds by the door.

SUSAN RICHARDSON

The Balers

TRICIA CURRANS-SHEEHAN

The combining was finished, the oats were in the bins and the straw was in straight plump rows when I heard the back door open and Dad call out, "Balers coming."

"When?" Mom asked.

"Tomorrow," he answered and the back door slammed shut.

Mom poked her head into the living room. "Get up," she said to me. I was lying on the floor, behind the couch, reading *Vogue*, which Clarice, the neighbor woman who worked in town, gave me when I delivered eggs to her. Every time I got a new one, Mom said that I acted like a mother cat going off to some dark place to give birth and not returning until it was finished.

"What are you reading now?" Mom asked sharply. It was Dad's rule that no one could read or do anything resembling fun until all the work was done.

"High fashion," I answered.

"Huh. What good is that going to do?"

"I can dream, can't I?"

"Not now." Mom's voice said not to mess with her. "Go pick a bucket of apples for pie and make sure you get the ones on the ground first."

I hated picking the fallen apples; they had bruises, worm holes or bird pecks — always some flaw. But when I was sure Mom wasn't watching me out the window, I'd pick one from the tree, a fresh one, a perfect one.

I trudged out to the orchard. Those balers, they'd wreck my day and the next couple of days. Mom'd have me cleaning, scrubbing and baking for them. I wanted to tell Mom that I didn't want to wait on them. Any of them. The old men and their sons, Daryl and Cletus and Gerald. They'd be at the farm, in the house, sitting around the long oak table with my five brothers and Dad, and I would have to serve them. The daughter always served the balers. If there was no daughter, the woman of the house brought in someone else's daughter.

I knew I'd have to put up with the sons' stares and the balers' bold looks. I knew what it was like to wait on balers. My sisters had done it before, and now that they were gone and waiting on their own husbands and balers, I had to do it. Take my sisters' place, that's what I had to do, and put up with the balers' gawking, looking me over like I was some heifer at the county fair.

The next morning Dad went out to check the straw for moisture. Balers never came until after nine o'clock, after the dew evaporated.

I waited with my brothers up in the barn loft. The huge loft door hung open, like a mouth waiting to be fed, I thought. Once a year that door was lowered, and it was fun to stand at the highest spot on the farm and see for miles. The elevator was positioned in the door ready to carry bales up there. Three of my brothers and two of the balers would take their places. When the bales came up, one after another, the men worked fast, stacking deep and high, sweating buckets and smelling of dust and oats.

Then they rested, while Dad drove the tractor with the flatbed wagon to the field to get another load. This was the time for stories and jokes, and everyone, even my brothers, sat and drank a Grain Belt beer, ice cold from the pump house. I always felt funny listening to their laughter, as if they were talking about me, so I'd climb down the ladder to the cool cow shed below and listen from there. I'd hear them snicker and giggle about somebody's daughter with big tits, and they said other words I had never heard before but I knew they were dirty. Once my brother walked over to the ladder, looked down, and yelled for me to get lost, like I was the one doing something wrong.

I watched for the red tractor and baler coming down the section road that ran parallel to the road that went by our farm. From our perch at the barn door, we all waited. Dad stood down below, next to the two tractors and flatbeds lined up, ready to go when the baler pulled into the oats field across the lane. I saw Mom poke her curled head out the front door and look toward the section road, too.

"They're coming," Bernard called.

I stood on tiptoes, holding tightly onto the side of the open door, and looked toward the tree on the horizon. All traffic came from behind that lone tree.

"I see them," yelled Gene and I at the same time. The red tractor and baler and the caravan of wagons and pickups came from behind the tree into the open.

For a second we watched, then Dad gave the command, "Let's get moving." My brothers hoisted themselves onto the elevator and, balancing, descended. They stepped high, a kind of dance, to avoid tripping on the metal dividers on the auger belt.

I heard Mom call, "Margaret, we have work to do. Come inside." I was too afraid to take the elevator so I scooted down the ladder and shuffled toward the house. I would have given anything to stay outside.

I pulled the long oak table apart and inserted three leaves. I pushed the table back together tightly, then I covered it with a thick flannel cloth because Mom said we had to protect the table from spills and scratches. She said this would be the only dining table she'd have in her lifetime, and she was going to keep it nice. Next I put a new flowered percale sheet over the flannel. These days all the farm women were using flowered sheets for tablecloths. They thought they were so smart. It cost less than a tablecloth, especially when they got it at a white sale, but who were they fooling, I wanted to know. I could tell it was a sheet and I imagined sleeping on mashed potatoes and gravy and pickled beets.

The dining room was an uncomfortable place — green walls with a framed picture on each wall. Each one was the exact same height from the ceiling; I'd seen Mom and Dad measure many times to be sure. On one wall the Good Shepherd looked down on Mom's place at the table, and on the next wall two swans swam in a turquoise pond with lots of too-pink flowers on the bank, and opposite Dad's place was a brightly colored picture of St. Agatha, virgin and martyr, dressed in a peach robe and carrying a plate with two loaves of bread.

For years I had heard the story about St. Agatha, thrown into a house of ill-repute, but she hadn't committed a sin; she hadn't given herself to a man. "St. Agatha died for her purity," Mom said over and over until I was blue in the face from listening. One day at school I looked up Agatha in the Catholic encyclopedia. It said that Agatha wasn't carrying two loaves of bread, but her own breasts. Well, I didn't think I'd go that far for my purity. When I thought of Dad eating his bread and looking piously at the picture three times a day, I grinned.

On the other wall was a picture of a vase with hollyhocks, which I knew was phony. Heck, everyone knows that hollyhocks close up right away if they're picked.

"Fill the pickle dishes." Mom crossed off another item on her list of preparations. One job after another, I moaned to myself as I went to the china closet and took out six fancy glass dishes. The beet pickles bled and had to be put in a bowl by themselves, but the rest of the pickles I could team up. Mom made pickles out of everything in the garden — zucchini, carrots, tiny ears of corn, onions, watermelon rinds, and green tomatoes.

"They're on their way in," Mom called from the front door and ran back to the kitchen.

"What's the big hurry," I said under my breath as I stood at the living room window and watched the balers pile onto a full load. They were a flock of blackbirds perched on top of the straw; their heads, covered with hats and caps, bobbed up and down as they went over bumps in the field lane.

I walked back to the kitchen and began filling all the bowls as fast as I could before they arrived at the back door. I had filled the bowls of mashed potatoes and green beans and creamed corn when I heard them tromping down the basement stairs to the old sink and mirror we kept there. I'd hung a clean towel on the wood roller and left two others hanging from nails because Mom said they'd get the first one soaked in no time.

As soon as I finished putting the basket of homemade buns on the table, I heard them tromp up the stairs and I scurried out of the dining room into the hall.

They sat at the dining room table loudly chewing string beans and baking powder biscuits and roast beef — too well done. I thought their sweat-stained shirts with tufts of straw poking from their collars, their matted-down hair (they'd left their caps in the basement after washing) and dirt-filled nostrils were just plain common. But their glaring-white foreheads bothered me the most because this skin, where daylight never touched, couldn't be washed away. It marked them.

"More gravy," Dad called out, and I hurried in and scooped up the bowl. When I returned I set it on the table, but I was careful not to touch eyes with them. I could tell about them though. Skinny Cy looked heavier without his 300-pound Wilma, and I knew that Albert, even in the house, spat brown stuff into a red hanky, and Ralph carried three packages of Juicy Fruit in his front bib pocket. Owen rarely talked; he ate slowly because he had no teeth and Mom told me to be sure and set the mashed potatoes and Jell-O in front of him.

My brothers, all five of them, and Daryl, Cletus and Gerald sat proudly at the table silently imitating the balers. They weren't allowed to talk yet; they hadn't earned the privilege.

Privilege! I lifted my chin. No damn privilege waiting on them.

"Have you seen all them cockleburs in Dude's field?" asked Albert as he passed the mashed potatoes while coughing into the bowl. He picked up that antique hand-painted bowl as if it were a bale of hay.

"Nope, didn't particularly notice them," Cy mumbled. "But I did get a look at Ted's wife mowing out front." He paused and took a bit of beans, then raised his bushy eyebrows. "In her swimsuit."

No one said anything for a few seconds. The statement hung in the air like pig manure on a humid day.

"Was it last Tuesday?" Ralph grinned, just before plopping a bread-and-butter pickle in his mouth.

"Yup," Cy answered. "Damn skimpy."

Ralph nodded in agreement. The others looked up at Ralph, caught his eye, then nodded, too.

"Well," Cy said in a serious tone. "I wouldn't let Wilma stand out front like that for all the world to see."

The balers nodded again.

I snickered to myself from my station at the doorway. These men were jealous of Ted's wife, Clarice, who came from the city to the country four years ago. I thought it was wonderful to see a farm woman with a suntan all over her body, who wore real sunglasses, not the clip-on kind, and who read *Vogue* and *Glamour*, not the recipe section of *Farm Journal.*

"Gophers are thick this summer," Dad said.

There were more nods.

"I got a mess of rabbits in my yard," Cy added. "Wilma's raising a stink about them eating all her gladioluses and zinnias."

"Drown 'em," said Owen quietly. All glanced at him, not turning their heads much. "Put a hose down the hole and drown 'em." I could see the potatoes squish out from between his gums as he talked.

"More potatoes," Dad called out as he turned toward me. For a second our eyes met and he looked irritated with me.

I rushed in and grabbed the bowl, being extra careful. Mom would kill me if I dropped it.

Mom must have heard Dad's call because she stood in the doorway. Ralph looked up and smiled wide. "Good grub, Frances." Mom got all smiley and skittery.

Damn them, I thought, for making Mom act like that. And to think she'd ironed her best dress and made her blue ribbon apple pie with criss-crossed top crust just to have them call it grub.

As I set the bowl back on the table, Mom motioned for me to pick up the empty pickle dish. When I ducked into the kitchen to fill the dish, I heard Albert say to Dad, "Give her some time, Johnny, and she'll perk up in the looks department. She won't be so homely in a few years." Out of the corner of my eye, I saw the other men nod, and my brothers and the balers' sons snickered uncontrollably.

My face burned and I fought back tears. If I didn't do something, I knew I'd explode. "One, two, three, four, five," I counted, spearing the pickles in the jar and piling them on the dish.

I took the pickle dish back in, set it on the table and waited near the door.

"Bring in that pie and ice cream," Dad called out. Dad had a thing for ice cream; he loved it on anything baked in the oven, but he would only have it on Sunday or when there was company. I guess he thought he was sinning if he had it on a weekday or when just the family was there; the family wasn't special enough to rate ice cream. We always saved the real good stuff like Lazy Daisy cake with coconut frosting or the chocolate cake with fudge frosting for relatives who stopped to visit on a Friday evening or Sunday afternoon. I figured that we gave company good food so they wouldn't know how poor we were, and they'd leave thinking that we had this kind of fancy dessert all the time. It was our secret that we had plain bread and butter with a sprinkle of brown sugar before bedtime.

Quickly I carried the plates of apple pie with ice cream into the dining room. Mom and I had a system where she grabbed the dirty dinner plate and I slipped the dessert plate right onto the same spot.

When I had finished carrying all the plates in, Dad said, "Bring in the bucket. We could use another scoop."

Mom handed me the ten gallon ice cream bucket that we had bought from the Schwan's man last week. "You do it," she said, pushing me into the dining room. I wasn't sure where I was going to stand to do this and how I was going to do it without touching the ice cream with my fingers in order to get it off the spoon. Lord, they thought they were big shots the way they expected to be waited on and to be able to have seconds and thirds of the good food.

I stood next to Ralph first and felt my hand shaking as I dug into the hard mass of ice cream. I felt everyone's eyes on me and I wondered if I smelled. I had put a dab of Avon Cotillion perfume on each armpit but it might have worn off. I didn't have any deodorant left and Mom wouldn't buy it for me. She said that if I just washed myself with Ivory soap, then that was all I needed to do, and I shouldn't waste my money on that Secret deodorant where I was really paying for the blue bottle instead of what was inside.

I worked my way around the table scooping ice cream for each baler and my brothers and the balers' sons. I had just finished giving Dad two scoops when Albert winked at me and motioned for me to come back over by him.

"Just plop it right on here," Albert said. He'd saved half of his pie for more ice cream.

I gave him one tiny scoop and I heard him mumble, "Don't be stingy. Toss another one up here." He pointed with his spoon to the top of his pie.

"Have two or three," Dad said and motioned for me to give him more. I knew that Albert had said the right thing, if he wanted more ice cream. Dad hated to be called stingy or cheap, even though he was.

The ice cream was two inches deep at the bottom of the bucket and I dug underneath it and lifted part of it out, using my fingers to balance the hunk on my scoop. It was the size of a half loaf of bread. I plunked the huge mound down on his half piece of pie, covering it.

"Slow down there, girlie," he chuckled, but his face was getting red. There were a few whispers coming from the boys at the other end of the table.

Then I decided to give him another. I dug down and got another giant scoop and plunked that down. He had a whole mountain range of ice cream on his plate and I couldn't see one bit of apple pie. It would melt fast if he didn't do something.

"Lordy, I didn't say I wanted the whole bucket." Albert nervously spat into his red handkerchief, wiped his sweaty forehead, and began scooping up the ice cream that was dripping over the side of the plate.

Everyone snickered louder this time and I felt good. They weren't laughing at me but at Albert whose face was a big tomato. He heard them laugh and tightened his grip on the spoon. I saw the veins in his temples jump up and down.

I felt Dad's eyes on me and I was scared to even look up. I got out of that room fast.

Mom was waiting for me in the kitchen. "What did you do that for? Good heavens he can't eat all of that himself. And it's staining my new sheet."

"He asked for more and you always say we should give the balers what they want."

"Don't be smart with me, young lady. You know you wasted that ice cream on purpose."

"But he asked for it and Dad said to give it to him."

"I should send you to your room. Good heavens. I hope he doesn't get sick on us. Nothing like too much of that cold stuff to give him a real belly-ache and then he won't be able to run the baler."

I peeked into the dining room and watched as Albert, red-faced and sweating, worked at spooning the mound of ice cream into his mouth. The rest of the balers were finished and every few seconds they glanced up at Albert as they dug into their back molars with their toothpicks. Balers had to leave the table all together, and Albert knew he was holding them up.

There was an uneasy silence as they all waited. Dad tapped his foot against the leg of the chair, and Cy chewed on his toothpick while Ralph unwrapped another piece of Juicy Fruit gum.

Albert kept at it as if he were shoveling out the hog barn, a nasty job, but you did it fast to get it over with. The white cream dribbled on his chin and stuck in the stubble of his beard.

Dad was sweating, too, and he wouldn't even look at Albert. "Turn on the radio," he yelled to Mom. "Got to hear the weather report."

Mom hurried to the radio; she plugged it in because the switch was broken, and turned up the volume.

After mom leaned around the doorway into the dining room, she rubbed her hands nervously together. She gave me a look that could kill and walked toward me. I was next to the stove. "Your Dad won't forget this, you know," she hissed and wiped her hands on her apron. "This kind of nonsense doesn't set right with him."

I hated to get Mom in trouble, but I felt I had to do it. Not just for me but for all the daughters who'd ever waited on balers and had to put up with being judged, as if we were a bad batch of pickles at the county fair.

The weather report was over, and I heard the chairs being pushed back from the table. Mom turned down the radio and I left the kitchen by the other door and hid in the upstairs hallway so Dad wouldn't see me. I heard the balers mumble "Good grub" to Mom, and I waited for them to go down the basement stairs to get their caps and then up the stairs and out the door.

When I heard the back door slam, I walked into the empty dining room and saw the pool of cream on Albert's plate and the gooey mess on the table-cloth.

I walked over to Dad's chair and sat down. The seat was still warm. I looked up at Agatha and studied the plate with the two mounds. The painter hadn't known either that those were breasts, or tits as the men called them out in the barn, because there was no blood and no nipples. I thought about what it would be like to have Dad carry the bread on the plate to me and have the bread begin to bleed and grow nipples that poked right up at him. Agatha watched me with that look that Dad thought was piety, but I knew now what it was.

A Mother Visits Hooters

MARY PIPHER

Recently our newspaper announced the grand opening of Hooters. Its full page cover picture was of a Hooters girl, the modern Mcbunny, carrying a tray of burgers and fries. I had read about places such as Hooters, Knockers and Melons, but I was surprised to hear of one in my town.

My husband and I went to Hooters for dinner. By 6:00 at night, the parking lot was packed. Outside two young women in shorts hula-hooped and greeted customers. Inside it was stimulation overkill—twenty two televisions, loud music, flashing colored lights, sports paraphernalia and signs with jokey, sophomoric messages such as, "Let your kids run wild at Hooters. They'll fit in with our employees," and "Not a bad view in the house," and "Men, no shirt, no service, women no shirt, free food."

A family with two pre-school aged daughters sat at a table by the beer sign display. A middle-aged man with a pipe, shades, and sandals looked like a Hugh Heffner wannabe four decades too late. But mostly the customers were college-age men with their buddies and, this being Nebraska, many wore Big Red shirts and baseball caps. The waitresses wore skimpy orange silk shorts, hose and tight little t-shirts and sat down at the tables of the men as they took orders. They obviously were expected to flirt, but they flirted really fast.

We were shown a corner table by a window that looked out on the parking lot and the western sky. The sun was sinking low onto the horizon and the trees were blazing from its light. Our waitress came over. Billie looked tired and stressed, and seeing a mild-looking middle-aged couple, she let down her guard. She wiped her damp forehead and said, "It's hot in here. I have a fever and should be home in bed. But the management doesn't like us to call in sick. It's hard to be perky and charming when I feel this way." She paused and looked over her shoulder, "I shouldn't be telling you this. Don't worry, I won't breathe on your food."

We looked over the menu and ordered "naked" chicken wings and burgers. Waiting for our food was a hard go. The lights gave me a headache and the noise made conversation impossible. This environment was designed for lookers not talkers, a testosterone-laden amusement park. Watching the young women with their heavy trays and forced smiles move among all these guys, I realized this place wasn't about sex as much as it was about declarations of heterosexuality. Coming to Hooters was a statement, fervently and publicly made, "I'm a straight, lust-filled, fun-loving, not politically correct, macho guy."

Since I am not an lust-filled guy, I noticed the airport-quality food, the underdone greasy wings and the cold, inedible burger, which contrary to the newspaper's picture, had no fries on the side. I could elaborate but what's the point. Hooters is not about food. It's about sexual hype for adolescent men of any age. And apparently there are a lot of them out there. Hooters is a blazing success, franchising all over the world and spawning a host of copy cat "breastaurants."

As we ate, I looked out the window more and more yearningly. I found something comforting about the October sunset, the orange clouds against the pink and blue sky, not garish colors at all, but subtle and calm. I debated the ethics of writing about this place. The issues were important. I had seen victims of domestic violence and sexual assault in therapy. I had worked with men whose lives were ruined by their addiction to pornography. Recently I had heard Gail Dines, author of *Pornography, The Production and Consumption of Inequality*, say that in this country we now have more adult book stores than we have McDonald's.

I wanted to make some points, that in America we are in trouble because we are teaching our young men to see women as objects, to disconnect their sexuality from relationships and to prefer large breasts to strong hearts and fine minds. And we are teaching our young women that we value their measurements more than their character structures. Plato wrote that education is teaching our children to find pleasure in the right things. Hooters was as good an example as any of teaching our children to find pleasure in the wrong things.

As I thought about writing though, I realized that to comment on Hooters was to help it. Its owners boast that controversy sells Hooters better than sexual titillation. With sadness I realized how complicated it is to protest in America today. Sometimes the fight becomes part of the advertising hype and strengthens the very thing we are trying to weaken. Hooters is in business because women like me don't like it. That's the point. If mothers liked it, adolescent males wouldn't go there. In fact the best way to put Hooters out of business would be to rave about how much I, a fifty-year-old mother, enjoyed the place. I should organize tea-ins at Hooters all over the country where middle-aged moms sip iced teas and chat with the customers about what sweet girls work there.

Jim and I paid a whopping 25 bucks for our pathetic little meal. We left Billie a good tip which we hoped she would spend on cold medicine. We walked past the little girls who seemed stunned by the place, not eating, just staring at the big screens with football players bashing each other. Billie slipped over and said to us, "I think the boss will let me leave early." Then she pasted back on her smile and jiggled over to another table. The Hugh Heffner wannabe re-lit his pipe and watched her behind.

We walked out past the line of guys waiting for their "good views" and expensive burgers. We breathed more freely in the fresh and quiet night. The air felt wonderful, cool and crisp, with a storm front coming in. Leaves blew at our feet. We heard geese overhead and looked up. Jupiter was blazing in the twilight. A wedge of geese flew over us, traveling south and searching for a safe place to land.

The Griffin's Daughter

JAMIE BACON

I have distinct memories from my childhood that are detailed in color, sound, emotion. I remember without a doubt the dresses my sister, Jeanne, and I wore for a birthday party in the house where I grew up. The dresses were a stiff satiny fabric with even stiffer lace petticoats holding the skirts out from our skinny legs and making them so much fun to twirl. Mine was tea green, my sister's, white. I can picture the two of us swishing our skirts from side to side in anticipation as we stood on the stairs watching my mother greet our relatives at the door. I can hear the sounds of the satin on the lace, I can picture my sister, just a toddler, prancing in her black patent leather shoes. I remember wanting my mother to retie my sash which was too shimmery a fabric to stay in its bow. I remember the way my tongue felt in the hole left by the loss of my first baby tooth

The problem is, most of these memories are not possible or are in the wrong places. The stairs I remembered were actually in our second house, the one that we bought when I was in high school. My dress was lavender, my sister's yellow. According to my mother, I was dressed to be the flower girl in a wedding, not to attend a birthday party. I try to get objective evidence from photographs, but my mother insists I've mixed things up.

Somehow my mind has collected bits of information from stories, from black-and-white photos, from baby books, and from true memories to create a new but fictional recollection. I think the experience I have of recalling happy anticipation is true, it just seems that the emotional memory got attached to some false or rearranged fact. Perhaps emotional memories need a vehicle to transport them to our awareness and it doesn't matter if they're right, only if they fit.

In the same way, the memories of previous summers have surfaced during this summer of record-breaking heat. The sweat carries them out to my skin where they dry and tickle. I recall sweating in my father's garden which stretched at least a quarter of an acre from the paved road at the front of our yard almost to the gravel road in back, leaving enough room for a big lawn and a swing set for my sister and me to play on. The garden was bounded on either side by two driveways, ours and the one belonging to our Eastern European neighbors, Willy and Yvonne. I mainly remember picking beans in late summer for my mother to can; that was my job.

During those summers, Yvonne would place a chaise lounge in the middle of her immaculate lawn and sunbathe in the tiniest little black bikini. I don't remember it. I do remember my mother teasing my father about his enthusiasm for mowing the lawn when Yvonne was out tanning.

My parents held wild Halloween parties each year, the adults going all out to costume themselves. I don't remember the original parties. I wish I did. I remember Jeanne and I being allowed to stay up to greet the guests, then being led off to bed in our footed flannel pajamas. I only know what the parties were like from old 8-mm home movies my sister saved onto video-tape. As the cameraman — my father, presumably — got presumably more intoxicated as the night went on, the camera focused for longer periods of time on the breasts and ass of Yvonne, who was wearing a skimpy black French maid costume. She played for the camera, bending at the waist and arching her back in her high-heeled shoes, her fish-netted legs squeezed tightly together to get the maximum effect from the ruffles and bustier. She primly tickled clean the clown noses and black-faces of any man within reach of her feather duster.

Does memory get more reliable as children grow older? I feel more con-fident I have the details of my later childhood down correctly although the times I got in trouble remain vivid but other times are confused. For instance, there was the time we were on vacation with my father's sister and her husband and it rained most of the days. The grown-ups were in one motel room playing cards, and Jeanne and I were having a vaulting contest onto the bed in the other room. One of the wooden legs on the old bed splin-tered, crashing the mattress to the white floor. Of course, since I was the old-est, I got the spanking.

Then there was the summer Jeanne and our cousin Paul spent most of their time hiding from me and the rest of the cousins so they could smooch. Those games of hide-and-seek were intense. It never made sense to me, why, if they could hear us coming, they didn't stop before they got caught.

After Paul and my aunt and uncle went back home to the West Coast, Jeanne and I found some pornographic photos hidden in the joists in our basement celing. These were actual black-and-white photos, not clippings from a magazine. In one photo, there was a blurry shot of a naked woman standing crudely in front of the camera, barefoot in the dry grass of a lawn, her dark hair vaguely like my mother's. Another photo was a close-up of pubic hair and a vagina . A burning cigarette drooped out of the vaginal lips and someone had printed in ball-point pen, "Does your cigarette taste a lit-tle flat lately?"

We felt certain that my uncle from the West Coast was responsible for those pictures. It didn't seem possible to us at the time that anyone other than a Disneyland-type of mentality could produce anything that grotesque and fascinating. We couldn't figure out, though, when my uncle would have gone down in the basement. When they arrived after their long drive to our house in the Midwest, it was an event. My mother bought special cold cuts and bread, special beer, turned us out of our beds for company. It didn't fit that he'd have gone down there, even for my father to show him the new sump pump or to discuss his never-to-be accomplished plans for turning the damp cement walls into a useable rec room.

I wonder about my memories of those pictures. The blurry photo transposes in my mind with a picture of my little sister standing outside our house on a summer morning in her baby doll pajamas. Both figures were standing straight on to the camera, squinting into the sun, only Jeanne is smiling and you can see she's lost her top front baby teeth. I don't remember the face in the other photo, just the small drooping breasts and the arch of her bare feet on the brown, wiry grass. She was obviously not a professional model.

My sister remembers things differently. She doesn't remember hiding in the weeds with Paul or finding those photos. She only remembers things I told her to do that got her in trouble. I will allow that I did that occasionally, but it was always in self-defense. I remember her as being spoiled and getting almost anything she wanted. She was the blond, darling baby. I was the clumsy, plain big sister.

More astounding to me are the memories she has for events that don't seem to exist in my mind at all. Where was I? How could I have lived in the same house with my mother and father and sister and not have known that my father was going into her room at night and touching her? Not simply touching. Molesting, entering, fondling, raping, blunt instruments of words that don't come close to describing the indescribable. He would come, my sister later told me, even on nights when she had a friend staying overnight. This other girl was the daughter of a close friend of my parents. Would that have kept her from telling on my Dad?

I always felt closer to my father than to my mother. My father had a beautiful garden and he loved words and books. He let me be, he didn't try to change me. My mother, on the other hand, would push me at boys or pick, pick, pick at my appearance. Her gotta-getta-man view of the world disgusted me. I couldn't ever trust that she had my interests at heart. And, it was obvious, she preferred Jeanne then and prefers Jeanne still.

Jeanne can be overly dramatic and tends to think of herself as never to blame for anything that happens. She's very convincing. Growing up, I always had to take that into consideration, whether I was trying to decide if I should believe her stories, or when things came up that would require my parents to arbitrate between us. I stopped wasting my time trying to sway them to my side. Birthday presents, choice of movies, a car when she was 16, an Ivy League college, she usually got her way. I held three part-time jobs to save for my state university tuition. I rode my old bike to classes and to the grocery store. It's not that I minded earning my own way, it was the fact that we didn't both have to work that hard. Then the money they gave me for room and board stopped abruptly and without notice when my sister transferred to an even more expensive university in New England. It was during that Christmas break when we were home from our respective colleges that she told me about what had happened to her.

I grew up thinking of her as the spoiled child, a liar and manipulator, the sucker-in of all resources, the princess to be kept happy at my expense, the preferred puppy at the only available teat. She frequently could not be believed. But I believed this. The Miss Marple in my mind demurely laid the evidence out from the unexamined narrative of my memory: my father silhouetted by the hall light through the door of my dark bedroom, staring at my best friend and me a bit too long as he scratched himself through the fly of his pajamas before asking if we wanted to order pizza. The dirty books in the storage room behind my bedroom downstairs all about daughters seducing their fathers. The day he came up behind me and grabbed me at about the level of my new and despised training bra ("training for what?" I grouched at my mother when she made me get it) and started to tickle me, the tickling ending forever when I literally put my foot down to stop it. I stomped on him hard and nearly broke his foot.

I remember the terrible game I invented to get my sister to stay in bed at night when I had to baby-sit her, about the Griffin who would get into your room and eat you up. The rules were, you had to lie deathly quiet, hardly breathing. If he knew you were alive he could get you.

I know with the depth of my experiences that he was capable of incest. I also know that my emotional world shifted in tectonic proportions when she became the chosen one with all that implies. There are no old photos that could have perverted these memories, no translocation of households to explain away the layers of slime. We were all involved, we all said nothing and continue to say nothing. Our adult households are distant from one another. My parents retired to Arizona, my sister and her millionaire husband live in California in their perfect house with their perfect children, and I continue to live on the prairie where you can see people coming from miles away and where the winters are cold enough to kill the vermin so common where my family members live.

I've always had the feeling that I saved myself from a terrible fate. I've also always felt myself as an outsider in my family. It's only since my sister's revelation that I see one as the price of the other. If I think too hard about it, I think, "In my family you either get screwed or you get fucked."

I also think of another image from the videotape my sister made from our old home movies. My father is a young man standing on the front porch of the house he built when my mother was first pregnant with my sister. He bends down to pick me up. It must be a chilly day. He's in a flannel shirt, and I am in a little snowsuit, my one-year-old cheeks glowing a healthy pink. He tosses me up in the air over and over, catching me and holding me close each time. There is no sound, but I look as if I'm crowing with pleasure at being launched into the sky. And my father looks so happy looking at me. I wish I could remember that. I wish I could.

Fall

GAYNELL GAVIN

The sun was warm, especially for so late in the season. It was Friday. I'd thought the day would go one way: meet the caseworker, make an unannounced home visit, take a quick look around the house to reassure ourselves things were more-or-less okay—that is, in compliance with court orders—and I'd head back to the office for mid-afternoon appointments. That plan lasted as far as the large and pleasant front porch of what had, in better days, been a large and pleasant home.

Inside, a dark-haired baby wailed on the living-room floor, which would not have been such a big deal except that he was underweight, underfed, hungry, and sucking an empty bottle, while his young father—in violation of a restraining order which "prohibited" him from entering the home—and younger mother watched silently, perhaps angrily, from the one piece of furniture in the room, a tattered couch, some indeterminate shade of dark green or gray.

The social worker, a kind, round-faced, no-nonsense Nicaraguan woman, nodded toward the back of the apartment. "We have to see if there's food, formula. We have to check the kitchen." There was another girl—the young mother's sister—with her own two toddlers in the kitchen. Did that girl really begin to wail along with the baby as soon as she saw us, or does the scene unfold that way only in memory? Almost certainly, at the time, I did not acknowledge any part of what I felt as shame. Maybe I didn't even feel it until later.

The social worker moved from empty cabinet to empty cabinet, opening each one. We worked quickly, efficiently, bound by some tacit communication. I opened the refrigerator. There was a little milk and cheese from WIC, the only food in the house. No formula.

I moved to the bathroom. Like the other rooms, it had holes in the walls and ceilings. I checked methodically, every move a statement in which I refused to acknowledge participation: You are nothing because you have nothing. Nothing in this country is yours. Not the home you live in, not even your children.

The bathtub was without running water. Sopping newspapers on the floor surrounded a leaking toilet. While the landlord apparently did as the landlord pleased, the girl had been ordered to provide adequate housing for the baby. As if she could choose where to live. As if anyone who had a choice would live here.

I could not get back to the air and sunlight on the porch fast enough. We paused on the steps, saying the same words at the same time. "We have to pick up the kids." The worker's hands shook for maybe a second while she lit a cigarette, but her clipped voice was reassuringly steady. "This is the part of my job I hate. The auto body shop guys on the corner have worked on my car. We can use their phone."

So she exchanged greetings with the owner, a stocky, bald guy who said, "Sure you can use the phone. What do you need to call the police for?" When she told him she probably shouldn't talk about it, he laughed. "It's all right. I already know it's got to be something to do with that fat little Mexican three doors down who's always violating his probation. And you two better be off this street by dark. It's okay now, but it'll belong to the Inca Boys then."

I called the office to have my afternoon appointments rescheduled while we waited. The officer was a big, calm, blond guy who knew and spoke to neighbors as they gathered near the squad car to watch us go into the house. Inside, the girls knew, of course, right away, when we came back in with the cop. They knew we'd take the kids. They started crying and pleading— they'd have food stamps and food by Monday, no, they'd borrow food money from their mom, get food right away, and pay her back Monday, they'd make the landlord fix everything right away, really, really they would—while the baby's father sat on the couch, hands dangling between his knees, staring at the floor and saying nothing.

The officer went back to his car and got on the radio for a long time. Inside, I guess we tried to calm the crying girls, telling them to just get food and start looking for a better place to stay, they'd have a forthwith hearing and probably get the kids back Monday. Then I went out to the car and said, "Look Officer, I know you have to be really careful about the criteria for an emergency pickup without a court order, but I've got to know your decision. Because if you're not going to pick them up without the order, then I've got to get into court for an emergency order this afternoon. And I'm running out of time here."

"We've decided," he said. "Let's go."

The crowd was small and quiet, watching as we took the wailing children from the wailing mothers. The baby was so light, so light on my hip. I patted his back, and he quieted, resting his head on my shoulder before I handed him over for shelter care where room after room is filled with waiting children.

In my car, I return to the corner which I am told will soon belong to the Inca Boys. Maybe so, but it does not belong to them quite yet, for in the moments that I wait to make my left turn, here is what I see. A slender man on the sidewalk, at the crosswalk, with a small baby in his arms. The man's straight, black hair sticks out beneath his denim cap. In the late afternoon sunlight, the baby is wrapped in blankets, bundled against that first edge of winter. And in that instant as I turn the corner, this man draws the baby closer to him and brushes his lips to the baby's forehead. He will never know how I keep and guard this moment, this picture he has given me to hold against nights of intermittent, sweat-soaked sleep and pre-dawn awakenings to a blank sky. He will never even know that I see him, but I do.

Raspberry Coat

(for my mother, who showed me what strength is)

NICOLE CHURCH

Dad writing home to Grandpa and Grandma in Nebraska:

September 1968, Tripoli, Libya

"...Karen is generally satisfied but feels the lack of freedom here due to the restrictive attitudes towards women in this country. Some Libyans actually lock their women in their houses when they go to work in the morning. A lone woman on the streets sometimes gets harassed (pushed, shoved, pinched). But the ones who fight back seem to get along all right..."

Mom liked to sing to us, songs she sang when she was growing up with her brothers and sisters. The one I liked best was called, "Sweet Violets," and she sang it to us a lot, especially when we were traveling. During long hours in the car after Dad got his degree and he drove across the mid-west to California looking for the perfect job. And during dull hours in airplanes, flying from Nebraska to our new home in Libya after he was hired by Amoseas.

> *There once was a farmer who took a young miss*
> *In back of the barn where he gave her a*
> *Lecture on horses and chickens and eggs,*
> *And told her that she had such beautiful manners*
> *That suited a girl of her charms,*
> *A girl who could take in his washing and ironing*
> *And then if she did,*
> *They could get married and raise lots of*
> *Sweet violets*
> *Sweeter than all the roses,*
> *Covered all over from head to toe,*
> *Covered all over with sweet violets.*

When Mom sang that song, I believed the expression on her face said she was happy. It made me feel safe and cheerful. I had no idea we were very poor before we went to Libya. Tony and Ben and I always had clothes. We didn't know that most of them came from cousins and second-hand stores, and that Mom made my dresses from scraps of fabric she collected. We always had enough good food to eat although we didn't know Mom grew tomatoes because she couldn't afford to buy them, and the dandelion soup she sometimes fed us was actually made from dandelions she'd picked in the field across the street from our house. I knew she worked nights to help out while Dad finished school, but I never understood why she was so tired, even though she stayed up when she got home from work because Dad left for classes in the morning, and somebody had to take care of us. She and Dad hardly ever went out for fun, and once in a while I'd wake up in the night to hear them yell at each other because they had no money.

As far as I was concerned, we didn't need more money. I had everything I wanted. Mom and Dad took care of us and kept us entertained. On warm summer evenings they piled us into the station wagon with our pillows and drove into the country where we opened the tailgate and lay watching stars in a huge, black prairie sky. Sometimes Dad took us for long rides on his bicycle, balancing Tony on the front and me on the back. And it seemed like Mom was always singing to us or telling us interesting stories when we weren't outdoors playing. Every day she read books to us that we collected from our bedroom. I don't think she ever got tired of reading stories. Her voice changed with the characters in the story, and she always gave in when we clamored for more.

When Dad was hired by Amoseas, it was the first time we had ever had money. Dad traveled to Libya several months ahead of us to work while we lived with Grandpa and Grandma in Nebraska. Dad found a large villa for us to live in with high ceilings and marble floors. He sent measurements to Mom and told her to buy carpet and draperies for a palace.

It felt as though we had been suddenly thrust into a foreign world before we ever left the prairie. My brothers and I pelted up and down the aisles of department stores while Mom selected colour-coordinated fabrics and carpeting. We squirmed in dressing rooms, hot and impatient as she outfitted us in brand new clothing and even tried on a few things herself. Mom had always made her own clothes. There was never enough money to buy a new dress. Until now, when she moved through the stores, cautiously, as though the money might somehow disappear in an instant and drop her back into the rusty, high-walled bucket of poverty.

Green was Mom's favourite colour. There was green in the bluish shag carpet she ordered and in the dark, ornate drapery fabric. Her new luggage was green, and so was the pretty, practical dress she chose as she moved almost gingerly through the women's department. A spring coat was the last thing she bought, a long coat of nubby, soft wool. The hem reached well below the knee to conform with the Libyan brochure that advised modesty in the appearance of women. It was dark pink, the colour of lips that have eaten ripe raspberries, and it made her green eyes sparkle as I watched her turn round and round in front of the dressing room mirror. Her Sweet Violets face appeared and her smile was positively lovely. Mom wore her new coat on the trip all the way from Nebraska to Libya, buttoned tight across her stomach growing big with Mindy. After we arrived in Tripoli, she had to wear the coat unbuttoned until after the baby was born.

Shortly after our arrival, Dad left to work in the Nafoora Oil Fields five hundred miles deep into the Sahara. He was gone to the desert frequently, which left Mom to fend for us as the breadth of her belly achieved startling proportions. He was working at Nafoora when her pregnancy reached nine months with still no sign of Mindy.

Our shipment of household goods, the carpeting and draperies, dishes and furniture was not due to arrive for another month or two. We'd been living for two months already with the barest furnishing of living necessities in a provision kit provided by Amoseas. It was wearing on all of us to have to share wash clothes when we were supposed to be rich.

A couple of days after Dad left for Nafoora, his boss stopped in the see how Mom was getting along. She met Jack at the door with her good-company-wife smile on her face, but it didn't fool him. He'd probably seen company wives in this condition before. All he said was, "My goodness, Karen, it looks like the pressure is really getting to you."

To my surprise, her bottom lip began to quiver and her voice was thick with sobs as she choked, "Yes, I guess it's been a bit rough lately." Jack steered her into the living room and said, "Tell me what I can do to help," as she dumbly allowed him to lower her into a chair. Tony and Ben and I stood and gaped as the floodgates broke:

"I don't have any dishcloths or enough silverware for my kids and I need a washing machine to wash their clothes. I only have four soup bowls and no plates and I'm all alone and what if I go into labour when Norm is in the desert and I don't even have a paring knife and the only pans I have are big enough to bathe a baby in and there aren't any rags to clean with and what in the hell was Amoseas thinking when they put these provisions kits together anyway?" Great, wrenching sobs spilled out of her and we all stared with mouths open.

After a minute or so, Jack stood up and said, "You just hang on, honey. I'll be back." Then he was gone, and we clustered around Mom, patting her awkwardly on her back and murmuring nonsense like, "It's okay, Mom, it's going to be okay, just you wait and see."

A few hours later Jack returned in a truck. In the back of the truck was a huge collection of household items, including an antiquated wringer washing machine, pots, pans, dishes, rags, towels and kitchen utensils. It almost felt like Christmas. Jack had borrowed a truck and gone to the other Amoseas families asking for anything they could spare to help the newly arrived Church family. Evidently those families well remembered their own hardships in moving to Tripoli. The donations were abundant. Mom was back in business. It took some practice to work the washing machine, and once she even got her huge stomach pinched between the two rollers that wrung the clothes flat. Tony and I were playing outside when we heard her scream. We thought maybe that would bring the baby who was already a couple of days overdue, but it didn't. The next day, Dad walked into the house, in from Nafoora a week early to announce that Jack had called him in and said he wouldn't be assigned to the desert again until after the baby arrived. Mindy was born two weeks later.

When Mindy finally came, she was sick all the time. Infections of her eyes, infections in her ears, intestinal disorders and colic through the night. Mom came home from the hospital anemic and tried to resume her former pace. Dad helped when he was home, but he was called to Nafoora frequently after the birth. My mother was pale and shaky and thin, and lots of times I saw tears in her tired green eyes. She cooked our meals and washed our clothes in the old wringer washer. She built kitchen cabinets and bedroom shelves and worked to make the villa look like a home with our sparse belongings. Without fail, toward late afternoon and evening, Mindy started with colic, and Mom walked many twilight hours up and down the long marble hallway while the baby screamed. Her doctor continued to pump her with iron shots, and she continued pale and tired. Tony and I helped where we could. I learned to cook a few simple meals, and I walked the baby in the hallway until my bedtime. Mom had no license to drive, so Tony walked to the little shops by the beach and bought groceries. It was ghibli season, and sand that crept into the house every day had to be swept back into the yard. In a letter home to Nebraska, Mom wrote:

"Tony and Nicci are looking forward to school's end a week from Friday. We're looking for ways to keep them busy — besides work — they get plenty of that. They can't be allowed too much freedom here although they do take hikes. They've all had incidents of Arab kids patting their pockets for money and occasionally getting rougher. It's something they just have to live with. Children adjust so much faster. I will never get used to being snickered at by men and boys (it ain't the lusty ol' American way). They think of women as repulsive, especially when they're uncovered..."

When summer was over and school began again, Mom enrolled little Ben in a preschool a mile down the road from the villa. This gave Mom five quiet mornings a week with only Mindy at home and, after a while I noticed she finally started to look like my pretty mother again.

Ben was delighted with preschool. In the first week he fell into a lively romance with a little Dutch classmate named Francesca Metricalli, who couldn't speak much English but that didn't matter to either of them. He called her Frawncis Mrs. Kelly, and he gave us daily reports on her welfare. He loved the myna bird that spoke with a clipped British accent. For a number of mornings that followed, Ben greeted us with a high-pitched "Good mohning my dahling!"

Mom got a lot accomplished in the villa during those first few months of school. Every day, it seemed we came home to a new closet or shelves or draperies. It finally began to feel like a home rather than some grand, empty palace. Dad built stairs up to the flat roof where we looked at stars and the desert and Tripoli through Tony's telescope. He made screens for the windows to keep Ben from falling out when he sat on the wide windowsills to watch the desert. This was a very good idea because Mindy grew to be a climber of the primate persuasion. During naptime one afternoon while Mom was working in the kitchen, Mindy escaped from her crib and crawled out of the house through the veranda door. After a frantic search, Mom found her perched twenty feet up on the villa roof, sitting silently like a little Buddha with curls.

Just before the Thanksgiving holiday, mornings blew a chilly prelude to the mild Sahara winter. Several hours after Tony, Ben and I had left for school, one of our neighbours, who had a short-wave radio, pounded at the front doors. She'd received a message from her husband at the office that a wall had collapsed at Ben's preschool. Mom asked her to get a message to Dad's office as she fastened Mindy into the stroller. She threw on her raspberry coat and started down the road at a jog.

The late morning was still crisp and clear, and the road was populated only by a few pedestrian men and a herd of slowly plodding camels. Mom avoided meeting the eyes of the men, but she could not prevent Mindy from waving her chubby hands and chirping, "Ciao, ciao," to them as she passed their unfriendly glowers. The collapsed wall turned out to be the rear garden wall that fell in an area where the children did not play. The garden was destroyed but nobody had been hurt. Ben was already gone; his teacher told Mom that Dad had just been there to take him home, unaware that Mom was on her way. Mom turned around and started home on a wave of relief.

There was no need to rush on the way back to the villa. She took her time and enjoyed Mindy's golden curls bouncing ahead of her in the stroller as the baby looked one way and then the other and babbled in her little singsong voice. Gradually, other voices invaded the song of the baby from behind. Low voices, Arabic vernacular but with inflections that are universally understood as lewd and threatening and insulting. Mindy stopped chattering and turned around in her stroller to see who was talking. Mom did not turn around. She gently turned Mindy's head forward and pushed the stroller a little faster. The voices became louder and bounced off the back of her mixed with harsh laughter. Still Mom did not turn around. She scanned the road ahead of her, looking for any friendly face, someone who might provide a deterrent to the voices that followed her. Only dark, glaring men walked the road before her. Not one of them would offer to help a white woman who showed her ankles and her hair and pushed a baby on a man's road.

A stone struck the coat on Mom's back, not hard enough to hurt but with a force that meant business. Mom turned around, still pushing the stroller forward. A group of six or seven men were following not ten feet behind her. They seemed amused at her frightened face. One of them yelled angrily and they tossed obscenities, gyrating their hips and describing sick gestures in the air with their hands. Mom turned around and faced forward. She dared not run with the stroller because she knew the men would chase her.

Another stone struck her with more force, and another and another. A shower of rocks came, hitting her coat, her head, her legs. She bent over the stroller to protect Mindy's golden head. Mindy continued to babble and watched curiously as rocks clanged against the metal frame of the stroller and whizzed past her curls. Another half mile to the villa. Just a few more minutes. The rocks hurt Mom's head but she didn't dare reach up to check for blood. Keep walking. Keep walking. Don't trip. Don't hurt my baby. The sunshine glittered in the baby's hair and clashed with the black fear of the morning.

A voice rose angrily above the terrible yelling behind her. An imperious voice, and the rocks stopped flying. The young men scattered, muttering and hurling a few last insults. Mom turned around to see a small, ancient man in a cart drawn by a donkey. He shouted at the young men and gestured arthritically for them to be gone. The young men obeyed. The elderly gentleman guided his donkey to stand next to Mom and the stroller. He didn't look at her. He merely switched the donkey into motion when Mom began walking again. He rode at her side all the way back to the villa. Neither of them spoke, and the man never even glanced in her direction. Mindy was silent as she watched him.

When they reached the villa, Mom found her voice to thank the man in the cart. "Shokran," she said quietly as she stopped at the corner of the villa. He didn't acknowledge her or check the pace of his donkey. The old gentleman continued down the road, clucking to his beast. Mom stood in the sand for a long time and watched him disappear into the dusty distance. Then she went into the house with Mindy where she took off her coat and gave Ben a great big hug.

⇜ Plains Wild Indigo ⇝

Flowering period principally May into June on gravelly and rocky sites. Plants break off at ground level and are tumbled by the wind, aiding seed dispersal.

Self, Portrait: Child

It is winter in South Dakota,
the icy air prickles her nostrils.
The child has tucked under her coat
the copy of *Wuthering Heights*
some kind woman has offered.
She stumbles on the front walk.
Her voice is too loud, the older cousin
reminds her to hush. When she opens
the door, she can see them all waiting—
solemn faces and chairs, Aunt Annie's black hat,
the strange minister, the coffin shut tight.
The dark pressing down.

JOANNE MCCARTHY

The Watering Tank

Do you remember —
we were seventeen,
stood on the dock,
dove off
into the dark hole
of the watering tank,
not knowing
what unseen fears
we might meet
below the surface?

When I need
to be brave
about death now,
I think of it like that:
you and I
standing on the edge,
hands joined,
leaping
together.

BARBARA SANDERS

Long Before the Window Light Dies

Maybe this is how it is before horses die.

She remembers her grandmother after the stroke —
Shut the blinds, all of them at 3 p.m. —
block out the night before rolling tight in a sheet —
the hot house, windows closed in summer.

So at 7 p.m., she shuts her blinds,
louvers up
to keep the light
from bending down.
She can feel the earth
pass her on Highway 2,
maybe catch a child's voice in dusk
outside her window.

TAMMY TRUCKS

Silent Protest

Looking for the kind of solitude
the Platte River provides,
the neighbors buy up all the land to the west,
dragging with them
yellow dozers, McCullough chainsaws
and a white picket fence.
They clear cottonwoods, hackberry, and elms
dreaming rezoning
and roads carved to the bank
where they will plant duck blinds
for hungry hunting clubs.

So when the moon calls me quick,
I slip through the trees
that know me well,
strip off my clothes and wade across
to islands shorn
and squat in their blinds
relieving myself

of any further protest.

TERRY SCHIFFERNS

Living In Larry's House

My neighbors see my house lights on late
across the fields. I've got drapes, but never
draw them. The blacktop's two miles away.
When Larry died, I bought this farm cheap,
moved here alone, and figured Larry'd died
a victim of our customs. Out here sometimes
a family picks one boy to do its chores
and never sends him to school. That boy ends up
as Larry did, an old bachelor, mad
in a rotting house after his mother died.
He scared the neighbors, driving the rutted roads
too fast, killing their dogs and cats. The chores
are no problem here: I haul water,
beat the woodchucks gnawing through the floor,
can tomatoes. But nights are trouble. I keep
a glass of sipping liquor near and stare
from my ex-husband's photo to
that deep band of red on the horizon
when all the life that's going to stir
is making its last move.

MONICA BARRON

Canyon del Muerto

In a trip into Canyon del Muerto we gather at the rim of Canyon
de Chelly. I drive to Antonito & follow the narrow gauge
railroad over Chama Pass into New Mexico. In Chama, I have
enchiladas & green chile with iced tea in a chipped plastic glass
in mid-afternoon. The café is dark & 2 old men holler a
conversation into the kitchen. I spend a long time alone with my
chipped glass. The cook brings the fresh enchiladas to the table
herself. After crossing the Jicarilla Apache reservation, we
meet on the rim, then descend into the canyon. Navajo women with
skirts pulled up wade the creek that runs the bottom. My first
glimpse of petroglyphs is through hands waving back & forth
across my face by a swamp thick with mosquitos. In my notebook I
record the trip into the canyon, the pages wet with river water.
Each morning from my tall blue tent I go down to the river with
soap & washcloth, wash my face, arms, & bloody pubic hair. We
leave the apple & peach orchard where my blue tent stands alone
against the cornfield that runs the edge of the steep black
streaked canyon walls, the Canyon del Muerto, where so many
Navajos died when Kit Carson came for them for the long march.
Farm implements & a tractor that is hard to start line the
cutouts at the base, out of the mist & rain that run down from
the rim. We climb high across several ridges to untouched ruins.
Ancient corncobs are piled high in a trash heap. Not even the
birds have taken them away. There is a black and white pot on
the ground, all the pieces fallen around the center where food
was stored. I can feel the space the pot has taken all these
years in the ruin, like its own kiva where voices sing. The rim
I could not cross, the ledge I was afraid of, it is all there in
the broken pot fallen away from itself that stands alone in the
sun.

Kyle Laws

Leave Me Alone

I had worn that
stupid bandana over
my face day and night.
But still the dust came in.
The coarse brown powder
whistled down the chimney
covering food faster
than you could eat it,
laying like a scum
on the nearly empty water pail.
So I boarded up the chimney
and lit a fire in
the soup kettle to cook on.
But still the dust came in.
I stuffed rags into the cracks
'round the windows and doors
then taped them tight.
But still the dust came in.
It sifted under the back door
(left un-taped for access
to the out-house
and to the barn to feed
what animals had not
already choked on the dust,
their eyes and nostrils filled
with it).
So I
brought in all the water
I could get from the well
and the only scrawny hen
that was left out of forty —
in hopes of an egg or two —
and sealed off the back door, too.
And still the dust came in.
I sat in the oak rocker
that came with us from Ohio
in the middle of the floor
and waited —
for the dust to stop
or waited —
for it to cover me, too.

And that's where they found me
when finally some neighbors
ventured out to see
how everyone else fared.
And more dust came in
when they took the boards
from the fireplace
and the doors
to make my coffin,
sealing it tight
in hopes of keeping
the dust from coming in.
They laid me in
the churchyard
beside my babies.
But still the dust came in —
the wind tearing at
the fresh turned soil,
churning it
across the plains
to torment someone else.
And more dust came in
to settle over me.

CHARLENE NEELY

Yom Kippur 5750

Dedicated to Rabbi Jules Harlow. Inspired by and derived from his compilation of the Mahzor for Rosh Hashanah and Yom Kippur

My sons' Jewish legacy
like the Dead Sea Scrolls
crumbles. I, the clay jar,
ridged with wheals, crack
from discomfort of difference.
The Aramaic letters my
forefathers used tumble
like autumn leaves.

My blue-eyed blonde sons
the sacrificial bullock
dare not see honeycomb
in the lion's jaw.

I lead them
from eons of curled
caftaned rabbis, from
the test of Isaac's
Binding, the Covenant
of Jacob, Isaac and Abraham.

On this day of Atonement
my head droops like a bulrush
my heart's dressed
in sackcloth and ashes.
I read, God is slow to anger
ready to forgive.

Still, I steer my sons
away from Bialik's
bellies slashed
men hung after death
like geese along a rafter
Minna's son suckling
at her dead breast
bodies bulldozed
into limepits.

On what wind shall
my sons reach, touch
the ash that was
their Zeida's hand?

MIRIAM BEN-YAACOV

Summertime

Bob, my neighbor, mows a bit then stops,
walks the few feet back to his open garage
where the blue nose of a sports car pokes out
like a wide-eyed turtle. "Robbie," he says, "I think
what you need...." His words carry or fall
as he moves in and out of the garage from one end
of the car to the other "...then re-fit the threads...
    be sure...."
His voice has reminded me of my father
and I accept its soothing tone, take
comfort in a good father's care and careful
teaching, the distant knowing of how
things work, how they come apart,
    what must be done.
I finish reading Molly Ivins on Kosovo
— her take and Vietnam reference
not untrue, but empty — objecting to bullets
    for peace.

A few more lines of Carruth's *I, I, I*
and a couple black-capped chickadees dart
to the window feeder behind my head,
    flit away instantly.
Four mottled finches twitter on the power line
fifteen feet from the house. All in a row
their slender bodies like thumbs up
turn this way and that. A red-headed male
soars and lights, hops in and out of the brown
chorus line. Over Vetta's yard,
a big-breasted robin puffs up his silhouette on a wire
and a flicker attaches to a high
    bare branch.

Bob's mower starts up again. Starlings
gather and scatter through the green
like phrases on the page, marks that I
read again and again and still can't
    catch the meaning.
The mower goes quiet and Bob ambles
back to the blue hood, "Should be another one
in back...like the one you did the last time...."

It is summer.
There has been rain. The world is green
and my father's work boots are worn,
his overalls faded and thin, blue sleeves
rolled to his scrubbed elbows, a Camel
two inches long deep between his fingers,
cupped hand rising from his knee, pausing
at his mouth then up over his white
bald spot to rub the back of his neck.
He looks up, out across the yard,
blows smoke.

DENISE BRADY

Calibrating Conscience

When his father, drunk and surly, struck him, and the urge to
strike back choked him, he left home and joined the navy. In
Vietnam he learned drugs and vandalism. In Vietnam he learned
stealth and dispatch.

*There would be a very disruptive effect if we entertained claims of actual innocence.
There is a need for finality in capital cases, and it would be an enormous burden to
the States if they were to retry cases based on new evidence introduced many years
later. We do not have to take every conceivable step, at whatever cost, to avoid con-
victing an innocent person.* (Justice Rehnquist)

*Don't ask if a second trial would be more reliable than the first but does the new
evidence show the result of the first trial to be sufficiently reliable for the State to
murder someone.* (Justice Blackmun)

What he learned in Vietnam he took home. It woke him in the
night and sat with him in the day. Sometimes he peddled drugs.
Sometimes he just sat. Sometimes he slept in his car.

*He is not innocent in the eyes of the law because he has been tried and found guilty.
In deciding between guilt and innocence in our system, the trial is the paramount
event.* (Justice O'Connor)

*The Eighth Amendment extends its protection even to a defendant who has been
validly convicted and sentenced.* (Justice Blackmun)

His brother had shot the policeman, but they looked too much
alike. How could witnesses tell whether the gunman was him or
his brother? He wrote a confession to protect his brother and his
brother's kids. He could not give evidence against his brother.
Who would do that? At least Vietnam hadn't killed that in him.

*If the system that has been in place for 200 years (and remains widely approved)
"shocks" the dissenters' conscience, perhaps they should doubt the calibration of their
consciences or, better still, the usefulness of "conscience-shocking" as a legal test.*
(Justice Scalia)

*I believe it contrary to any standard of decency to execute someone who is actually
innocent.* (Justice Blackmun)

His brother's son gave the evidence after his father died. Before he died, the father had taken his son's hand and said it, said maybe he was wrong to let his brother take the rap, said tell them the truth, said if the law needs to kill someone for the crime, the almighty is already doing that, said tell them don't kill my brother, tell them it's even now, tell them he did time for them, and I'll do the death part. Or do they think only they can execute someone? Ask them what kind of even the law wants.

ARTIS BERNARD

Buffalo Dreams

It was morning,
cold and damp.
Hooves beat on frozen ground.
Time had come,
my time.
Shadows arrived to retrieve me.

Homeless, hungry,
cheeks moist with salt.
Men on horseback
led me with leather
to their way of life.

Forced, I turned my back
on my Self.
I turned my face to the corn
of White profit.

Children taken from old ways tradition.
With new haircuts and clothes,
their voices stolen.

They want similarity,
an example of their decency.
They may as well ask me
to stand on a street corner
with a sign stating:
"Witness As I Sell My Soul"

They watch me,
forced to reject the mountain,
reject the river,
the sun.
They force me to embrace shadows
that will never understand
that in my dreams
buffalo run,
feathers cut through wind.
In my dreams, I am enough.
Sun guides me,
Moon lulls me,

Wind carries me on currents.
While they walk straight lines
with one eye closed.

So I sit now,
enslaved by righteousness.
Tongue has forgotten word.
Hands have forgotten touch.
But I will always dream of buffalo.

TIGERLILY ERNST

Awaiting the Bombing of Serb Forces in Bosnia and Herzegovina

Standing outside, the woman stares above,
her head leaning on the man's shoulder,
watching for the northeast meteorshower.
The tail splashes into sparkling stars —
but her neck begins to hurt, her mind dizzy.
Even with perfect eyesight stars mesh,
become falling ones if they're not.
She says good-bye to him, not having made a wish,
runs inside, away from mosquitos, away
from his last kisses, so she can be alone
to think of those who may not be so lucky
seven hours ahead, at sunrise, east of here,
looking up into the sky, seeing planes
dropping bombs, like a shower of death.

BILJANA D. OBRADOVIC

My Father Tells Me He Loved My Mother

My father stands beside a glass case
in the National Portrait Gallery,
listens through headphones to poets.
I read inscriptions

until he pushes the earpieces
toward me. I press them close
still warm from his ears,

hear Robert Creeley tell me
Be natural,
wise
as you can be,
my daughter.

I know my father
needs to say
these words to me.

I also know
he intends more:
listen

to the middle notes:
Remember
your mother,
the way you came,
the days of waiting.

I know my father means
to tell me the whole poem,
connected
through earphones
in the hub of a small room
in the heart
of the large
museum.

STEPHANIE PAINTER

Her Story

The photographs are black and white.
In a dress too dull to be anything
but brown, a watch pinned like a medal
to her flat chest, she frowns,
backed against the brick wall
of the world. It is 1938
and I can taste the fine dust of despair.
She will leave home, refusing to marry
the man her father has chosen,
and go to work. On a blind date
she will dance with my father
and say "yes." A church-bell rings
alone somewhere,
but she stays where she is.
How did she fly entirely whole
into the next photograph? Crouched
beside a greenhouse, in a white
dress with a barrette in her hair
she curves one arm around a baby
whose face flowers from the bonnet.
I find her when I look into myself.
I am her egg burst into skin and flame,
her tongue cut out at the farm.
I follow her every move
as she aches to read into my life
proof of the girl she left behind
whose mama feeds her children
on into the middle of the night.

CAROLANN RUSSELL

My Mother Never Knew

that she was pretty
Big brown eyes Black hair
Her mother came at eighteen
from Moravia Gypsies maybe
Maybe that's how come
I can tell fortunes See things
Everybody says we look alike
I shake my head She's tiny
I'm big-boned She's dark
I'm blue-eyed

But both of us worry
about money disappearing
flying off on its own wings
We'd take a key
and lock it up
My Fair Lady I want to say
Show her pictures
Pretty skin Beautiful smile
Sometimes a little cocky hat
Pretty Pretty I want to say
You were I am
We are Beauties

BARBARA SCHMITZ

Keeping My Mother Warm

I gave a down shirt: rib-knit collar, snaps,
forest green.   She says she wears it in the house.
I gave a jacket: royal blue, zipper, hood, premier
northern goose down. When she scrubbed

makeup off the collar, she bleached
the color out but she said she doesn't mind.
I gave a black cotton sweater, a jillion red roses
embroidered on the front, heavy as chain mail,

elastic in the cuffs. She said she washed it,
dried it in the dryer, said it held up
pretty well. I gave a sleek wool blend, gray
with white cables.   Perhaps it flaps

on her washline even now. Maybe it tumbles today,
cuffs over crewneck, in her dryer.
I should make her a quilt. A quilt
for the quiltmaker. Last night I slept

under a quilt she sewed: gorgeous prairie,
sea of many colors. Red velvet triangles,
yellow satin trapezoids, purple silk
parallelograms, dark shining rhombuses—

her feather stitch holding every crazy thing
together. Thanks, Mom, for that beauty.
May your loneliness go south for the winter.
May your old friends bring you cake. May you

beat them at pitch, pinochle, hearts, and gossip.
May the mail arrive early with gifts. May
hummingbirds remember where all your
windows are. May your feet be warm as

waffles, warm as buckwheat cakes, warm as
sweethearts. May your fingers limber and
bend above any patch you ever want. May all your
pies be chocolate. Love, Me. Love me. Love me. Love me.

MARJORIE SAISER

A Bird of the Shoreline
-for Elizabeth

My daughter tells me she doesn't believe in God.
Her words pour onto the supper table like milk spilling.
In measured silence
she waits for what I will say.
The evening news mumbles in the background,
dog scratching at the door.
I look out the window to September sky opening
its dark blue skirt of night. I tell her,
the Piping Plovers will be leaving soon, if they haven't
already.
Asking her, do you remember the first time we saw them
through binoculars,
on the broad sandbar near McConaughy?
You were eight or nine.
How you were the first one to spot the bird, its
pale sand color.
You knew to look for the black tail spot,
the whitish rump.
How you loved the story of their "broken-wing" act,
when Mother Piper, frightened,
pretends she is crippled, leading intruders away from the nest.
How all the way home we made its sound, *peep-lo, peep-lo,*
laughing at our silliness,
happy because we loved a new thing.
This bird, becoming more rare,
like this woman-child, eyes
gray-blue pools of shiny rain.

SHELLY CLARK

The Sixties

A huge glass peace sign
hung on the beam in our living room.
We didn't allow you to have toy guns or G. I. Joes.
Your best friend was a girl. You went fishing together,
sold lemonade on hot afternoons.
I showed you how to make origami cranes,
sent you to your room if you hit your brother.
Once, when I found you in the backyard,
staring down at a frog you'd killed,
I made you bury it and say a prayer.

Now I worry that you don't have the killer instinct.
You'll be standing on a battlefield somewhere,
and there will be that second
when you look away from the enemy
and up at the sky, at the clouds I taught you to name.

SONDRA UPHAM

Sarah's Response

Research is what she promises to do for me,
right now, immediately, she knows whom to call,
where to go, or she'll find out, I'm not to worry,
what there is to know we'll know. And soon?
I beg, far worse than any child terrified
of disappearing, held down only by the thread,
her voice, pulled through the wire at 20,000 megawinds.

She calls when she finds out the bad news and the good
to promise a package: tradition mandates gifts
to make it better. A kiss is what I want, her hand
in mine. But this is what she sends: a box.

The huge carton is heavy, cardboard walls they
let me batter until I get to what's inside
intact within a web of tape and swaying,
entire six foot stalk of brusselsprout,
a hundred knobs or more, each perfect head,
enfolded pattern. I know her message instantly.

In the world that gave us life, or takes it from me,
beauty so precise and orderly if seen by microscope,
or cell biopsy, or tissue through the light
is what divided cell from cell and made her mine,
and him and her, and you, dear reader, whose gel-filled eye
reads out this message written two years later by my pulsing hand
to honor her, my harmonious daughter far away
whose play is radiance. Let her live.

HILDA RAZ

The Bumblebee Bird

The last day of his visit, you drive
your son through mountains of magpie,
juniper and lupine when a black and gold bird,
scarlet-capped, signals you to stop.
You could become roadkill, hopping
from the car where there's no shoulder,
on a curve sharp as the bird's colors.

But you two have known too many seasons
of depression's dark wings coming for him,
too few of following a single beauty.
And now you fear you won't see it,
that it's flitted away like too many wishes.

Suddenly, the cottonwood opens her hands,
a sorceress delighted by her own trick,
releases the bird that vanishes again
behind the scrim of leaves, reappearing now
and now and now until it seems
there is no end to hoping.

Back at the cabin you still need to find it
in your book, as though saying *western tanager*,
you'll taste again its magic colors,
and something in you will be released.
Your son sticks to the name he dubbed it.
But there is no argument between you—
only two names for that startled recognition,
for this one love.

JUDITH SORNBERGER

For My Daughter

You are from strong women who left home
and family to go into the unknown, perhaps
afraid, lonely, weeping for that left behind.
But they came.

From a great-great-great-grandmother, burying
two husbands, a son neighbors called
crippled, sleeping in a dugout on a treeless
plain. Like a mole burrowed in for safety.

You are from a great-great-grandmother bearing
14 sons, one daughter. "She delivered them herself
in the outhouse," an aunt told me. Her husband
came in from the fields to a baby in the cradle and
dinner on the table.

From a great grandmother, driving a team and
wagon loaded with furniture, a new baby on her lap,
15 miles across Dodge County in a snowstorm;
the baby was fine, but Elizabeth almost died of
pneumonia three days later.

From a great grandmother, living on the Wyoming
frontier, finding a rattlesnake under the wash tub.
With a broom, she flicked the snake out the door.

From a grandmother learning to smoke in the
blackouts of World War II Hungary. "We liked
to watch the red tips glow as we talked in the
dark," she said.

From another grandmother married at seventeen,
parent of three by twenty; no running water, no
electricity, no indoor plumbing; a farmer's
wife, her place in the kitchen.

You are from a mother who learned lessons late in
life; seventeen years of marriage a harsh teacher;
scrambling for money, for time; wondering if
one lifetime will be enough.

CAROL MACDANIELS

Daily Grace

"This is a wonderful image of God, no? I think we are neither in the raw cotton or the thread, but in the twirling."
Michael Siefert

It is in the padding of your daughter's feet
down the hallway after lights out. In her hand trailing
the foot of your bed, in her whisper, "You forgot
to give me good dreams." It is in the contraction
    of muscles you use to sit up, to rub

your hands all over her head, catching curls and
snarls in your fingers. You pull out the bad dreams, roll
them into a ball, toss them into the trash. It is in the moment
when there's room for good dreams only and no bad,
    in the moment when you whisper

a whirring, whispery sound that becomes only a few
real words. Words like "friends," words like "play," like
"chocolate," "rainbows," and "laughter." It is in the kiss
from Cupid lips, the quick turn of her tight body skipping
    back to her own bed, packed full of good dreams.

It is in your son at the breakfast table
making you read his favorite comics in just
the right order. In him saying, "Get it?" after you read each
one. It is in you asking him to wait when he begins
    to leave. It is in his waiting. It is in that whirring,

whispery almost-sound that passes between you. It is
in the bones of his hands when he gives you the sculpture
he made in art class. And in your smile, because you get it.
It is in the quick kiss in the vicinity of the lips,
    in the sunlight that shines on his dark brown hair

as he runs for the school bus, in your daughter's
small hand waving. *Good bye! Good bye!* And it shines
    oh it shines like the wild love you feel for them.

KAREN GETTERT SHOEMAKER

Ashes

I. Gap

Lapsed, she used to say.

Fallen, I'd reply
Retired, recovering

as her mouth clamped down
on an unchristian anger.

II. Truce

As I remember it now
we'd stopped fighting about the Church
before she was sick.
If this is false memory, I welcome it
and will not seek the truth.

As I choose to remember it
I'd stopped the baiting
long before she noticed
though the habit would flare when we discussed
a wedding or baptism or Christmas

she'd suddenly bite back
at something I hadn't said
or had said years ago and
sometimes it was hard to
calm her down.

III. Wind

I was moving the day we got the results
a very hot May Day
car loaded with boxes
and freaked-out housecats
but I waited for the call
with my brothers and sisters.

We sipped on bubbling raspberry water
ate up all the sugar in the house
watched children run from door to door
with baskets made from wallpaper
newspaper, white paper doilies
spilling out flowers and innocent treats.
Children know nothing, really, of May Day
of celebrating the Mother
and how holy she becomes
when she's about to go.

IV. Party

The year of her dying, I drove back to town
and took her to Mass every Sunday.

Sometimes we'd get wild
go to the Russians
where a handsome young priest
sang Mass in a baffling tongue
or to the rebel Latin church
like and not like what I remember and we
tried not to giggle under borrowed altar veils.

In February, the Polish church threw a Polka Mass
and nothing could keep her away
though it almost did.

V. Pain

This is where I learned
the bones in my mother's hand
and how not to wave goodbye.

VI. The Sacrifice We Do Not Choose to Make

By the time Ash Wednesday rolled around
she couldn't leave the house.

I went to that Mass alone
unreconciled and hungry.
In the crowded back pew I made a decision
to give nothing up
proved it with a pound of bridge mix
driving home through the dark March night
window down, radio blaring

forehead crossed with my
bitter burnt offering.

MAUREEN HALLIGAN TOBIN

Tulips for Michael

My son inherited
my love for gardening.
Though it's been six
years, and two moves,
he remembers picking
June strawberries
with me, dropping them
one by one into the red plastic cup
I knew would fit
his three-year-old hand,
remembers how we'd eat them
straight from the bed,
squinting against sunlight.

This week he asked if geraniums
were in garden shops yet.
Every year we plant them
in the cinder block
wall. Last spring
I gave him pots
and money for his own flowers.

In fall, we planted tulips—
50 new bulbs,
and Michael worried them through
a long winter.

When it snowed
three days last week,
they'd been ready to bloom,
but were beaten to the ground.

The snow will melt
and water them, Mom.
Such optimism
not from my gene pool.

But this morning, three
red tulips have opened
wide in the sun, and the others
are about to.

KAREN FIELDS

Discount

When a child cries
in Wal-mart,
I always wish
I'd gone to walk in woods.
I'd sit beside a tree,
a cottonwood, perhaps
(they like us).

And I could watch
the shifting leaves
make whispers
as they turn again
like schools of fish
that sail beneath
the surface of the water:
this way,
that,
their undulating rhythm
soothing rifts,
establishing connection.

I always cringe
at Wal-mart
and wait for angry words
from frazzled parents,
fret about the ways we widen
accumulated family chasms.

GAIL JOHNSON SUDMAN

The Black Velvet Horse

for Me and My Mother

I don't remember what you
stuffed it with, but do recall
the cloth left over from my lace-
collared dress, and the twig hooves
we chose in the backyard that summer
deep in the shadowy cave of the elm.

It was one of our few times together
(I wanted a horse so bad)
in those years of sickness and
babies and diapers.

I wanted a horse so bad you said you'd
make me one, carefully stitching
the doe-skin velvet, looping and tying,
looping and tying the white yarn mane,
snipping the shock of tail, fitting
in hooves, the knots of the twigs
forming perfect fetlocks.

I wanted a horse so bad, but
there was nowhere to ride, nowhere .
to feed, nowhere to tether. I rode
through the yard on the whip of the wind,
my hair a wild mane, legs green
in the gallop, the whinnying shrill
in my nose and my ears.

And now that I'm tamed and you're dead,
this black velvet horse with raveling
forelock cocks his head
almost as if he knows
who galloped off with those years.

IMOGENE BOLLS

Myrtle

What if she'd been happy?
What if she had drawn the sleeping child?
Myrt-dear she was called
her prized firstborn son
heard his father call her
"Myrt-dear"
so this was the name for
the gentle sweet-scented woman

"Myrt-dear" stuck
through all the rest of her life
a life intermittently and continually
held distant in a clear dry martini
later in more refined wine glasses

What if she'd been happy?
what if I pretend she was?
what would I remember
instead of shouting
arguments
sodden face
by day so pleasant and nice?

What if she'd sketched scenes
she newly saw each time
they tore her roots and moved?
what if the living portrait in oils
of the man she followed
from port to port
had been but one of many works?

What if she had claimed time?
drawing painting
grasping life
what if Grace had watched the littlest one
while she with sketch book and charcoal
captured raucous sliding gulls over spiky
harbor in front of new quarters?
What if somber pastel eucalyptus trees
and gray ocean breaking on rock
had been just two

in a full portfolio of art?

What if being Myrt-dear were less important
than being …

Myrtle?

EILEEN DURGIN-CLINCHARD

tradition

for amoreena

your new diploma blowing down a highway,
eighteen
you fly away
without warning
or thanks for the wings
unfurled and glistening behind you.

when you arrive at your destination
a blonde blue-eyed bad dream
you call collect
say you didn't want me to worry.
this is our family tradition
three generations of daughters
slipping out at night
so as not to disturb mothers.
i say, if he ever has you against a wall
remember there's a door in it.
you call me no matter what time
i'll get you out.

after we disconnect
i do what my mother always does
i take down the atlas
trace the blue and red roads to bullhead, arizona
my new arteries and veins.

JOSEPHINE JONES

Monday, Snow

Through glass in the living room,
where the view is flat sky tangled with limbs,
songbirds crowd the feeder.

I perch on the sofa's back watching
with two granddaughters, wide-eyed,
attentive, like cats, all eyes and ears.

Though they are young, the girls know
these birds mostly by name, most of them black:
red-winged, starling, grackle.

The birds bunch and jump in the cold weather
as if uncertain of their next meal,
cackling for survival, while

the girls chortle and point,
all arms and legs.   They're growing at a pace
swifter than I can comprehend.

I recall my mother telling of
her youth, so many mouths to feed it meant
some nights going to bed hungry.

The blackbirds flap-rise in an abrupt swirl
as if to thrill this small audience: shrieking,
falling back over the cushions.

Cardinals dart in for a meal, sparrows, too —
Harris and white-crowned — snow a steady
reminder of an indifferent world.

O my sweet ones, these are matters of life and
death, aren't they. I wish for you what all my mothers
wished: for air, for wings.

TWYLA HANSEN

Second Chance

She remembers his eyes
that day in February
when he left for boot camp
dull, lifeless, like the eyes
of street people

How can it be she wonders
that someone so far gone
can come back
as if from the dead?

Six weeks later
those same eyes sparkling
his face animated, clad in his navy blues
taking in his commanding officer's every word
even his eyebrows at attention!

ARDISS CEDERHOLM

How We Met

I drove out to town's edge
to walk the sun down.
Parking on gravel near two pale ponies,
I kicked rocks and scuffed my shoes for
a quarter mile maybe, chewing big pulls of air.
Pressed my back to the roadside ground,
watching pine against cloud against sky.
The sky over the field darkened
as I moved in the soft light towards the car.

You pulled up
with cans of dusty grain
and talked guardlessly to the horses,
nickering their names.
My presence bobbed their heads; they pranced.
I didn't mean to startle your horses, I said.

We talked,
noted the appearing stars,
shared what little we knew of them
and agreed that stars twinkle, planets don't.

As the horses vied for feed
I told you about
the buried, cave-in feeling
(when ceilings threaten to collapse
and the air in the house is thick paste)
that only walking roads like these relieves.
You said you lost your only son
and nothing has relieved you since.

Twice we moved to go
but talked longer;
about the ponies' loose winter coats;
their soft and shameless faces.
You showed me which one your boy loved best
before girls and cars turned his head.

The mare, she let me
spread my fingers through her loosening coat,
quivering under them like something incomplete.

Tonight at home I thought more of you,
whether you too turned our talk over in your palms
and wished a little we'd talked longer.
Still with your horses' names on my breath,
the deep smell of their warm necks on my hand
I checked my own sleeping young ones,
nickering their names.
One stirred, I blew softly to her.

A part of me walks your field tonight
with the horses lit now by moon,
roots the ground for overlooked grain
and startled, shies back
from the twinkling apparition
of your son in full gallop
across the hardened ground.

KELLY MADIGAN ERLANDSON

The Circle Dance

The great circle dance at the September powwow
is about to begin but
this family has lost a child
over the summer and the grief must be combed
from their hair before they can enter
the circle. The mother walks the grasses
to the west side of the circle. The father
walks the grasses, then the other children,
then the aunts and uncles of this family
who has lost one of its children to accident
over the summer. They stand just outside
the circle, and the old people come with

finger combs and begin running them through
the hair of the family, combing the grief
from the mother, the father, each sister and brother,
aunts and uncles, combing out the grief
like snarls, casting out grief
in tangles. On the north side of the circle,
my scalp tingles. It is grief caught
in my own hair, and I must comb it out
if I am to join the circle. I, too, use my fingers
as a comb, pushing the hair up from the head
and away so the grief can loosen.
This combing takes some time,

and the family begins to cry and the old people,
too, begin to cry, and I on my side of the circle
begin to cry. Tears and grief spill
over my shoulders and run down my legs.
Tears and grief spill over their shoulders
and run down their legs.
The earth receives it as rain, takes it in
as if it were her own because it is her own.
From it she has already begun to fashion
new children to send to us. We
bow to the wisdom of the old people,
enter the circle that we may dance.

MARY K. STILLWELL

Spring Coming

but still a long way off,
and on some highway
a line of cars, headlights shining
in the bright daylight.
We two, talking—
when we saw him last
how we never would have thought it
he so young, and then the children.

All the way from St. Paul
remembering
the priest, the joy in his eyes, that smile—
but he a man of arms stretched wide
and maybe he knows.

You said how it might be like birth:
the fear, some pain, then separation,
but oh, the world!

Then turning the corner
to the old dirt road,
and on either side of us,
horses
running back and forth
from trees to lane to fence,
manes and tails like wings of cloud,
running for the unhaltered joy of sky
and grass
and muscles moving.

That long slow drive
and at the end,
sweet Lord, the horses!

LUCY ADKINS

Yearning

Patsy coveted that stump, liked the way it roiled
and twisted and threatened
to burst from its wooden frame.
Wouldn't it be pretty in front of the house
she asked Jake. *Won't you go get that for me?*

Jake guffawed and went out to the feed the cows.

Patsy shifted her inflamed foot on the couch
and sold some Avon.
All the gals understood.

In a land of red dirt and scrub brush, everyone
built a rock garden: rose quartz, pink agate, petrified wood
plucked from dry creekbeds and nestled
among swirls of driftwood.

Her boy Craig mashed his tan Stetson
on his head and went outside. Patsy saw him roll
out of the yard on the tractor and float up the ridge.

He returned in the hot midday,
churning through a sea of grasshoppers and dust,
the stump pitching on a chain behind. He deposited it at the edge
of the lawn—not where she wanted
but who'd move it now?—and headed for the barn.

At home in Patsy's yard, the stump coils
like a stranded sea serpent,
surrounded by petunias.

AMBER DAHLIN

What This Means, Being Cottonwood

Stand near the river with your feet
slightly apart. Push your toes down
beyond the mud, below the water.
Stretch arms and head back
deliberately, until straight lines
no longer matter—until the sky
from any angle is your desire.
Let the skin go grey and split open.
If you die a little somewhere
the wind will carve the branches back
into an alphabet
someone will try to remember
how to read. Stay this way
half a century or more, turning leaves
in the half-note tides of the air.
Inside, with that blood so slow
no one hears it, set buds for spring
by each late October.
November, December, dream what it means
being owl...or star.

KATHLEEN CAIN

Owl Sound

How I would gather it,
whole armloads, from under the trees,
carry it home by the basketful.
Soft owl sound,
still slightly moist
and fallen like feathers.
How I would hug it close,
pick up the rhythm,
the rise and the fall
of the breath that intoned it,
get it to hum again
in the core of my spirit.
I would tie it in bunches
with bright ribbons,
arrange it in nosegays
throughout the house,
wrap the kind solace
of owl sound around me.
Day and night what is sylvan
inside me would listen
to the round, hollow lyric,
and even in sleep
my hand would reach out
for the feel of it.

MARILYN DORF

Sumac Scattering Like Bones

When a sheepdog goes off alone to die,
do you suppose he believes his survivors won't suffer?

Maybe the dog and all pets comprehend their presence.
The message in their eyes and tails—almost human—

commands us; their primary flaws lean to excessiveness
and unquestioning loyalty.

Mostly, he was all hair and wagging. Even when he heaved
blood throughout the basement, we couldn't bring ourselves.

He chose the fern bed, cool and damp, where for years he'd
dug and trampled. Where mosquitoes could do nothing more.

We buried him beneath sumacs. Cinnamon ferns,
true to their ancient spores, unfurled again from loam.

Each fall the backyard, having flamed, drops its leaves.
All winter from inside the house we gaze out over ribs.

TWYLA HANSEN

Dirt

MARILYN KRYSL

Dirt. As a kid I liked its soft, powdery feel between my toes, and the way you could dust things with it—earth's talcum. Summer days I wandered my grandparents' wheat farm, tossing up small tornados of dust in the corral, sitting and sifting this fine stuff through my fingers. Stunned by heat those long afternoons, I stirred water into a pan of dirt. Magical, this mixing of two elements. So unlike each other, dirt and water, they became together a third thing, new creation. Stirring suggested food, and the combine's flat lengths of tin looked like cookie sheets. I laid out my delectables and left them, baking.

Dirt and water: this was the primal goo, the basic material of the universe. One day I mixed up a pan of mud and made Adam and Eve. Arms, legs, hair. She had breasts, he had a penis. I remembered though that they were innocent, they couldn't see each other's nakedness. So I gave them no eyes. Their mouths cried out in the wilderness of dark. I mixed up a pan of brownies.

I fed my creations, and while they ate I began the long contemplation. The Bible said dirt was what people were made of. *From dust thou comest, to dust though shalt return.* Everybody came originally from dirt, I thought. Every *thing* came from it. Dirt was everywhere, it was what the earth itself was made of. It made sense that everything came from this substance. Dirt was precious stuff, our basic material. Elemental, magical. Dirt was not dirty, it was a sacred powder. I began to construct a philosophy of dirt.

Dirt was sacred stuff, the earth was sacred ground. Holy. I piled dirt in a cracked blue willow bowl, set it on top of a box, lit a candle beside it. I knelt before this altar, murmured devotional incantations. The air agreed with my procedures. Water running underground seconded my motions. I had made a shrine, I held services. At the close I stood and sang *America The Beautiful.*

Digging graves was all right. It was right to bury the dead, it was fitting to put them back where they'd come from. I understood that leaves and dead people decayed, these things returned to the elements. When my Adam and Eve began to crumble, I scooped out a hole and laid them in, covered them. I stood over this funeral a long time with the hose, watering. I thought how Adam and Eve were losing themselves, becoming ground.

Gardening too seemed a permissible way to work the earth. Fat worms drilled their passageways through topsoil, giving the roots of plants an airing. Loosening the top of the ground with a spade seemed to let the earth breathe. When I turned earth over with a trowel and crumbled it in my fingers, it fluffed up. You could tell dirt liked being handled. Handling would feel to the earth the way it felt to me, like the good roughness of my grandmother's hand rubbing my back.

I had doubts about tractors though. They made a terrible noise and their blades sliced. These brutally clean cuts weren't the same as my digging. I thought this was an important distinction. It seemed important because I thought the ground could feel what we did to it. Dirt felt my hands in it. It liked being handled, as I like being hugged and held. On hot days it liked my mixing it with cool water. I talked to dirt, told it stories and sang it songs, stories and songs, those things I like so well myself. *Do unto others as you would have them do unto you.* I tried not to hurt beetles, I was good to grass. It seemed self-evident that we owed the ground every consideration.

I was not in favor of building dams, and I didn't approve of oil well drilling either. The dynamiting of perfectly good hillsides upset me. I didn't think men driving bulldozers should smash down fine stands of wild grass and weeds, leaving behind the imprint of tire treads. "Why are they doing that?" I asked my grandmother. "They're just building a road," she'd say. Did we need another road? How many roads did it take to get from one place to another? One, I thought, was plenty.

Stories of the Gold Rush made the miners sound like men gone mad with greed. But even before I heard those stories I felt uneasy about mining. I didn't like to imagine picks hacking away at a mountain side. Hacking rock seemed brutal. It hurt the mountainside. The rock could feel it. Rock was sentient, not quite in the same way animals and plants were sentient, but in its own way, rock's way.

I felt in the features of the landscape a resonance. Earth's electromagnetic web? I felt vibration. I was a sounding body for the Schumann resonance. I stood amidst the trilling presence of my surroundings. I stood amidst a field, like the field around a magnet. I was alive amidst myriad live presence. I registered the sentience of lakes, hillsides. And I worried. We were hurting things, I thought. I worried about the sensitivity of leaf, hollow and stone.

My grandparents had a mulberry tree and on good days I climbed this tree and looked out across distance. I swayed on my branch like a girl at the top of a mast, and I thought I could see the curvature of the earth. I could feel it, way out there, starting to curve down. Anything that big had it's own plan, I thought. It wouldn't do to try to move things around on the globe as if they were furniture. Let things just lie there the way they are, I thought. If the earth wanted to move things, it could make an earthquake or a volcano or a flood. If the earth made a cave of the winds or cut out a channel for a river, it knew what it was doing. Those things were earth's business, I thought. Let earth do those things. Who were we to interfere?

There was nothing to do with these feelings of mine. No one I knew shared them. Eventually I learned not to voice them. I worked to tear myself from these feelings, I tore myself away and was torn. But at the time, in my solitary moments, I registered earth's irritation and wondered. When no one was watching I held a rock to my ear and listened, calling the universe for news. And sometimes I knelt and laid my ear against the ground. I heard, far down, a grumbling, like thunder in the distance, but round, a spherical grumbling, vast in its dimensions, a sound as large as earth itself. It was, I thought, the moan of a creatureous thing, the audible irritation of a great being. I'd been right, I thought. We shouldn't be bothering dirt with bulldozer and dynamite. Like anyone, the earth needed soothing. We ought to be patting and smoothing, watering and blanketing. We ought to be talking to and singing to the reassuring our ground.

I did not know, as a child, the true extent to which the earth had reason for irritation. I mixed dirt and water and did not know about the Trinity test, about Hiroshima and Nagasaki, about testing of the hydrogen bomb in the Marshall islands. I did not know of these events, but I heard and took note of the earth's muttering. Now I think what I had then was a wonderfully irrational wisdom. Ancient people felt metals had a life of their own, like animals. Stone was the concentrated power of earth. Precious stones were frozen nectar, the life force crystallized. Thales, a Greek physicist, believed chunks of amber were alive. Native Americans know mountains are living beings, wind caves are the mountains' lungs. They breathe; this breath can be recorded. We have measured the breath of caves at the base of the San Francisco peaks in Arizona. They inhale and exhale at 30 mph in six-hour cycles. Smohalla the Dreamer said, "The white man tells me *plow the ground*. Shall I take a knife and tear my mother's breast? The white man tells me *quarry stone*. Shall I dig beneath her skin for bones?" Claude Kuwanijuma, a Hopi, said, "The stones remember. If you know how to listen they will tell you many things."

In my lifetime physicists have been among those listening. Physicists have been listening to rocks, and what they hear is what Claud Kuwanijuma heard. Listening to parts, they hear the whole. They hear the whole, David Bohm's *that-which-is*. Physics has noticed that the basic bits of the universe are not truly particulate. What is going on in and around us is not the still presence of chunks of inanimate matter, but a process. As Gary Zukhov writes in *The Dancing Wu Li Masters*, the basic "unit" of the universe is an event. And events in one place mesh with all the other events in all the other places. As John Archibald Wheeler declared at the 1981 Nobel Conference, this universe is a participatory universe. And we are in it, alive amidst liveness. We're alive, and here we go, here we have been going. What there is that whole, that-which-is. Whether we like it or not, we are of the whole. We are bound into each other and into the world. This universe is a matrix of sentience.

Playing rock telephone, it seems, wasn't so silly after all. My notion that dirt liked watering on hot days was a notion wiser than I knew. I lacked knowledge, but I had wisdom. I was paying attention or, as Buddhism teaches, being mindful, not with a child's arbitrary fantasy, but in an important, vital way. I was paying attention to what went on in me and around me. The elements were like me—I was of them. The elements and I were made from the same stuff. Waterfall and volcano, parrot and pickerel were like me, I was like them. And I could deduce from the way I felt how fine dirt felt getting sprinkled, how well grass liked being left alone to flourish. How birds fluffed up with well-being when they were sung to, how crickets and beetles profited from storytelling. And how the trunk and branches of the mulberry tree appreciated bodily contact as much as I did. How light needed our prayerful attention. How darkness rested in our sleep.

Our lives depend on such attending. Not attending can hurt us. What we know now is how little we know, we who prided ourselves on being realistic. We held up reality as an absolute, the final arbiter. We imagined we knew, pretty much, what reality was. Now we know that our ignorance is vast and dangerous. We don't know where and when to touch or not to touch. "Look—see that flame? The stove is hot." We know about as much as the child who hears his mother say this for the first time.

Knowing we are ignorant may be useful. There is knowledge and there is wisdom. We are ignorant but we may still be wise. Ignorant, we become cautious. Ignorance transforms us into watchers, listeners. We sift dirt through our fingers, feel its texture, become attentive. What will constitute wise attendance?

There is doing and there is being. Wise attendance is wise being. It is more than disinterested observation, as we are more than recorders, collectors of data. We are part of the data. We are sentient creatures, of the mesh, of the whole, that-which-is. In a very special, important way we are what we attend. When we hurt what only seems to be outside us, we hurt ourselves. In the most vital way imaginable, we are not disinterested but interested.

Sentient beings, we wander the earth, drink the water, eat the fruit, sit on the ground. Knowledge of our ignorance brings us down to ground level. Ground level is human level, sentient level. There are no microscopes at ground level, human level. There are no instruments. Sitting in the dirt, without instruments, we begin to see.

We see mite and sprout, feel heat and light. We hear wind and water. We pick up handfuls of dirt, we begin to wonder. Sentient, we notice we're here, in and of the universe. From this perspective, everything is as important as everything else. Sitting in the dirt, we are at last in a position to become philosophers. Finally we understand deforestation hurts the forest, the granite upthrust registers the blast.

I would mix again some dirt, some water. I would fashion another Eve, another Adam. I would give them genitals again, those necessary parts. But this time I would also give them eyes. Let them sit on the ground and gaze at each other. They compare, they notice the differences between them. And they notice as well the similarities. Both have hair, both have legs, arms, fingers, faces. A nose, a mouth. Ears. And those eyes.

When they have looked their fill at each other they notice where they are. They notice the earth beneath them. Eve picks up a handful of dirt, feels it. Adam picks up a rock, puts it to his ear. Eve's fingers register the texture of dirt, its fineness. In sunlight the dirt looks bright. Suddenly, a sound Was that a sound, over there where the leaves moved? Eve pokes Adam. He takes the rock from his ear, looks where she's pointing. Leaves. A bird?

Sunlight, a breeze, insects, flowering shrubs, grasses. These things are a felt field. There is something in the air, an animation, an expectancy. The clearing where they sit has a life of its own, their own.

They look around, they listen. Now Adam too picks up a handful of dirt. There's something here, he thinks, something it seems important to notice. He pours his handful of dirt into Eve's hand. They examine this dirt, they notice in it some quickening energy. Isn't it bright, this dirt, and alive inside its texture. They feel the life stuff sparking in it as they sift it through their fingers. They begin to notice they are not alone.

Plain Scared, or: There is No Such Thing as Negative Space, the Art Teacher Said

S.L. WISENBERG

In a college art class I learned that negative space was the nothing behind the figure you were looking at. But years later another teacher told me that this was not so. There is always something there, he said. If you look, you will see it.

Kenophobia is the fear of empty rooms. Fear of empty places. Agoraphobia is the fear of open places. But it is not the agora, the market-place, that frightens me. I am not afraid to leave the house. I am afraid to leave the city. To be more precise—to venture from the SMSA.

I live on the North Side of Chicago. I find the word "kenophobia" in a book in the main library of Evanston. About twenty years ago, I lived in a dorm room in Evanston. The room was empty when I arrived and empty when I left. I remember one June I kept a university library book almost until the minute the taxi came to take me to the airport. I wanted to keep, as long as possible, some connection with the place I was leaving empty.

I am afraid of being erased. One night in a lover's apartment, after he told me he didn't want to see me any more, I left this note in his desk: I was here. I was once a part of your life. He has since moved to San Francisco. I do not know what became of the desk.

We are all afraid of being erased. Our names in water writ. Of the earth disappearing. We are small and the night looms.

The night ends. The prairie goes on forever. A sameness, for the unini-tiated, the way all the seasons in Miami seem alike to newcomers. I am uninitiated.

We all fear the blank page, the blank mind dry of thought.

In and around Chicago, experts are replanting the prairie. I think this involves both public and private funds. I like reading about such things. I don't mind walking through these prairies if they are small and surrounded by city. It's the big areas I don't like; I don't like to hike. I like to walk through cities, looking in store windows.

I grew up in Texas, came to the Midwest at 18. I grew up with ranch houses and sidewalks. I loved taking the bus downtown and walking among abandoned railroad cars, buying old records in a shabby pawnshop. I'd eat lunch at Woolworth's and buy make-up at Neiman-Marcus.

In my 20s I moved from Illinois to Iowa to Florida back to Illinois. In Iowa I liked the pale green bowls of hills along the highway. I admired them from behind the windows of cars. The hills looked like paintings. In Miami in the newspaper office where I worked, we worshipped the sun from afar.

During particularly dramatic sunsets, we reporters would stand near our desks, looking through the windows closest to us, facing west, waiting, watching.

My only forays into nature are very tame—residencies at artists' colonies. I have to pack along piles of little white tablets made of cortisone. When my asthma's bad I take the pills for eight or nine days in a row. I'm allergic to nature. Ragweed, grasses, mold, spores, hay, milkweed—things I can name and things I can't name.

The first artists' colony I went to had once been Edna St. Vincent Millay's retreat a few hours from Manhattan—strawberry farm, hills, pond, trees. At Millay, I learned what foxglove was, and phlox, learned how to spot jack-in-the-pulpit and ladyslipper, all veins and sex. The colony's assistant director told me about a New York artist who had come to the colony and had walked around the grounds a while. Then he'd fled inside and reported that he'd seen an animal. What was it? she'd asked. He didn't know. He couldn't tell whether it was a squirrel or a deer. During my residency, there were two painters who gushed over the landscape. They tried to match the colors of nature with the colors of paint. Cerulean Blue? they would ask each other, pointing at the sky. Havannah Lake?

It is land. It is only land.

The assistant told me that the pioneers from the East feared the flat open land of the West. For some of them, the horizon was too large. They couldn't see themselves in it. They were diminished. Some Easterners returned. Some carved themselves into the Western landscape.

I am not from the East but I understand those Easterners. I don't like limitless horizons. I don't embrace endless fields. I like nature with borders.

The plains scare me.

I am plain scared.

I am terrified of the universe that has no end. I am afraid to step behind the curtain, ask, What is the system behind this solar system? And behind that.

There is no negative space, only positive space having a bad day.

Franz Kafka was born in a city and was buried there. In 1912 he wrote: Ever since childhood, there have been times when I was almost unhappy about my inability to appreciate flowers. This seems to be related in some way to my inability to appreciate music.

I like flowers. A flowerbed is not the same as a field. Which life depends on. Wildlands are beautiful, they say. They must be saved. There is music in the prairie, they say.

Kafka is less foreign to me than Wendell Berry. I feel closer to Mikhail Zoshchenko's Moscow of the bureaucratic 1920s, than Larry McMurtry's Texas.

I find myself inside books by writers who write in fast, urgent sentences with no time for landscape. Writers of closeup conversations—internal and external—writers of the life of streets, cafes, stores, restaurants. Writers who rent. But there are others, so many others; I am not always curled up with my own kind. But I skip the parts, all the parts, about nature.

When I was younger, my friends and I would find books with sex in them. We would read those parts aloud, skip everything else.

Therefore, nature is the opposite of sex.

I know two women in Western Michigan who like to read farm novels. One of them has tiny plastic cows and horses super-glued to her dashboard. I don't think I've ever read a farm novel, though I imagine myself finding pleasure in following the slow quiet rhythms of crops pushing their way skyward, in descriptions of the dirt and sweat and dampness of stables, the lowing and groaning. Pure, sweet tiredness after you latch the door, blow out the lantern.

I was at the late Kroch's and Brentano's bookstore on South Wabash Avenue in Chicago. A street with the same name as a river, believed to be taken from the Miami Indian word for "gleaming white." At the bookstore I picked up a book, *A River Runs Through It*. Originally a sleeper of a book reissued, glamorized by Hollywood. It is my friend K.'s favorite book. I never talk to K. any more because he met his ex-girlfriend through me. Somehow that is a problem though we were never lovers. These are the sorts of things I write about—things that happen indoors. I like K.'s writing, respect his judgment. But I didn't buy the book. I was afraid I would not enter it, afraid of some flatness of surface, nothing to hold onto. Like being afraid to enter into a conversation with a person who has a difficult accent or an unfathomable expression; scratch and scratch and still there may be nothing there. (But so many other people liked the book. K. loved it, and he's from Manhattan. He likes to fish.)

Or like being afraid of sex, afraid to enter its raw territory, afraid I will find myself in the middle of it, not want to be there, and feel alone, terribly alone, too aware of my surroundings.

Many years ago I had an internship in Downstate Illinois at the Quincy Herald-Whig. I made friends with a young reporter there from a smaller town. She told me, All cities are alike. She didn't see the point in going to more than one of them.

I use free address labels from the Sierra Club and Nature Conservancy. I am not a member. Over the years I've joined the National Trust for Historic Preservation and the Chicago Architecture Foundation. I used to love the before and after spreads in magazines on restored opera houses, movie theaters saved from the wrecking ball and transformed into quaint shopping malls. I loved reading about the resurrection of inner cities, led by young urban pioneers, before "yuppie" was a bad word, or maybe even a word at all.

In Chicago once I met a lawyer who worked for the National Trust. Soul mate, I thought. She said, I'm really an environmentalist, I don't really have a feeling for architecture. I was appalled. This was hard for me to understand. I told her over and over: You must see the Victorian Gothic apartments at Chicago and Wabash. The building is in danger. It is beautiful. It must be saved.

They say you'll see everybody you know if you stand long enough at the corner of State and Madison. I see Louis, that is all that matters. I am talking about a building. I am talking about Carson Pirie Scott designed by Louis Sullivan. The green and rust filigree ironwork. The design is inspired by organic shapes, the same energy of nature that animated Whitman. This ersatz vegetation fills my heart, the way that Sullivan's first view of a suspension bridge shook him up as a boy. An exhilaration. The same feeling I get from walking down a certain street in my neighborhood, Roscoe—the pedestrian scale of the two-flats and three-flats, the undulation of the brick fronts, the Italianate eyebrows on windows, decorative carvings on graystones—the way someone must react to the undulations of corn, clouds, furrows.

Or the straight vastness of the Great Plains with their wheat, earth, sand, clay—whatever is on them, in them.

I liked *Charlotte's Web* — and it appears to have been a farm novel. I fear the Other.

I am afraid nothing is out there but God and landscape, and he doesn't exist and land can't talk. I don't know the language of it.

I like crowded civic and political events during which everyone believes something important is happening.

We city folks go to therapy.

We fantasize about strangers on the El.

We fool ourselves into thinking we have a shared destination. We fool ourselves into thinking we don't.

This is the secret, the secret I have always known: that the bare open plain is my heart itself, my heart without connection; that the bare cinder block room is my soul, my soul without connection—the place I fear I will end up when the fear of loss of connection overrides everything else.

I long to receive this benediction: May you see that something is always there, have hope for the heart to rise up for, come to a feeling of settlement, find a light way of walking on the earth.

Spring Shows Up at the Crooked Heart

CONSTANCE BROWN

WEDNESDAY. 4:59 a.m. The first cattle truck of the season pulls into the yards at Crooked Heart Ranch, engine growling, 119 calves aboard. Wind has sheared off the snow from the gravel drive and the ground is frozen enough to bring the truck right to the corral gate. Yellow caution lights outline the Silver Star three-axle pot-bellied trailer as it backs up to the loading chute that Bob has set up. Silhouetted by the headlamps of his Ford F250 pickup, my husband directs the driver with hand signals. The cattle truck's aluminum siding is clean of manure, and the young steers, brought down ten hours from Billings on a midnight ride, are calm and dry. They bawl softly, tired. Feet moving in the compartments sound like hail falling on a tin roof. Ping, slap, ping. Dressed in Key coveralls and manure-covered mud boots, the trucker opens the back door onto the chute and begins pushing yearlings out with gentle prods and hissing sounds.

Notepad and pencil in hand at the ramp, collar turned up, I begin my job. I count as each compartment in the belly of the whale is emptied: 17 calves in the first wave, 18, 15, 18, 15, 13, another 13, then 10. Black calves, red calves, black and white brockel faces, a lone gray Charolais. No limps, no weepy eyes—good. They move quietly down the chute—reminding me of kindergartners on their first day of school—and into the dark corral, then up the alleyway to a loafing barn and small pasture where they'll stay for a few days to settle in.

The night sky is turning from black to navy blue as dawn approaches, and a raw breeze coming from the creek bed below the corrals chills my face. Bob and the young trucker exchange small talk, brand inspection papers, and load weights. These "light calves" were born a year ago. Their average weight is 505 pounds. Now, as yearlings they're ready to put on another 300-400 pounds grazing our rangeland this summer.

The yellow light shining from the kitchen window guides me as I return to the house to put on more coffee and breakfast bacon. We moved right into the tiny bungalow farmhouse a few years ago when we brought a small herd of cows up from Colorado to this 1910 homestead ranch on the high plains of eastern Wyoming. Soon enough we discovered winters here to be fierce, with ten-foot drifts closing the barnyards, not a good place for a year-round operation. So we sold the mama cows and now run a seasonal grazing business, pasturing stocker cattle on hearty rangeland.

6:10 a.m. Back in the corrals after breakfast, Bob and I open the gate from the creek paddock behind the barn, letting in our four horses confined out of the way during the cattle delivery. The sun rising over the eastern hillside shines down onto the round-bale hay feeder like a laser, melting frost from the feeder's sides in silver drops. The horses snort steam, nosing at feed pellets in their rubber pans. Two pairs of quacking mallards streak down the streambed to the duck pond, beginning their morning reconnaissance. On the hill south of the barnyard, the yearlings have already broken through an electric fence and come down into the lee of the loafing barn and are sleeping with bellies full of hay, protected from the south wind.

8:37 a.m. Tom and Ed from the Natural Resources Conservation Service office in Lusk pull up to the farmhouse in a federal-issue blue Ford Ranger. In the kitchen, we drink coffee and sample my "black banana" bread while we wait for Gerald, a bulldozer operator driving over from Douglas. We talk about last week's fire at the Mule Creek Junction cafe.

"The whole place was gone in two hours," says Ed, who's a volunteer fire fighter.

"Now there's no coffee stop between Lusk and Newcastle," says Tom.

"Glad it didn't blow up the gas tanks," says Bo.

All three of these men, like us, make their living from the land. But their connection is not as obvious as ours. Tom is the local NRCS manager, schooled in resource management. Ed works with him as the technical expert, designing land and water projects. Gerald is a ranch son who had to find another way to make a living 30 years ago when his older brother took over the family ranch. He's been digging and plowing his way across northeastern Wyoming as a one-man excavation company ever since and last summer built us up a road out of the two-track that comes into the ranch from the gravel county road. He'll build the earthen dam Ed has designed for us in a deep draw a couple of miles west. Its purpose will not be stock water, but rather "wildlife habitat enhancement." We're getting some cost-share funds for the project from the feds and Wyoming Game and Fish.

We plan to dam up one end of a spring-fed woody draw to create an acre of year-round water for wildlife. Wooded stands and draws are in short supply on the high plains of northeastern Wyoming. In our county, for instance, they make up only 12,000 of a million and one-half acres. Yet they provide critical food, shelter, and cover for both wildlife and livestock.

The March breeze kicks into a cold wind as we head out in two pickups to the piece of state land we lease along the Hat Creek Breaks. The Breaks, a western extension of Nebraska's Pine Ridge country, divides watersheds in our region: the Cheyenne River basin on its north, and the Niobrara River basin on its south. We're headed to the Cheyenne River side. No trees grow in the short-grass pastures that spread out beneath the spine of the Breaks, but scattered ponderosa and bunch junipers poke out of it. We're not discussing ecology or agriculture today; it's all engineering and dam building: emergency spillways; anti-seep collars; core trenches; backhoes and crawlers; catwalks and slant-inclined headgates; angle iron phalanges. Costs will run around $13,000. While Bob and the others relish the details, I walk deeper into the draw with our dog, Doc, seeking shelter from what is now a cold north wind. A lab-and-border-collie mix, Doc is always in motion and always in water. He heads toward the draw's boggy bottom, already showing green from meltwater seeps. Down here it's silent and still, and I hear a meadowlark singing for the first time this spring.

THURSDAY. 9:53 a.m. Another bunch of Montana cattle arrives from Miles City and Glasgow. Only sixty-two head come off the truck here; it will continue on to Torrington to disgorge the rest of the 50,000-pound load for the sale barn's auction. Two dozen of the new arrivals have horns. We'll need to cut them off, but for now they join the growing herd on the hill top corrals as Bob and I replay the familiar cattle delivery ritual: counting heads as they unload down the portable ramp, looking for visible health problems, noting how uniform sizes are, exchanging brand and weight papers with the driver, filling his coffee mug and waving him off to his next stop. The Glasgow arrivals cause us alarm. They're gaunt, lethargic with their heads down, covered in their own shit. Somebody has sent us some cull cattle, and they've been in transit for close to 24 hours as the truck picked up parts of its load—way too long to be without water. Calculating the load weights, Bob figures each one has dropped 28 pounds since entering the truck. Bob is in for a lot of extra care to get them fed up into better condition; otherwise, they'll likely catch pneumonia and die.

2:15 p.m. Three of us ride out to check on the growing herd in the holding pasture snaking west along a ridge to the south of the barnyard. We'll confine the cattle here and feed them hay until green-up in two months. In mid-May when the grass has had a chance to emerge and grow a bit, they'll begin a four-month pilgrimage back and forth through five different pastures in 1,700 acres until they leave in late September.

Bob is riding his muscular Hancock-bred Quarter horse, Snook. I'm on a graceful Arab named Cadence. Our friend, Penny, has bred and trained Cadence, but she's riding a sorrel and white paint for me, a 12-year-old we've named Grady. He arrived at the ranch last fall on a horse trade. Horse trading—buying, really—is risky business. We've now discovered that docile Grady has a serious problem. A perfect gentleman in the riding arena or with a bunch of horses like now, he's wild and dangerous when alone working cattle. Called "buddy sweet" by some and "barn sour" by others, he's fiercely herd bound. The challenge now is to ride him through the problem. That's a job I can't do. I'm not a strong rider and have managed three broken arms in the past two summers flying off bucking horses. Middle age has settled in and I can't risk another. Penny, a professional horsewoman, is diagnosing how serious Grady's problem is.

Horse and rider are out of sight behind several swells in the pasture, but Grady's shrieks and screams of fright and frustration are carried on the wind. Bob and I catch only glimpses of the pair. In a far corner where two fence rows cross, Penny is on the ground walking Grady round and round in ever-tightening circles. Then they're cantering wildly up a hill, his head up, toward clouds skimming the top. The next time we see them Penny is astride Grady, backing him up and down a gully. A good hour passes before we finally head to the barn. Grady's head is drooping but he's still worked up. As we come off the hill into the corrals, Penny again turns him around and backs him all the way in. "He won't be so anxious to come home if you back him in," she tells me.

His coat is soaked through in sweat and standing in tufts. Mouth wide and bumping on the bit, nostrils bulging, he looks like a carved wooden carousel horse.

"Don't ride him alone, Connie," she advises. "He's not safe."

"Can we work him through it?"

"It's so deep in him he may not get fixed."

"I can't have a working horse out here with those problems, Penny." What's the future to hold for Grady now, I wonder. There's a real problem.

TUESDAY. 7:10 a.m. Several more loads of steers have come to the ranch and are settling out in the holding pasture. Today six neighbors come over to help us process them. By early afternoon we've worked 350 through the squeeze chutes for shots, brands, ear tags, sorting off horned cattle and bulls to be castrated. We finish the job and mark our accomplishment with a big meal I've prepared at the house.

THURSDAY. 5:27 p.m. It's been snowing since noon and already dropped four inches, falling thicker as Dick, the Lusk vet, drives out at the end of a long day to do some doctoring on the Glasgow cattle. Horned cattle get discounted in price at the packinghouses because they don't fit in standard loading and handling equipment. These yearlings were supposed to have come to us already castrated, but some always get missed. Graupel snow pelts us at the squeeze chutes as I assist him in castrating the first calf in line. I hold up its tail, pulling it forward hard along his back while Dick grabs two testicles and snips them off. The tail hold prevents pain, he tells me, by numbing the whole area. It seems to work—not a sound or a shudder comes off the shaggy animal. We work through 22 more yearlings, doing a few more cuts but mostly lopping off horns. Dick is skinny as a rail at maybe 150 pounds, so he uses his whole body to achieve leverage against the Goliaths—one way to stay in condition.

Shrieks and groans coming from the de-horned steers have started Doc howling in the backyard, and the horses running in panic outside the corral fences. Dick allows as how this procedure does cause some pain. "It's short-lived. They'll be fine by morning." It's fast anyway. He squeezes a steer in the chute and puts a nose thong in its nostrils that's attached to a rope. I take the rope and pull it tight around the side of the chute to hold its head steady. Light is fading in the dusk so I hold a flashlight on the horn as Dick lops each one off at the skull with a double handled pruning tool. Pop! Circling his finger in the bloody stump he locates the vein and pulls it out. "Like a piece of spaghetti." Each horn cavity gets a dash of No Bleed, a caustic that looks like talcum powder, which stops the bleeding and the surgery is complete. By 7:00 p.m. he's packed up and driving home in what is now a spring blizzard.

SATURDAY. 8:03 a.m. The two-day storm has been good to us. More than a foot of snow has fallen with little wind. No tall drifts to plow through when feeding the cattle, and the moisture will melt directly into the nascent pastures for green-up. The new windbreak we planted to the west of the house will get lots of water for its conifers to send out new growth, too. Rising temperatures today will help the Glasgow calves to strengthen up. I think about how much I like young cattle, and how much we like our new life. The seasonal grazing operation suits us—there's no midnight winter calving, either. From the kitchen window I watch Bob in the British-red Massey tractor up on the hill. He's rolling out a half-ton round bale of hay for the yearlings, and they're jumping around behind the tractor like the kids they are. In the barnyard, the horses are feasting on scrap piles of hay the tractor dropped on its way past, and a dozen meadowlarks are diving into the piles too, feeding on the grass seeds within them.

Farm Auction

SUSANNE GEORGE-BLOOMFIELD

All morning the neighbors had been going in and out of the house, help-ing Dad carry the boxes of household goods into the farmyard. The screen door creaked and slammed, creaked and slammed, creaked and slammed. Long tables, borrowed from the church, had been arranged in rows from east to west and consumed the space all of the way from the chicken house to the milk shed.

Out in the lot behind the old horse barn, the farm machinery waited beside the loops of rusted barbed wire, stacks of hedge posts, and crates of tools. The pitchforks, scoop shovels, and spades, their handles polished from years of labor and linseed oil my father had religiously applied to keep them from splintering, leaned against the hay wagon like hired hands taking a noon break. Buckets of cow kickers, the old block and tackle from the hay-mow, wrenches, screwdrivers, hay hooks, and rows of faded red Butternut coffee cans brimming with assorted nuts, bolts, screws, and nails crowded the top of the wagon. I wandered among the clutter, surprised that so much had been found to sell at the auction.

I climbed up onto the metal seat of an old sickle mower that had been rusting in the weeds behind the granary for as long as I could remember and pretended that I held the lines to a team of horses, and we were cutting alfal-fa on the north forty. "Gittup, Belle! Gittup, Annie," I clucked. "Gee, now. Haa! Whoa, easy girls, whoa now," and tried to remember whether "gee" meant right or left.

Thunk. I felt a thump on my back as a clod of dirt exploded into dusty pieces around me. "Terry!" I yelled without turning around. I jumped off the mower in time to see my thirteen-year-old neighbor from across the section loping around the corner of the barn, his long, gangly legs carrying him out of range and sight. Rounding the corner in pursuit, I stopped short, for the yard had begun filling with strangers who were milling about the now-laden tables, thumbing through cookbooks, turning over plates to examine their water marks, and holding my mother's aprons and dresses against their clumsy bodies to assess the fit.

Beside my parents' dresser, chest of drawers, and mahogany headboard tilted the iron bed that my mother and I had painted coral when I finally had persuaded her to let me move into my own room, the old storage room. The coral lace curtains we had bought at the dime store draped unevenly from the top rail. I didn't even close the gate as I raced to the house, weaving in and out of the farmers and their wives until I reached the kitchen. Aunt Ruth was sweeping up the dust where the stove and refrigerator had stood, and a cir-cle of friends was consoling Grandma.

"Where's Dad?" I asked, but nobody seemed to hear.

I sprinted upstairs to my room and found it empty, except for the coral roses on the wallpaper, the ones that I had counted, cluster by cluster, row by row in the moonlight the night that my mother lay dying in the next bedroom. I heard a shuffle of steps behind me, turned, and saw my father. "My bed," I cried. "Why are we selling my bed?"

"Honey," he started.

"Tom, what do I do with these arrowheads," a voice from below said.

Dad and I looked at one another, both of us remembering our days of hunting them each spring when the frost heaved them to the surface of the fallow wheat fields. The hill east of the home place was a traditional stopover for the Sioux Indians on their return trip from the Flint Hills of Kansas. Every spring, the Indians would rest their horses on our hill and begin shaping the new stone into tools and weapons. And every spring, a hundred years later, we would walk the fields, searching for the butter-scotch-colored points.

"I'll take them," my dad replied. We walked together downstairs, and he handed them to me. "Put them in the basement, honey. We don't want to sell these, do we?"

The auctioneer arrived at noon to sell my childhood to the highest bidder. I stood, alone, beneath the old cottonwood tree where Dad had built a hitching rail for our horses. Cars and pickup trucks lined the driveway and both sides of Highway 10 in front of the house for a good quarter mile both ways. Men in stiff new overalls and women in starched aprons trampled around the yard, and children raced up and down the aisles of tables, playing with my outgrown dolls and picture books. Even though I was twelve years old, I felt an urge to object, "That's mine. Don't touch it," but I knew I couldn't. I didn't like dumb old dolls, anyway.

The auctioneer stood at the south end of the yard. I was too small to see him, but I was tall enough to hear the bid. "WhadamIgive for this fine set of dishes. Twennytwennnytwentytwenny do I hear twenny dollar?"

I felt a hand on my shoulder, and I turned to see Terry. Our parents had been best friends, and we had grown up together, survived childhood, so to speak. Now, a smile stretched between his sunburned ears, and his blue eyes said, "Follow me."

Silently, we stole out to the old cow barn in the far northeast corner of the farmstead. We were not allowed to play in that old barn, for it hadn't been used in years. Ancient cow dung, hard as cement, layered the floor, and the whole building slanted south, rafters crippled from too many Nebraska winters.

Terry strode inside and disappeared between the dimly-lit stanchions. Soon I heard the rhythmic scrape-scrape of his boots as he climbed the wooden slats into the loft, then silence. I stopped at the entrance, at the line where the shadow met the sunshine, afraid to step across. Paralyzed, all I could hear was the roar behind my eyes. Then, the cool darkness calmed me, and I stepped inside. I could see Terry through the broken boards of the ceiling as he walked carefully on the joists to a solid section at the north end of the haymow. I climbed the wall like a spider into the loft, where sunlight filtered through the untended shingles.

Terry was sitting in a pile of dusty straw beside the hayloft door with what looked like a dried chamois in his hands. As I eased myself down beside him on our little island of wood, he showed me an old rabbit pelt that he had found. Someone must have cured it in the barn and forgotten about it. He studied it intently, his dark-rimmed glasses sliding down his slender nose. I focused on him, his carefully tended crewcut, his always-too-short blue jeans, and his familiar scuffed work boots.

Abruptly, he stood up, turned the wooden stop that fastened the loft door shut, and pulled the door around to the right, its rusty hinges creaking. Our eyes squinted in the sunlight, but soon we could see for miles across the brown and green and yellow patchwork plains, the orderly roads meeting at perfect ninety-degree angles, over and over again. The white dome of the courthouse rose out of the cluster of trees that was Minden, and to the west, we could see the white silhouettes of the grain elevators at Motela, Keene, and Axtell. Then, slowly and carefully, he tore the rabbit skin in half and shared with me.

The bidding done, the cars began their snail-like procession north, growing smaller and smaller until they disappeared into the trees. We watched together in silence, each stroking our piece of fur, so stiff and sharp and soft.

Sis

DIANE-MARIE BLINN

Sometimes a person comes into your life whom you cannot comprehend. You reside in the same place and time, but carry some other place, other time inside. That gap stands between you when you speak. My mother-in-law Sis was such a person in my life.

Sis was a child of the Sandhills. She loved the treeless prairie vistas, the endless billowing wind, solitary wildness. Her father had been a real cowboy. In his youth he rode the range, knew the animals, made a living off the land. Later he sold feed cake in town, provisioned the reservation with government surplus. Her mother grew up in a small soddy her father built near the Snake River during a drought and later in another, six miles north of Valentine, Nebraska. A child of the depression, Sis counted a coyote head as one of her dollies, learned to want little and manage with less. She could make pies from molasses, transform quilting scraps into a dress for the Saturday night dance. Her mother died of a brain tumor shortly before Sis turned eighteen—the death a long time coming, and hard on them all.

The daughters reacted differently. The older girl headed East to find her fortune, but Sis fancied a local boy with a mechanical bent, full of ideas. Frank saved what he made working at Earl's Bakery so he could marry Sis, then bought a dump truck, hauled rock for the crew cutting out the Donner Pass. The truck held up long enough to make some money. He bought a second and a third, but found no drivers who understood machines like him. The more trucks he had, the less money he made. Finally he sold them, started over with a beverage franchise, went bust again.

Still and all, Sis remained full of fun and the couple found time to dance. After Pearl, Frank volunteered to go armored and Sis traveled with him to Fort Knox. She returned to Valentine pregnant. He shipped out, crossed the ocean, fought his way through France into Germany. Sis found ways to offset the worry, keep things going on her own. She taught her son Loren to read, coaxed rides out of their ailing car, learned to cook eggless cakes, wrote letters to her husband.

Frank returned when the war was over, moody and preoccupied. Kept his feelings close to his chest, sat on the porch and stared into space. He took another go at the beverage business with poor results. Sis bore a second child, Melissa. With another mouth to feed, they needed a new start, moved to a larger town on the interstate. This time it was different. Frank had a bigger market in Grand Island, a better brand. He put in long hours, was friendly, lent a helping hand to others when he could.

He paid off the loans, bought a cozy house on Elm Street. They had Oleo on the table now. Frank was loading trucks before dawn and when he finally came home, his khaki pants were stained with grease. Tired by nightfall, he hadn't much left in him for anyone else. The war was won, business going good. This should have been enough for Sis. It wasn't.

I had met Sis only once before moving to Nebraska. It was my wedding day—a second wedding, private and simple. No pictures in the New York Times, no flower girls or salmon canapés, no view over Central Park. None of this mattered to Loren. Newly returned from a second tour in 'Nam, he didn't give a rat's ass about any of the wedding details, wanted to elope instead. He made his guest list small, too small—didn't invite his mother. Loren said it would make his dad uncomfortable and she wouldn't come anyway.

I argued that since she wouldn't come, the invitation couldn't hurt. I was convincing but wrong. Sis bought a bus ticket from Nebraska to New York City, stirred up difficult memories for his dad and my husband.

"Say goodbye to your Mom" was all his white-knuckled father told him. At fifteen he wouldn't have admitted it to his buddies, but Loren was still close to her. He asked her, "Can't I come too?" Sis turned her reddened eyes away. She knew it would take a father to handle him now. She settled his little sister Melissa into a seat, stowed her suitcase. As he waited, Loren's voice acquired an edge. "Why are you doing this?" he asked. Sis tried to gain some semblance of composure before looking his direction. When she turned back he was already walking away. He didn't look back. Sis didn't call after him.

His dad got drunk that night, too hurt and embarrassed to explain. Loren heard the next morning how his mom had been fooling around with some guy and his dad found them out. He cut school, stopping home only long enough to throw his thirty-ought-six into the trunk of the car and drove after them. Loren laid an ambush, waiting for the stranger who had destroyed his family, sure he'd show. But at sunset he still hadn't.

The principal reported Loren missing by second period. Frank came out of shock enough to know the boy was in trouble, but not what kind. It was Sis's brother who figured it out. He checked for the boy's gun, took off for Valentine without telling anyone. The uncle found the boy, told him the lounge lizard had already fled, convinced Loren he'd best come back.

In the Army, Loren learned to buffer the emotional drain of family with physical distance. So after we married, it came as no surprise that my new husband applied to an international company. By the time we were ready for a child, we were living overseas—Sao Paulo, Panama City, Hong Kong. We moved on the average of every eighteen months for twelve years. A convergence of events brought us back. The company planned to close its Asia-Pacific office. Loren's dad decided to remarry and said it was now or never for taking over his business. Our son, Andy, was ready to start school.

I wasn't sure peddling pop on the prairie was for me, but Loren convinced me to view Grand Island, Nebraska as my latest foreign post. He worked long hours, didn't come home till the last truck was in, often eight or nine o'clock. He needed to learn the routes, prove himself to the drivers, help his Dad make a graceful exit. All at once. He swallowed a lot of Maalox.

For me, there were new relatives: father-in-law and wife, cousins with kids and mother-in-law. Sis was living in Grand Island too. She had not fared well in the trailer park after her second husband left. A neighbor called Loren's sister, told her to take her mother away, dry her out. Melissa did. Then she found Sis a place to live where she wouldn't be isolated: a tall building just around the corner from my son's new school.

The hallway smelled of old-fashioned cooking—meat and potatoes, cabbage, fruit pies. Andy broom-broomed his Hot Wheels along the grab rails. Sis watched from her door, short hair peppered with gray, skin leathery from the sun. She led her grandson across a faded carpet to a well-worn sofa facing a T.V. still left on. A metal ashtray piled high with butts sat atop an end table. The coffee table had been cleared of *Reader's Digests*. Two shoeboxes of photographs sat on it now.

Sis squatted at Andy's side, waved me toward a lounger, footrest already extended. "Have a seat, hun," she said. Then her attention returned to her grandson. "Don't tell your dad I showed you this," she whispered in his ear, pulling out a naked baby picture. Their heads touched as the two of them giggled. "Look Mommy," Andy said, "here's Daddy in a cowboy suit!" Sis told him how Gramps had given Loren a .22 when he was eight. Her hands were nervous, working a stray curl, a cigarette. I watched her twirl the cowlick on the back of Andy's head, so like his father's, and tried to imagine abandoning my son, losing my family. I couldn't.

From Sis we learned how Loren climbed up a bear's cage, circling round the opening atop, running faster and faster; how he and his buddy set the garage on fire when they filled a rocket full of powder and launched a mouse. Her stories were funny but also made me uneasy, displayed an inclination to danger I disavowed. Sis also taught Andy how to play Scrabble.

The only "deluxe" thing in her apartment, her edition featured a turntable and wooden letters that clicked against each other in their velvet sack. Andy was more interested in turning the board upside down and examining the mechanism that made it spin than in spelling words.

We got busy in our new life, stopped visiting Sis so often. As our visits became rarer, shorter, Sis began to ask for favors. What she asked was little enough: pick up her milk, drive her to the doctor's. But when her cough became persistent and she was sick to her stomach a lot, I spoke to her physician myself. Sis had emphysema but was still smoking. Her liver was pretty far gone from cirrhosis. She was suffering from malnutrition too.

I confronted Loren, expecting he would do something about her. But he only explained how he felt about Sis. She had been a good mom when he was little, but after she left everything went bad between them. Even when he was in 'Nam getting shot at, she complained to him long distance. He had decided that she was a tar baby. "Once you touch a tar baby, you get stuck," he warned me. "And the harder you try to get away, the more stuck you get. Best to keep your distance."

The last time I saw Sis was a bitter cold day. I gave her my gloves to wear to the supermarket. Sis appreciated the way they cut the wind chill, but assured me she "couldn't possibly" keep them. I added comfort food to her meager shopping cart; treated her to saltines, soup, Jell-O, ginger ale. I carried the sacks upstairs for her, made a cup of tea as she tucked herself under a crocheted afghan to watch T.V. "Call you soon," I said as I left. "I'll be fine, hun," she replied. "Don't you worry about me. I'll be just fine."

We both lied. Sis's neighbor knocked one morning before I'd called again. Came back at noon and called the super when Sis didn't answer. He opened the door with the passkey, found her on the bathroom floor.

Loren went over himself to clear things out. He was surprised how little time it took to pack her possessions. Surprised how hard it hit him. He sent the pictures to his sister, saved the Scrabble set for Andy, took a cookbook for me, yellowed, spattered with stains, interleaved with recipes torn out of Family Circle.

One thing Loren couldn't account for: a nice pair of binoculars on her windowsill. He inquired from the neighbor whether they might be borrowed, found out Sis had bought them to see the playground behind the school. She'd learned the recess schedule, knew when Andy was out, watched him from the window climbing the monkey bars, sitting alone on the swing, playing chase with a friend. She had followed her grandson's comings and goings, silently, from afar. As Loren told me this, he bit his lip.

At the funeral home, I stared at Sis's childhood picture displayed among moss roses. Attendance at her service was sparse, her friends far away or long gone. Someone needed to say a few words in eulogy. Sis had no church, no minister, and her own family was at a loss. I couldn't say I knew her, but I gathered my thoughts: Sis left her grandchildren a legacy that was neither obvious nor tangible—a fierce spirit of independence, pride in the prairie roots of their family, a knowledge of hard times, the desire not to take advantage of someone else . . . and finally the lesson that none of us can truly read or judge the heart of another.

Then I stood up to speak.

Feathers

DENISE LOW

Great Blue Heron

When my sons were ten and eleven, we canoed a muddy reservoir filled with crayfish. Above, flocks of river gulls chattered, and we marveled at blue herons in the distance, lords of that waterway. But the great wading fishers are leery of people, and if they spot a human within a quarter mile, they rise on prehistoric wings, make a clattering alarm, and disappear, perhaps folding sidewise into the clouds themselves. They are enormous, with wing spans of six feet, and their feathers are a luminous charcoal-blue. They could be ghosts from the past or angels of the future.

We had just startled one such heron as we paddled across a small bay and watched it fly beyond reach. My son called out to stop the boat, and he pulled a huge blue feather from the water's surface, unmarred by the element water. Fresh oils kept it dry. The bird effervesced into lake ripples years ago, but a token of its reality remained.

I kept the feather in my office at Haskell Indian Nations University, the Native American college where I teach, for some months. One student in particular asked about it, but then she appeared to lose interest when she found it was a heron's plume. The Native American Church uses water fowl in its imagery, and I have heard of both an egret or a goose as part of this, their tradition, but not a heron. Some Great Lakes tribes have crane clans, but I do not know of a heron clan. Through the years I have not seen pow-wow regalia made of heron feathers.

Some months later I noticed, like the elusive heron itself, the memento of that afternoon excursion had vanished, but I remember its shade of fog blue. I recall that moment of grace within cold choppy waves and tedium of oars, when the natural world opened itself for a brief encounter. Perhaps it was a random occurrence, a statistical intersection of so many canoes and so many herons crossing paths, and one particular lake and one long summer's afternoon. Or could it have been more: a sign, the landscape in dialogue with an observant young boy.

Red-Tailed Hawk

A second feather fell from the sky years before, when I was about ten, in the Flint Hills of Kansas. I was playing with friends—girls and boys mingled together at that age and in that place one hot summer, and the sun beat down in pure yellow shafts of light. The west wind fanned the heat across our faces: sun and air were greater forces than parents or church or any other authority. I looked up and saw a hawk for the first time, and friends told me it was a "chicken hawk," a folk term for red-tailed hawks. It circled above us, riding the updrafts of air for hours, it seemed. The hawk navigated a great height, and it gave my child's mind a new scale of measure. Where the sky had been an undifferentiated mass of blue, now I saw the range of a hawk's flight.

Then I looked down and in the grass found a speckled feather, as though it had been laid out for me. It was the largest feather I had ever seen, as long as my arm, newly dropped and in perfect condition. Ridges of brown herringbone designs mottled the tawny background. I do not recall carrying the feather home, though I must have, and I must have put it in my room. All I remember is that moment of recognition, of truly possessing it by bringing it into consciousness and never forgetting it.

The hawk population of Kansas has increased the last ten or twenty years, and I see the birds every winter, roosting along roadways. Last week, a late winter afternoon, I saw a large female with a long strand of bluestem straw in her beak, flying in front of my car, left to right, which, according to some people, is lucky.

Hawks continue as a quiet presence throughout my life, directional points on the outdoor ceiling, like gargoyles come to life, distant but still part of the same realm. Conversely, the great raptors must sense me as slow, hot flesh ambling about far below, on the basement of their world.

Years ago an Osage friend gave me a red-tailed hawk feather that had been blessed. It was as though the feather of my childhood had returned. Though this individual feather may disappear again, another, in some form, will take its place.

Owl

This winter two owls lived in our neighborhood, and when we walked by their roost, they hooted a particular call, not an alarm, but the same regular sequence of hoots. When we were at a greater distance, the owls were silent, and I came to believe that perhaps the owls—the male tenor and the brighter female voice—called out to my familiar lump in its range of vision, neither food nor danger, but just a familiar creature every nightfall, in that particular hunting ground. One of my birder friends said this was indeed possible. I wrote about our connection:

This winter a great horned owl roosts on the neighborhood water tower. My husband does not speak of it because he thinks I might have superstitions about owls, like Appalachian people. I do not speak of it because night birds might be bad signs for his Menominee people.

The giant bird calls out in the night when I walk the dog. It seems to recognize me. Its echoing tenor mixes with wind in the trees. Sometimes I wake up and hear its voice beyond my roof and feel that darkness has a kind voice.

One February evening my husband and I walk together. Its hoot-hoots penetrate surrounding trees and houses. The dog knows its voice and keeps trotting, fur unruffled. And at once we both talk about owls, how far they can see. When it rises, its open wings become another name for "night."

Weeks later, as the maple tree flowers with knobby red buds, I hear only silence from the air above.

The sound of hooting became commonplace, until one evening the next fall I realized I had not heard from the neighbors above for quite a while.

The eerie silence was worse. It reminded me of the one time the owl flew near me. It was twilight and I was in the back yard watching fire flies for a few minutes before going inside. A black hue swept across my field of vision and was as suddenly gone. There was absolute silence, not even a whoosh. This was the silent killer who reaches into rabbit dens and mice holes in the patio rocks. This is the angel of death.

Goose

I cannot explain how, when a friend was dying of breast cancer, she began to dream of geese.

She was city bred and had never noticed geese before. At the next hospital visit in Kansas City, deep into the urban neighborhood, she looked up and saw geese flying above the building. At her next doctor's appointment in Lawrence, Kansas, she looked up and again saw geese above that hospital. The dreams continued. She and the birds did a minuet, tracing parallel promenades above and below, conscious and unconscious, through the final months of her illness. Sometimes they were in dreams and sometimes actual winging vees over the hospital. The realities interchanged.

I do not know why this happened, but the geese, distant specks in the sky, entered her vision, both night and day. Their visitations eased her suffering.

Geese mate for life. Geese move between wind and water; north and south; spring and fall. Perhaps they also move, in the same loose wedges, between life and death.

Eagle

Many times feathers have not fallen from the sky into my hands, and often people have died alone. I have canoed through reeds along the river without seeing herons or wood ducks or mallards. But then some piece of the usual world shifts, and I become aware that I share the same magical rain and wind and sun with other species. None of us understand why we are in this universe of gravity and moisture and finite edges.

My most recent moment with such awareness came at a shopping mall. This urban market has one-way windows and overlooks the Kaw (Kansas) River, about fifty miles above the confluence with the Missouri River.

210

Eagles roost along the dam every winter, during zero weather when water is frozen farther to the north. Environmentalists fought the mall construction and lost, but they insisted upon no foot traffic during eagle season as well as installation of one-way glass. Ironically, the store hallways have become the best place to see eagles for miles around. The eagles seem to survive their new situation, since more of them come to the dam than ever before. Last night I saw my hometown eagles featured on a Kansas City news channel, with dizzy footage of the feathered acrobats.

The University of Kansas, on a hog-back ridge at the edge of the Kaw River floodplain, is the site of a research museum that saved eagles. During the 1950s the pesticide DDT permeated the surrounding fields and runoff. Researchers found eagles ate so much of the bad fish the eggshells became too thin, and the fledglings broke their shells too early and died. In the 1960s, I never saw eagles. In the 1970s I bundled my children in snowsuits and drove them twenty miles up river to view a few distant winter eagles. After the poison was banned, the population began to increase, so now eagles are off the endangered species list. They have become regular migrants downtown, and several couples nest in the nearby reservoir. They are now urban eagles, like "urban Indians," indigenous people who live in the cities and retain their identity.

One cold, cold Sunday afternoon I walked into a mall staircase, over-looking the sandbar and dam, and there on a tree, inches away through the glass, hunched an enormous eagle. I was inside the human cage, and it sat in the open. The bird examined the gushing water, which sometimes carries stray fish. It was like a small, tough man or woman—even with wings folded, the bird fit a human scale. Up close, the bony structure beneath the feathers impressed me most, the finely wrought architecture, the amazing house—body, as finely constructed as a turtle and its shell melded to spine. The animal wore its flying machine attached to its torso, as if it were an Icarus who flew to the sun and transformed into this state. Its face was fierce in concentration.

As I watched, the great bird spotted a carp on the ice and glided, full-winged, no longer like any human, or like anything else but an American bald eagle, filling the sky.

I still see the focus of its eyes.

⇌ Scarlet Globe Mallow ⇌

Throughout the Great Plains in dry soils. Dakota
medicine men chewed the plant into a paste
which they rubbed over their hands and arms,
making them immune to the effect of scalding
water.

Memory Thefts and Transplants

PAMELA CARTER JOERN

The girl joins her father to watch the Nebraska sunset. His right elbow is crooked, his arm resting on the corral fence. She moves to his left side, squeezes between him and Jack, an old black dog. She centers her gaze between the split rails of the fence. Slides her fingers into his palm. His large and rough hand folds around hers. She turns her head to look at him. He tongues a matchstick from one corner of his mouth to the other without touching it with his hands. His skin glows like a new penny. His overalls pockets carry Juicy Fruit gum, her favorite, a pocket knife to remove splinters, a brown leather coin purse with a gold snap-clasp. His wire-rimmed glasses sparkle in the sun's slanted rays. The pith helmet on his head sits like a lampshade, the crown soiled with sweat. She can stand on the steel-hardened toes of his workboots, laced with long and square-edged sinews of cowhide, while he dances her around a room. Now, they do not speak. She turns her head in the twilight. Together, they watch the sky.

Like my father, Isaac Newton must have spent a lot of time looking at the sky. He was a lackluster student at Cambridge University. The classics didn't interest him. Alchemy, emerging theories of mechanical science, and biblical prophets did. He floated on a path of sunlight from an open casement window to an unmade cot in the corner of his room. Out of that observation, he designed his most famous experiment involving two sheets of paper with pin holes and two prisms, proving that white light is dispersed into homogenous colors. Even that might not have happened had fate not intervened. The plague forced the shut-down of the university for two years, and Newton retired to a solitary laboratory in the small village where he grew up. At the age of 20, Newton trusted his vision of the sky, the relationship of moons and planets in elliptical orbit, and he developed his laws of motion.

Everything that seems at rest stays at rest; everything that seems in motion stays in motion—unless acted upon by an outside force. See how he finds a loophole. Laws he is writing, intractable and pervasive, but something warns him. Some star flickers in an inexplicable way, some shaft of light bends in an unexpected direction, and Newton, in his private laboratory provided by the intervention of the plague, adds the qualifier: seems.

I wonder now when I first became aware of the hedge of seems. When did I first suspect that things are not necessarily what they appear to be? The earth looks flat, but isn't. Caterpillars look destined to die as fat hairy worms, but don't. My hand looks solid, but is instead a mass of quivering atoms.

Marriages I thought were stable have busted up. People in the prime of health drop dead of heart attacks. Failures turn out to be stepping stones. Dreams fade once the hand closes on them.

Once, when I was four or five or six, I awoke thirsty on Christmas Eve. I stepped into the small living room of our home, startling my father who scurried out from behind the Christmas tree. The room was draped in electrical cord and triangulated by three silver-coned movie lights. Dad filmed every Christmas morning with an 8mm camera, the forerunner of the modern video camera. No sound, but moving pictures. Designed for outdoor use, the camera required elaborate lighting to film indoors. Dad rigged the whole apparatus every year to film movies that turned out more or less identical, except the kids grew older. Mom always got a purse. I always got a doll. My brothers unwrapped cowboy gear and cars and trucks. Miraculously, year after year, we all seem surprised.

On that Christmas Eve, I was not surprised to find my father stringing movie lights. Nor did I believe in Santa Claus. Yet, when I asked Dad what he was doing, he said his back hurt and he was lying under a heat lamp. "Can I lie down with you?" I asked. So Dad rotated one of the movie lights on its tripod, and he and I laid down under it. I remember looking up at the bright light, the sun captured on a stick, and nestling into my dad's shoulder, where I must have fallen asleep and he carried me back to bed. All these years later, I still cannot understand why my dad told me that particular lie. Whose innocence was he protecting, his or mine?

My father's life is lost in the hedge of seems. My memories of my father have been replaced by gleaned fragments of knowledge. Later experiences, overheard snatches of conversation, impressions from other people, knowledge I have uncovered like a spy on a mission has given me a more complex picture of my father, but it has robbed me of my memories. I remember how I remembered him, but the memories no longer seem true.

Here's a moment that I seem to remember, but I don't know if it happened. I am three years old, and my family is Christmas shopping. We are in Scottsbluff, a town 25 miles west of our house in the country. We don't own our house. It's intended for migrant workers. We have electricity, but no running water. Our address is rural route #1, and the town we are attached to is a small town on the North Platte River in the panhandle of Nebraska. Scottsbluff, this big town, has stoplights and a Montgomery Ward store and a Sears. Snow falls in lazy lacy hunks. The clusters sting my cheeks and tickle my tongue. Colored bulbs stretch kitty-cornered across the intersection. A plastic reindeer rides the corner post. The light turns green, and Dad bends over and scoops me up in his arms. He's wearing his town hat, and his neck smells of after shave. I turn my face into the warmth above his collar. I look over his shoulder at other kids, the lights, the snow, the fake Santa ringing a bell with paper poppies bleeding in his hand, and I stretch my hand like a queen to her subjects.

While Newton gazed at the sky, he must have encountered the wandering stars. He watched out his open casement window and observed that certain stars appeared to travel backward, a little slip, a momentary zigzag in the wrong direction. Newton would have known this was an optical illusion. Newton would have listed this phenomenon in his category of seems. Newton would have explained it to a younger cousin or a later student in his classroom as a mirage created when the earth catches up to another planet against a backdrop of distant stars.

Newton's knowledge of the wandering stars did not prevent him from making a few zags of his own. He suffered throughout his life from fatigue and depression, possible symptoms of chronic mercury poisoning contracted from three decades of alchemical research. Like other alchemists, Newton was determined to isolate the philosopher's stone. Not a stone at all, but a liquid hatched in a beaker called the philosopher's egg, this elixir of life, when poured out like miracle syrup, would transform any common substance to purest gold, infinite wealth. Newton, like other alchemists, was not so concerned with the gold product. He wanted to harness the miracle of transformation, to understand the mysteries of birth, death, and life. Like other alchemists, he was doomed to disappointment. He chased an illusion, no more tangible than the ghostly zag of a wandering star.

My earliest memories of my father have fallen away from me like a distant echo. When I was eight, my dad went through a transformation none of us would ever understand. One day the father I knew went away, and some other man showed up in his place. This man's mouth twisted, and his voice got big. My mother said, "Dad's not himself," and I believed her. I was afraid of the stranger who was my father.

One bad morning I wake up early. I sleep in a crib in the corner of my parents' bedroom. I'm too big for a crib, but there's no other space for me in this house. I sleep with my back to the wall because the scary monster that lives under their bed comes out at night and haunts the space between their bed and my crib. A Sunday School plaque hangs on the wall above the crib. Tan with white carved words, Jesus loves me. Mom's green plastic jewel box sits atop Grandma's old dresser, along with a tiny wooden chest. Inside the chest are locks of baby hair wrapped in wax paper, mine and my two older brothers'. Clothes hang on a rod that juts from the back of the door. There's just room enough for Dad to stand at the foot of the bed and take off his overalls. He hangs them on a hook on the wall. This bad morning, I hear noises. Light streaks under the drawn window shade. My dad is sitting up in bed, and he is hitting my mother. His face is twisted and mean. She is turned over his knee. He hits her with his flat hand, more than once, he hits her. I remember it now in slow motion, his hand moving through the air as big as the wing of an airplane. I cannot see myself in the picture, but I hear my mother crying. I cannot see myself because I have shrunk into something small and prickly and ugly. I cannot see myself because I do not move to help her. I cannot see myself for a very long time.

My father's slide into mental illness lasted only a brief period in my family's history. For my mother, it was a temporary detour, hardly consequential against the larger orbit of their life together. For me, it was a defining period of my childhood. Perhaps two years after this episode, after other violent outbursts, after many paranoid accusations against my mother, after desperate jaunts to various doctors around the region, my father seemed to trade his emotional unrest for physical deterioration. His hands shook; his feet shuffled. He remained passive and gentle unless he tried to handle the pressures of a job, when he would again become restive and accusatory. Eventually, he didn't work, and my mother took up the burden of support. When I was sixteen, Dad was diagnosed with Parkinson's Disease. Almost nine years had passed since his episodes of violence, and we never knew whether they were related to his declining physical health. He died a week before my thirtieth birthday.

When my mother, my brothers and I try to talk about Dad, we sound as if we are four separate skygazers expounding theories on a wandering star. My mother claims that Dad was a strong and wonderful man who got sick. My oldest brother, faced with the model of a non-working father, shrugs and says, He was a hippie before his time. My brother, the middle child who shares my mother's practicality and resented the hardships Dad's limitations imposed on her, declares that Dad was a stubborn son-of-a-bitch when he was living and a stubborn son-of-a-bitch the day he died. I, the youngest, the only daughter, the one who rode high in his arms like a queen and then awoke to witness his madness, cannot find a definitive answer. I am undone by the unsolved mysteries of transformation. I observe his trajectory across my life, and I cannot distinguish the true path from the phantom zag.

Newton must have watched the sky out his open casement window, the ordinary sun and stars, the planets and the moon. He studied the constellations, and let the winged bow of Orion carry him farther and farther out into speculations beyond his immediate sphere of observation. Beyond the then-known world of science. He looked at the sky and imagined a bold theory of the universe. He must have known that it could all blow up in his face.

When I approach the past, I am in danger of spontaneous combustion.

My mother would like to perform a memory transplant on me, cauterize the gashing wounds and replace them with sweet dreams. She interprets my resistance to a happy childhood as an act of deliberate defiance, and she takes it personally. I want to help her out. I want to be a good daughter. But like Newton, my vision of the sky is all I have.

I have had to readjust my memories of my father as I have accumulated information. From broken shards, I assimilate and discard, building myself a man. Over and over, I have proved myself wrong, or if not wrong, then partial. New pictures supplant old ones, until I am no longer sure what I remember and what I have created. This fuller picture is not the one my mother wants me to carry. It's not the picture she has chosen to assemble. It is my picture of my father, and against it, I have made undeniable choices about how I will define myself.

The man I remember loved the sky. His theme song might have been "Don't Fence Me In," sung by Bing Crosby. He never drank, never smoked, peppered his everyday speech with hell and damn, and had little use for small talk. He graduated from the eighth grade and took correspondence courses from the University of Nebraska in engineering. He invented a few things, farm implements, gadgets, and owned at least one patent. He never made much money. He couldn't bear to let a thing go, rigging up an outdoor stand for our used Christmas trees until they turned brown and brittle. Although he didn't read music, he wrote a few songs and believed, at age forty, that he could abandon farming and become an overnight songwriter. One of his songs, Sweetheart, Say You'll Be Mine, was published by a vanity press, and our family holds all ten copies. The sheet music is mint green with a purple silhouette of a woman against the moon and stars of a nighttime sky.

It is my wedding day. I thought my brother would walk down the aisle with me, but Dad insisted. He looks nice in his new black suit. He's stooped over, he shuffles when he walks, he looks much older than his 63 years, but I'm used to it. We've practiced this. All he has to do is walk with me to the end of the aisle and sit down by Mom. No standing, no words, no required movement. I walk down on his left arm. A mistake, since Mom is seated on the left, but it never occurred to any of us. We reach the end of the aisle. I take Brad's arm and face the minister. We are waiting, I don't know why, when Brad leans down and says, "Your dad can't step over your dress." I turn around. He doesn't want to step on the dress. He can't step over it. He doesn't know what to do. I sweep the dress out of the way. Mom reaches out for him. It's over in a moment. I have no idea then that I will carry this memory with me all of my life.

Sacred Recollections

DIANNE YEAHQUO-REYNER

We are born to a place. The place that was given to me is the vast plains and rolling grasslands of Oklahoma. Rising out of the Southern Plains is a mountain range that stretches across landscape. Rounded boulders soften and contrast the harsh land that surrounds its base. Each mountain peak once told its name to our people. This land of our ancestors whispers their memories against our ears and we are taught to listen, carefully.

Every other summer, for as long as I can recall, the Queotone family has gathered on the allotment of my grandmother's father. The land has never supported the farm this allotment was supposed to produce. To the North, a hill we call Raintop rises to meet the scarring sun. Jimmy Creek, named for my great-grandfather, emerges as if from nowhere and its icy waters pool before they stream southward, cutting through the rocky terrain. Lining its banks are trees, which spread their canopy across the flowing spring in order to protect and keep its water cool as it moves along its journey. In the arid heat of Oklahoma summers the woods behind my great-grandfather's house provide a welcome refuge and a doorway to our past.

After the stories from our current lives are told, and all the new babies have been held and kissed, there comes a pause. We all know, as if told by the last breeze that brushed by our ears, that the time has come to listen to the stories we've really come to hear. The threads of our lives are woven into one fabric that binds our past and our present as one. We know who our people were, and from their lives we draw our strength.

Qualo was the son of Tahn-tsain, which means "Found a horse." Tiedle, which means "Big White," was the son of Qualo. Tiedle was my grandfather, although by the time I knew him, he was known as Edward Yeahquo. He would sit in the shade on the porch that wrapped around the house he had built for my grandmother. Facing south, you can see the Wichita Mountains as they move along the horizon. Their rocky points reach into the sky as they spread across the land, gathering the people in their arms. The mountains provide a constant reminder, that as Kiowa, our future is held and protected from harm. In the time before, the buffalo lived in abundance and there were no white faces to threaten our life. When they came to settle our home, pushing us aside, they killed and wasted our brother, our life. Our Uncle Saynday saw what was happening and he called to the herds. The face of Mt. Scott opened to admit the few survivors to its safety. They would return to the world below and wait. Wait for another time, another hope. When the great mountain closed around them one lone calf was left on the outside. His cries, filled with longing and pain, were lifted and carried by the winds to every twist on the earth.

When the sun beat down upon the land and the hot summer wind transformed the dry wheat fields into a golden ocean that swept across the red earth of Southern Oklahoma, we would gather around our Grandpa, and patiently wait until he was ready to speak. Edward was a tall man who always held himself with pride and great dignity. Each morning he would pay special care to his appearance as he wrapped his silver braids with long black ribbons. I remember his tan felt Stetson. There was a dark ring around the band, an impression left by the sweat gathered along his brow. I remember his sunglasses. They seemed to shield the mystery he held in his eyes. Every button on his starched, white cotton shirt was secured and the collar lay high across his neck. Edward had long been blind from diabetes yet as he looked out upon the scorched sea of grain, and he breathed in that sweet red dust, he would focus on something just past the Wichita Mountain range. When his vision moved into clarity he spoke.

"A long time ago there was a group of men. They rode south. Long past those mountains they went on a raid to capture horses. With them was Tau-ankia (He's Sitting in the Saddle), the son of Gui-pah-gah (Lone Wolf). He was your relative. You remember this. Always know who your relatives are. When they got there, they were surrounded by soldiers and had to run to get away. But Tau-ankia had been wounded the summer before and his leg did not work well, so he was left behind. When his cousin, Qui-tain (Wolf Heart) looked back and saw Tau-ankia was limping, he rushed to help him. Qui-tain drug him to the safety of a ravine but it was no good. They were both killed. Then their friends ran away. This is a shameful thing. The other men made it back to camp and they told Gui-pah-gah and his brother Red Otter that their sons were dead.

Gui-pah-gah and his brother Red Otter had just come back from Washington where the government had tried to persuade them to make peace. Overcome with grief for his only son, Gui-pah-gah cut his hair, killed his horses, and burned his buffalo robes. Tau-ankia's sister, Tay-yah-day cut off her finger as she cried for her brother. Gui-pah-gah and Red Otter went on a raid to avenge the deaths of their sons. They found their sons then properly laid them to rest. They were buried along with the finger that had been sacrificed for them. From that time on, Gui-pah-gah was not a friend to the white man."

The stories Edward told always linked us to our past. They told us who we were and the people we had come from. As he told us of the great sorrow felt by Gui-pah-gah, we cried with him. We felt the loss of our relative. For us, it had just happened.

At times Edward stayed in town with my Uncle Carl. When he was so close, we would all rush to finish our chores, much faster than usual. Bursting from our homes, my brothers, cousins, and I would run down the street and across the park. We always found him sitting alone on the screened-in back porch of my uncle's house. He never knew when we would be coming but he was ready. When we arrived, he would reach into his worn black leather coin purse and pull out just enough dimes to place one in each of our hands. With our new wealth we'd run to the neighborhood market. We took our time choosing the perfect pieces of candy. Returning we would all take our place by his side. Each hand would be wrapped tightly around a tiny paper bag. Holding our treats, we felt rich.

I remember Grandpa laughing. His laughter came easily. As he teased, asking what we wanted, he would reach into one of our sacks. Then he'd smile and place a candy in his mouth. He would begin to talk. He told us of great raiding parties into Mexico, when the Kiowa first saw the ocean, and a land where little hairy men lived in trees. In these lazy afternoons, we even learned how to milk a horse. We became part of the great Kiowa journey and it gave breath to our lives. We learned of our beginnings, our relationship with the earth, and our relationship with each other. We learned what it meant to be Kiowa. As his stories ended, we were changed. We had become part of the past and taken our place as part of the future.

Glaring Oklahoma skies can darken quickly in feverish spring afternoons. A warm gentle breeze can rapidly transform itself into a frigid aura that folds against the land. On a day such as this, my father and uncles would stand frozen as they searched the skies. My mother and aunts would gather up the children and quickly herd us into the cellar. A doorway into the earth opened and we descended into a damp and earthen cradle. The mix of kerosene and rich moist dirt hung suspended, and it filled each breath. As we climbed onto the tso-sain, covered with soft quilts, we settled in to wait. The men remained on the outside and we were content in the knowledge that we were well protected. An eerie hush lingered as the door closed behind us.

We lay quietly behind our mothers as they began telling stories of people we had heard of, but never met. These people would join us, and as we listened to the details of their lives, they became a part of our own memories. The voices of our mothers were soft and sweet. Hearing the winds above us rumble across the surface of the earth, I would snuggle closer to my mother's warmth. With my nose buried in the folds of my mother's skirt, I became part of her and the scent of her blocked all fear. When the door to the cellar finally opened, the bright sunlight would pierce through the darkness. As I watched the growing light, I was always reminded of how the Kiowa emerged from just such a place. Crawling through a hollow cottonwood log, we traveled from the center of the earth guided by the voice of our Uncle Saynday. I wonder, were we so hungry for the sunlight that we left this loving womb? What trade was made that we gave up this earthen embrace? As we journeyed to the surface I could hear the birds singing their welcome; we were called to emerge once again into this radiant warmth.

I hold these memories close as I make my way through life. Regardless of distance, this land will always be a part of me. It is the home of my ancestors, and it is the center of my being.

The Light in the Alley

JAMEY M. GENNA

I hold his little head in my hands, his hair soft and fine, dark, his tiny body small and alive. I do not feel motherly toward him, because he is my brother, but I do feel a need, constant and even slightly annoying. His head, sweet and delicate, his tiny mouth pulling at my pinky until I stop the joke and pop his bottle in his mouth. It's strange how quickly he can drink then fall asleep in mid-gulp, so quiet. His breath is even and solid, one breath catching up with the next.

The dining room where his playpen sits is dark except for the glare from the TV across the way in the living room where my mother is watching TV. It is my turn to feed the baby. It is my turn to take up the yoke of caring for the younger children. Each of us in turn bears the brunt of my mother's wrath when things aren't done right. "Why isn't this done?" is my mother's favorite phrase when she gets home from work and sees the dishes haven't been washed, the floor not vacuumed, the clothes not folded—my father not home from work yet or else from the bar. We are the largest family in the community. Doreen, Paul, Mary, me (Jody), Shane, Louise, Jude, Jimmy, Rob, and Kelly—we recite like a catechism when asked. This baby's name hasn't yet made the list.

This baby is a nuisance, the last child, and we are all complaining daily about his presence. "Why did she have to have another kid?" and, "I'm the one who'll have to take care of it," we say to each other.

Yet in the dark of the dining room, I can't help but notice how perfectly his feet are folded inside the soft fabric of his pajama, how evenly he breathes, how beautiful his strands of black hair are. None of the other children in the family have black hair. We five girls are all blonde, the five boys either straight-haired blondes or curly-headed redheads like my mother. Only my father has black hair, so we are all hoping this baby's hair will stay black like our father's.

I look down at the baby. His bare arm closest to my body is curved up inside my T-shirt now, against the soft skin of my ribcage, his other arm flung sideways in a curved arc out into the space of the room. His head has dropped sideways onto the bone of my arm, his mouth fallen open in the sweetest almost feminine "o" that is the way all the babies in our family have. I get up cautiously from my seat in the dining room and place him down into the playpen on top of the light blue crocheted quilt my Grandma Skinner already made for him. I pull the yarn quilt around his body. I'm tired and ready for bed and I don't want him to wake up if I carry him all the way to his crib in my mom and dad's room. I know that my mother will take him into his proper bed when she gets tired of waiting up for Dad. I slip past my mother sitting in the dark of the living room and walk up the stairs to climb under my own large quilt that my grandmother made for me out of light green polyester and corduroy. As I fall asleep I can hear the sound of the television set blaring up the stairs, my nightly lullaby.

I am asleep, and I am dreaming that my mother is screaming. She is yelling something in a long *O-o-oh*, then a *No-o-o* that goes on endlessly. Then she starts over with *Oh* and then *No* again. I'm not sure if I'm dreaming this because I think I heard my mother on the phone a few minutes ago, below me. It's early in the November morning because it's still dark outside, but it feels like it is about the time my mother goes to work. It is cold in my room because we had an early snowfall this year, and I am still partly asleep under the quilt. Then, I am sure I actually hear my mother crying. I sit straight up in bed when she does that, but then I hear nothing. I look through the green fiberglass curtains hung bunched up against the sideboards of my bed.

Sometimes when I go to sleep, I lie at the bottom of the bed with my sister Louise lying at the top, and I gather these curtains around my head and I look out at the streetlights in the alley while I listen to the train pass on the tracks across the highway. The stars here are always clumped in great clusters and they come out in the zillions, so I look at them and wish for a certain boy to fall in love with me at school. Outside now, it's still dark and I can see scattered patches of the early snowfall glimmering under the alley light. I can see my father's blue and white pickup truck parked under the light. It is hanging on the edge of the alley at a makeshift angle, so I know he made it home last night. Not that he hasn't ever made it home, it's just that now I am getting old enough to start worrying about whether some day he won't make it.

My sister Mary comes in from her room next door. The boys sleep in the basement since my parents remodeled after the fire we had when I was in fourth grade. I tell Mary how I heard Mom scream before she actually started, like I had had ESP or something, but she pinches me and tells me, "You did not. Shut up. Shut up, I want to hear."

Then I for real hear my mother screaming and crying and my oldest sister Doreen runs out from her and Mary's room and down the stairs as fast as she can in her slip pajamas. It isn't like Mom hasn't made loud noises in the middle of the night before. She yells at my dad when he comes home drunk. But this noise is different. It is sort of painful to hear and she sounds like she's asking a question, but she doesn't want an answer. By now, Doreen is down in the kitchen and I can hear my mother's voice frantic and angry. "No," she shouts, then, "No, no, no," and the last with the long o-o-h on it again like before in my dream.

I am afraid of my mother so I don't go downstairs. I wait. I think maybe

Doreen and Mom are arguing about Dad, but then pieces of the conversation float upward and I hear, "Give him to me," from Doreen and, "Let me see ... let me see," urgent-like from her, and my mother saying, "No," and, "No," again and again. I don't wonder where my father is now because I can tell by some heavy scuffle below that he is up and moving around the kitchen, somewhere near the phone, moving toward my mother's voice. The no's and pleading continue and then I hear some deep sound coming from below that is my father's voice, but I can't make out. It sounds like he is saying something, but is not using words. It sounds like he is someone who can't talk, someone who is deaf but can make strange sounds that sound like words.

More sounds, and then a feeling of some circuslike movement around the L-shaped kitchen, along the padded tile floor, then near the bathroom and the phone below me again. Then a sound of shifting weight as my sister says again, "Let me see." I hear the word "blue" and then "spots" float up—my sister's voice, sounding scared. My father's voice still only sounds like silent sounds, and something my mother is saying very loudly now, "I should've went to check. I heard him in his crib, a minute ago. I was on the phone to Aunt Joyce. I heard him just a minute ago."

That's when Mary goes down to help or see. I want to go, but I think I am too young. I haven't crossed that line yet into what was something only grownups were allowed to deal with. So I stay upstairs in the cold room.

I hear the sliding glass door to the cement patio open. Then through the window, I watch my father carrying a bundle, tucked up against his chest, folded away from the cold. He strides across the dirt lane to the pickup truck, my mother hurrying after, barely holding his elbow, her coat lifted out behind her as she passes through the dark and into the pool of light pouring over the truck. I sense then they are going to the doctor.

You know how when something bad happens, you pray and pray for it not to be true. Or sometimes you lose something important like a ring or a new necklace and you wish and pray to just be able to find it? I didn't pray. I didn't really think it was true. It felt like a dream I had concocted in the middle of the night. I kept wondering how my mother's heavy wool coat could fly out like that, the dark wool thrown up behind her like a tarp cast up for leaves, and I thought I dreamt snow falling and puffs of breath coming from her and my father's mouths as they rushed to the truck in the darkness. I think I dreamt there was a streetlight in the alleyway shining over them, and that I saw a look of fear cross both their faces and an awful worry too deep for me ever to erase. This image lasts forever and stays imprinted like light on a photographic plate.

It's almost magical, that time between the doctor and the funeral because of the suspense, the waiting, the specialness of change, and not having to go to school. We all of us secretly wondered at our part. What had caused this, we whispered. What part had we played by not wanting him, by complaining, by arguing over whose turn it was to feed him or change him? We had said it right to our mother's face. Years later, she carried her own vigil into the bar with her chant—"I smoked," she said, and, "If I had just checked on him, I was on the phone, I had to go to work, If I had just gone in to check on him . . . turned him over."

I remember his little head in my hands though, his bottle on the floor by the playpen. His black hair like my father's.

After the funeral, we go back to our house in town, and then many people come over to the house—Grandma and Grandpa Skinner, Grandma Anderson, Aunt Joyce and all her kids, Mom's friends from the hat factory and Dad's from the packing plant. There's watermelon pickles from Grandma Skinner and cherry pie from the Piggly Wiggly store someone brought, a casserole dish filled with scalloped potatoes and ham, and some kind of dish made from eggplants and cheese laid out in glass Pyrex. Aunt Joyce makes us some new kind of drink which is instant hot chocolate and only needs water, so me and my cousins are all excited about this. We wait in line for our Styrofoam cups and then scurry toward the stairs, our hands cradled around the cups, our elbows sticking out and stiff so as not to spill. I glance back at my mother as I turn the corner and she is sitting at the table with her head propped in her hands. Her fingertips are up around her eyes, her elbows resting among the jars and dishes, but her face is expressionless, empty and waiting—for what, I don't know. She isn't crying anymore.

Upstairs with our girl cousins, we make a game of I'll show you what I've got that you haven't, and then we're laughing and running between the two rooms, flipping the light switches on and off, and yelling "Hey," at each other in the dark. Suddenly, my cousin Judy who is crouched down on the other side of a vanity dresser from me asks me in the dark, wasn't I sad about my brother's dying. And I feel then that I should be sad, that I should not have drunk hot chocolate. I think that the tears I cried at the funeral were only to imitate my older sister Doreen, that I did not have the right to cry. There was nothing I could say to Judy's question. I did not answer; I did not yet have the vocabulary to say that I was filled with guilt. I did not know what the meaning of sorrow was, only the meaning of pain. We changed the game in the dark to hide-and-go-seek, and I hid behind the green curtains then and looked out onto the back lot where my father's blue truck was parked rightly in the lane.

Tata and The Queen of Roumania

JANE ST. CLAIR

My mother died when I was four years old, except she did not die. She was taken away to a state mental institution, screaming and babbling in Roumanian. She was dead for all purposes as my mother, but occasionally when her spells were over, Tata would bring her back into our house again, only for her to die again and again and again for me —I who needed a mother.

I suppose we each needed her, Tata and all six of us children, but we told everyone she was dead. I remember being quite ashamed of what was left of her. When high school friends said, "Wasn't that your mother, the crazy foreign woman, the one I saw in the streets, trying to take her dress off? So shameless! It was past midnight last night, I saw her." I would say no, my mother was dead. She may as well have been. She had no purpose but to humiliate me and remind me of my loss.

I know I took it harder than the rest of them. I looked for her in all the wrong places: in the hearts of the teachers, in the faces of my friends' mothers, in the social workers, doctors — I looked for my mother in any older woman I met. But finally my heart hardened and I learned to live without her. I went to school, my hair wild and uncombed and my face unwashed, the buttons on my dress not fastened correctly, everything about me lacked the mother's love, but I stopped wanting her to be well enough to take care of me. Even when they brought her home, I would look into her face and know she was not there, not at all, not the way I wanted her to be.

It was the Depression times then in Nebraska. We hardly had enough to eat. My father would not let us fight over the food: we had to share and divide every morsel. We had chickens, and to me they were never animal companions. I would watch one hungrily as he picked off corn from the ground, and I would think it was all right for him to eat now, because soon my father would wring his neck and then we would eat him back. I was bloodthirsty for chicken in those days, watching them fatten as if I were a stealthy coyote.

My first sister was twelve when my mother died. She quit the seventh grade, and it was she who took care of me and my baby sister. The two in the middle, both inbetween boys, ran wild all day, until my father came home from work to control them. My oldest brother lied about his age and joined the Navy.

My father worked eleven hours per day at the meat packing house, the big one owned by Swift Meat Company in Omaha. He who had been an aristocrat in Roumania now worked sorting parts of pig off a conveyor belt. The slaughtered pig would come and Tata would sort its insides, especially the long intestines that had to be carefully picked for sausage casing. The hooves and the tail, the tongue and the liver—all of it, even the lesser pig parts, were eaten. The lesser parts went to the people in my neighborhood, people who were living behind the stockyards in coal-tar roofed shacks. The better parts, the choice butt and belly, these parts were cured into ham for the people who lived on the top of the hill. Even during the Depression, these people were not hungry. They could contently wait while pig meat aged to ham.

The room at the meat packinghouse where my father stood all day was chilled to forty degrees to preserve the pig. My father wore fingerless gloves, a white coat, and hip length boots. There was blood everywhere, sometimes up to his knees, and that is why he wore the boots. He said the boots were good to protect his shoes, because shoes were expensive. The coat by the end of the day was stained with blood and black pig gut. His fingers were stiff from the cold; both his gloves and his hands always turned the same color red by day's end from the eleven-hour soak in the cold red water. When he got old, my father's fingers stiffened completely and one day they refused to move again, the way they usually behaved back then only at the end of the day—stiff and wooden and immoveable—they permanently behaved in old age.

He could never be warmed in the winter because he was chilled too much to the bones. He came home in the darkened time long after most people's dinner. One such dark night there were two social workers waiting for him in our house. My sister had opened our door to them. These women, dressed in black silk and furs, and carrying black notebooks and black leather purses, were talking to my sister and me and taking notes about our family. I touched the first woman's hair, because it looked so very soft and silky fine clean, and she also let me touch her face, which was so very clean and smooth and sweet-smelling—I imagined it was a face made out of talcum powder. I thought the social workers were wonderfully sweet and caring—they asked so many questions about our family and even about me, whom everyone always ignored.

But Tata took one look at them and his face stiffened to match his cold wooden hands. He would not speak English to them—he told them he had no English, even though we children knew it was a lie. Tata had six languages, including Greek. He apologized and showed them to the door, and told them to bring someone next time who could speak Roumanian. It was a big farce to us: he must be playing a joke on these Grade A Fancy women.

When the two went away, he told my sister and the inbetween boys and me that there was danger in these women. They wanted to take us to a home like where Mama was kept, and we would not be a family anymore. Immediately, there were things we had to do. The inbetween boys would have to go to school each and every day. And if any of us ever saw these women, we must lock the door and hide under the beds and pretend that no one was home. If the baby cried, we must stick a handkerchief in her mouth to quiet her so the women would not hear anything, not even a small cry.

Tata scared us with this story, because many times we had visited where our Mama was. It was a state-owned institution, with bed after dirty white bed in irregular rows. The people in the beds were sometimes tied down, and everyone was screaming and yelling. The smells were worse than our outhouse, and no one was clean—no one, not even the nurses.

Our mother had no doctor, as there were none in Nebraska who could speak Roumanian. Educated doctors who nonetheless could not speak other languages existed in this so-called modern country, and so none of them could help her. She had no drugs, but only ropes to bind her madness. I could not bear to see her like that, with her hair matted and her dress stained and unpressed. The earlier recollection I had of her, my baby recollection, was that she was sweet-smelling and immaculate and sang in an angel's voice. Our Navy brother who remembered her the most of all told us that Mama had to have everything perfect: she ironed towels and sheets and she sliced carrots in meticulous pieces all the same size.

The social worker women did come back to our house many times, but we did as Tata told us and hid from them. Still with their white papers and long envelopes and legal language, they succeeded partway. I was only four years old when I and my baby sister were taken to the big Settlement House near the meat packing plant, and the inbetween boys were made to stay there after school. My big sister got a job with my father at the packinghouse, and that was good in the money sense, but I missed her.

The Settlement House nursery was awful to me. I never saw the light of day: I was left there still half asleep, at five in the morning, taken to school, and not picked up until dark. They had a piano there, but only a few keys worked; nevertheless you were spanked if you touched it. There were metal chairs and tables and a rug on the floor, and it was heated with radiant reliable heat, not stoves. There were many, many children—all immigrant children who spoke between them maybe fifteen languages. We had very few toys to play with and only one teacher, who did her best to teach us nursery rhymes in English. We had very little to do and it was maddeningly noisy.

There were other rooms in the Settlement House besides my nursery. My baby sister was in one of them, but I was not allowed to see her. There were rooms where schoolchildren came after school and the social workers taught the girls how to cook and sew, and the boys how to whittle and tool wood.

On Fridays at 4 p.m. green and white flags were hoisted on the roofs of the packinghouses, and all the women in the neighborhood would walk to the packinghouses to pick up their husbands' salaries. This was done so that the wives had first hands on the money, before the men could spend it at the local taverns. My father had no wife so he went to the tavern. The cheering that the children made when the packinghouse flags went up did not apply to us, the way so many things did not apply to us. Fridays at 4 p.m. was not even the end of our week, because Tata worked Saturdays too.

I begged my father to let me out of the Social Settlement house. He did not have the luxury to observe a day of my child care, so he accepted my judgement. Tata took me to my brothers' school and he enrolled me in the first grade. He claimed again that he could not speak English and could not fill out their papers in writing, but he did swear to them that I was six years old, not four. I was now with my brothers, and only our baby and our mother had been left behind in state institutions.

I learned English quickly at the public school, but my mind was still in Roumanian. When I came to our house at night, I thought in Roumanian words and it is always the language of home and love and everything that is warm to me and not institutional.

The first day of public school my father celebrated my education by killing a chicken and making soup. He always gave us children the meat of the legs and the breasts, and he told us his favorite piece was the neck. He would make a great show of sucking all the meat out of the delicate bones in the neck. Later when he was very old, we held a family reunion and he made chicken soup. It was only then that he told us the truth: that he never wanted the neck at all, he was just being a father to us.

During the Depression we celebrated Christmas in the religious way, not the material. We gave thanks for our health and blessings, and we prayed for the less fortunate. On Christmas morning, each of us found an orange in our stocking and one or two candies. We shaved the chocolate from the candy so it would last as long as possible, and we sucked the oranges slowly, piece by fabulous piece. We'd take turns throwing the peels in the fire, so the house would be fragrant with Christmas orange for maybe six days.

The gift I really wanted, of course, was a Shirley Temple doll. There was one such doll in the window of the tiny store near my school. The tiny store, built in an underground basement in an apartment building, sold candy and little toys and school supplies, but I would stop in only to visit the doll. The store was owned by a Roumanian family, and the woman liked me and so she would let me hold the doll whenever I wanted, because she knew I was a careful child. To me, holding the doll and visiting her was almost the same as owning her. They never really sold that doll: no one in our neighborhood could afford such a luxury so she stood in that window long after I graduated from high school.

In our house we had two beds. I slept with my two sisters, and the inbetween boys and my father slept in the other one. It was so cold at night in the winter, that we liked having so many people in the bed. When the boys grew too big, my father slept on the couch.

What I recall most from those days is Tata, and how every night he would lie down with us on the foot of the bed and tell us stories about his youth in Roumania. We would beg for certain ones, the way you want certain phonograph records played over and over again.

Tata had been the only son of a rich man in Roumania. He lived in a great house with many rooms, and it was surrounded by farmlands and his family owned it all. He had his own whipping boy, who came to America with him and was loyal until the day he died from pneumonia the first winter he stayed here. If Tata made a mistake when he was a child, that whipping boy took the consequences and Tata's heart would bleed for him.

Tata ate off fine china and carved wooden tables, with tapestries on the walls and soft rugs on the floors. Uniformed servants would bring each beautifully crafted dish of steaming food to Tata and his father, and Tata was allowed to throw away any food he chose not to eat. Tata had not one, but two dogs of his own: there was plenty of food for even the dogs in Roumania.

Tata had his own private tutor: his teacher was a handsome young Greek who taught him languages. The two of them spent their days outside just reading and chatting about books. Tata had little use for mathematics or science and neither did the tutor: the two of them cared only for history, literature and language. So to this day Tata is deficient in some areas of his studies. The Greek scholar was dismissed when his father realized what was going on, and Tata at age fourteen was sent away to a very strict boarding school in Paris.

There all his classes were conducted in French, and his fellows were rich men from all over the continent. On holidays Tata and his friends went into Paris and pretended they were older than they were, so they could watch the Follies and have women friends. They ate at the best restaurants, and drank the best wines, and the best time of all for everyone young in Paris was spring—when there were blossoms everywhere and everyone was in love all at once.

Tata was only twenty when he met our mother. At first he heard only her voice because she sang songs all day long: in her angel voice, she sang. She was a peasant girl with the gift of music, and my father's family was willing to train her voice for their own amusement. They were not willing for their son to fall in love with her.

Tata told us when we were old enough to understand that his father wanted him to have this beautiful singing girl for his own, but not in the married way. Tata would not listen to his father's counsel, and made plans for the two of them to run away to America. They were married in Roumania, late at night in a country church in a tiny ceremony without the wedding glamour that would have satisfied my sisters' and my own imaginations. Just ten days after the secret ceremony, they ran away to America with Tata's whipping boy and several others from the manor.

Tata actually had other disagreements with his father besides his choice of a woman. His father had been stern, domineering to a fault, and oftentimes cruel. They had fought over the coming of communism, and the necessity of monarchy. His father, a friend and counsel to the Queen of Roumania, would not countenance such blasphemy learned in Paris boarding schools from theoretical professors and from a lazy Greek scholar who knew nothing of real life. His son was throwing away his future by not following his advice. But to the son, it was only a matter of time before Romania was taken over. Roumania had constantly been conquered throughout its history by Turks and by everyone else, and to Tata's way of thinking, the future of a landed Roumanian aristocrat was uncertain. Some twenty years later, Tata was proven correct. But when he and his bride boarded the clandestine boat, he could not have known that. Still he never looked back and his father stubbornly never sought him.

We asked over and over about the land and the great house that was somehow our legacy, and couldn't we go back and claim it? But Tata would close himself up when we started those kind of questions as if the answers were none of our business, even though they meant everything to us during the Depression.

So there were two things I was proud of when I was a little girl: my brother in his immaculately white Naval uniform with the colored stripes and visored hat, and my father's aristocracy. If my dress was faded and torn, and if my feet were cold from cardboard in my shoes, and if my mother embarrassed me when they brought her home, I would cling to the thought of the family manor in the Old Country, and my father's whipping boy and the grand dinners served by personal waiters. I would hold the Shirley Temple doll at the school store, and think that if only he had stayed in the Old Country, the doll would really be mine to own.

World War II broke out when I was a teenager, and my two brother joined the service. Only we sisters and Tata were left to follow the war and worry about Gold Stars in our windows. We finally brought a map of the world and put pins where our brothers and boyfriends were fighting.

Yet to me the War was somewhat of a good thing. It brought three regular checks from the United States military to our house, and it brought a good job for my eldest sister. She quit the packinghouse and went to work for Strategic Air Command. She no longer had to wear the bloody coat and boots: now she had a coordinated wardrobe and thirty-two hats. I loved to watch her draw the long straight lines up her legs with her eyebrow pencil every morning. She would say as soon as this darn war was over, she was going to buy some silk stockings. That made me feel rich when she said that. She was only sacrificing for the war, of course; she would be buying herself silk stockings this minute if only they were available.

So the war brought money into our family, though Tata told us it was blood money. But even with our new clean brick house and five salaries coming into it, I could never forget the Depression. Once you are poor, it stays with you, and I have poverty in my bones to this day. In that way the Great Depression will never be over for me.

Once when my brother came home from the Navy to visit, I told him about the stories about the Old Country that my father was telling us. He just shrugged and did not want to hear them. I begged him to tell me if our mother had told any stories too, but he would not talk about such things. He who had traveled and seen the world seemed to dismiss what was most important to me: knowing about our past wealth. He did show me a picture, a newspaper clipping he had put away in a box, with a picture of Tata and the Queen of Roumania. She had come to Nebraska and visited the Roumanian community here, and Tata was in the picture. I could see it myself clear as day.

I showed Tata the picture and he said that the Queen had wanted to see him and brought the message that his father was dead and buried on their manorland. He and the Queen of Roumania had talked much during her brief visit, but it was strained because she had known about their quarrel and was much attached to our grandfather and took his side.

I kept these words in my heart and it was only after I grew up that my Navy brother told me that I was much too serious about such things. Every immigrant in the United States had been an aristocrat back there in the Old Country. Every Pollack will tell you that if their last name ends in "ski", it means they are aristocrats, and how can everyone in America have been an Old World aristocrat? Likewise every Italian, Swede, Chinese or whatever; he could assure me of such things for he had traveled.

So I asked him then—is it true what people outside the family said about Tata: that we were poor because he was a drunk, and that he drank because he had no woman?

He just sneered at me, and said I was still not seeing the truth in front of my nose.

I had the picture of the Queen with my father, and I had my father's knowledge of six languages. I had the memory of my mother's singing voice, and I had all Tata's stories with their minute details. But a thing is either true or it is not. A thing that is true has no purpose: only a lie has intent and purpose. On the other side, the side of lies, I knew Tata could lie when he needed to, such as when he lied to the social workers and the school registrar.

It is strange that it was my baby sister who grew up and made the trip to Roumania after Tata died. She had needed the stories from the Old World the least of all of us, because by the time she was ten or so, our family was rich with five salaries and a brick house. Still, when she was an old widow, she was the one who went to Roumania herself. At that time the Communists were still the conquering rulers, and she was not allowed to travel freely about their country. But she was able to view the old man's grave and the manor house. In Paris, she found the ecole where the rich Roumanian boys were sent to study languages.

When I asked her for the truth, she would not tell me. I pressed her again and again, but she would only say it was impossible to tell me for sure what I had to know. Just leave it be, she said, only leave it be, as if I were the baby and she were the big sister. What's there is there, and the rest is not. But for me who needed to know for sure, that was never enough.

Never!

Said to Sarah, Ten

And Scribes wrote it all down.
Gilgamesh

There is no one to say why
this face on the scrap of newsprint,
The Times, is not the face of my brother.
No one to say why her cat wastes
in a nest on the sofa, shawl and heating pad.
It yawns and gapes and whines
and arches its back.

How long will it last? she asks,
meaning grief, and I haven't the heart
to say a lifetime. Daughter.

Epistemology, I said in the dark
to her father, my head on his arm,
is my favorite subject, how we know what we know.

It will take so long, she says at intermission.
We hold each other in our common arms.
Mother and daughter, we are bound by mucus
and blood, the spilling of waters, flesh,
and the uses of smooth muscle.
I don't have the answer. It wasn't wisdom
brought her to life. I did nothing.
Now we sit in the dark watching
the orderly art of the body. Dancing.
People sweat in service.

I tell her in the dark,
when we're gone, when they're gone
under the earth, when all our names are forgotten,
this will continue, this dancing.

HILDA RAZ

Subdivision: The End of North

The westbound truck has backed out of the drive
with everything the yard sale didn't claim.
Jon sits beside me on the floor, patting
my hand, trying to smile, watching my face.
And Ben, so often lashing out in rage,
is crying softly just inside the door.
Their dad arrives; his U-Haul fills the drive.
My sons begin to hollow out their rooms
these boxes packed three times in eighteen months.
I choke out *Call you every week!* and wave
until their matching faces blur beyond
the windshield's glass. They disappear, eastbound.
I toss on sea foam carpeting all night,
awaken to strange voices in the yard
debating when to hammer on the door
and will me from this rental I still hate.
They hover in a circle, mops in hand
as if I've left the place in disarray.
The loudest says, *Look how she's left the yard!*
There's not one single thing that's blooming here!
I drop the keys into her hand, assert
Completely empty now, then drive away.

PAT HEMPHILL EMILE

Dreams She Tells Her Father

The way she tells her father is at the kitchen table.
"Corn?" her mother asks, "Do you want corn?"
Yes, corn is fine.

She wants to tell her father that reading never
matters if it's not learned, and sometimes it falls
from her head, through her ear, she believes, and enters
someone else, just when she needs it most.
"This is all someone else's dream."
"This is where I am, father. I'm in Nebraska, and the books and I are divorc-
    ing."
"Did you get some corn?" he asks, strong face down in the plate.

But in Nebraska, her friend uncovers a shell with his walking stick.
What the hell is this doing here?
What has it learned coming all this way, far from the river?
What do they know?
They are just two Indians walking
to find Michigan and Colorado
between the wide oaks and swallowing sky.
We're fighting this all too damn hard,
she thinks, just too damn hard.

TAMMY TRUCKS

Hailstorm

he stands at the foot of the porch
facing west
smoking a cigarette
hands thrust in his jeans pockets
and watches the hail
hammer
his wheat crop
golden, ripe, ready for harvest

the five young children
shriek and run in reckless abandon
relishing a game of tag

while she stirs gravy in the kitchen
quietly weeping
and wondering
what to say

TERRY WIECHMAN

Abandoned Farm
for Renee Peterson

Nothing kisses wind in empty rooms.
I hear a river,
snow water and cistern,
gentle piss of girls squatting in grass.
In the mouths of cows
cud becomes a blue thread of milk
unwinding, crows
turning air around the barn.

We roll over and over in the hay,
swinging on the knotted rope
out the window.
Whatever we want, we dream —
horses, boys, red velvet dresses.

The white farmhouse is far from town.
At the skating rink we get inside the music
racing what we know
around the concrete, fenced-in field
we think is heaven
but is an emptiness we fill
like our mothers and grandmothers
for a while, in a small town.

CAROLANN RUSSELL

Heirloom

Today I washed by hand the peach satin
embroidered kerchief my father brought
from Thailand before I was born.
It looks worn. A few threads have run,
I fear, beyond repair
It has aged suddenly, like a face.
Like my mother's the year
I did not visit. Thinner,
imperceptibly graying as the maple leaves
die beside the lake.
I begged her for that kerchief.
When I was ten it meant everything
I didn't have. I stroked it
like skin. Buried years
in the trunk Grandmother gave
"for hope" she said
even though I eloped
and announced I'd never bear a child
but would go to college forever
and have real conversations
with people I didn't know.
Or love, I should have said.
Now, held up to the light
I see what it means.

CAROLANN RUSSELL

Sweeping

The girls tell me of a treasure,
and though their hands are empty
now, they want it.
Please, Momma, please,
a snake skin, Momma,
by the garden fence
all in one piece
and it rustles
when we touch it.
Does it sound like paper?
Like book leaves turning
when we read a story?
Or is it like little voices?
Does it rustle like little voices?
Like a child sleeping
warm under the quilts?
My questions won't
stop them.
They know my fear
of snakes. Teasing, they giggle
and squirm. Their boots
leave swirls of mud
on worn linoleum. I
tell them
it makes no difference,
this house holds so much dust,
so many shadows and dreams. Surely
one more will fit.
But if I
could stretch my hands
to the ceiling, crack my skin
along my spine, coil and
uncoil,
slither free along
the baseboards
toward the door.
Would I?
Would I?
Long ago?
What keeps me here
sweeping farmhouse dust

from room to room?
the moon above the chicken coop?
the calf waiting by the fence?
the little voices from upstairs?
the silence?

DIANE HUETER

Measuring Up

I tried to get him to the doctor
as soon as the pain started but he wouldn't go
said he'd tend to it after the corn was picked
if he wasn't feeling better

I think if he'd been a man of words
he'd say his life didn't measure up
to the tall stick he gauged it by

things were good in our early years
he didn't seem to mind much
when the first baby was a girl

when the second one failed him too
he smiled and said we'd try again soon

but when the third his only son
pounded his way out early
like he thought he had to be here
for planting season
and died before the next full moon
he said we were finished trying

we never let flesh touch flesh again
in that way

my days became frying up his chicken
crispy but not burnt just as he liked it
digging boiling mashing potatoes
'til I felt like a potful of white mush myself

the girls pleased me—Ruth and Maggie
we spent mornings home-schooling
studying Paris and Seoul and Santiago
from a rambling house with a rotting porch
on a half-section of dirt in a corner of Nebraska

my husband just laid down the measuring stick
after his boy died gave up hoping for anything
crawled up onto the seat of that blessed tractor
and worked the Land

as if he could unearth something better than us
in the fertile soils his disc turned over

you're working too hard I whispered
one midnight when he crawled in
and wrinkled up the ironed sheets
on his side of our passionless bed
"God formed man from the dust of the ground,"
was all he said
as he turned away
moonlight shining off his silvering hair

I have no regrets   things weren't great
but they coulda been worse

as for him   seems regret's
the only tune he knew

even now I don't s'pose he's too pleased
about resting in a corner plot
of the city cemetery —
hated going to town
even just for church or for seed

the girls wanted to buy him
one of those fancy headstones
with a tractor on it or a farm scene
but he's down there in the corner
with a 12 by 18 inch flat marker
where no one will bother him
I think that's how he woulda liked it

LU CARTER

1950-1992

A baseball unraveled is
Two leather figure 8s, red string for stitching.
Miles of thread wrap
a hard rubber core.

If our parents' college formal had been called for rain, or
If our dad hadn't been so blond and tan, or
If our mother's hair wasn't so soft, or
If the sweater she knitted had been pink instead of blue.

With a less attentive father, throwing, catching, coaching,
Scott would have played outfield instead of catcher.
Or stayed in his living room to watch the World Series
Instead of still trying to master the spin at 42.

If we hadn't hurried through so many cold suppers
Crossing two counties or more
To towns named for Indian chiefs and Civil War generals
To watch him play in fields paid for by dirt farmers' oil wells.

Without a father who hit dirt clod home runs
With a stick he found by the fencerow,
Scott might have been in air-conditioned safety
Instead of kneeling behind home plate.

How many miles an hour
Did the ball travel?
Stitching, at the right spin,
Unwinds a carotid artery.

Like sandpaper letters
for a child who learns best by touch,
I trace numbers on granite to
train my stubborn mind.

RITA SHELLEY

Cataloging Actions Never Taken

Familiar as an old mistake
And futile as regret
Edwin Arlington Robinson

I sort my collection of regrets
the way Aunt Susie fingered
through her quilted button-box
to brighten up a rainy afternoon
for her brother's child
Mother-of-pearl or glass
or stamped-metal disk
each one keys a memory
Charlie's white kid baby shoe
Sister Etta's wedding dress
Grandma's cloak store-bought
for train-travel clear to Texas

Keenly I regret
a half-dozen mountains
I meant to climb
Backpacked in three times
to the lake below Split Mountain
and never made the summit
Galls me worse than pack-straps
when I look up from Big Pine road
toward Split's double peak against the sky

Down my long list
check one more regret
Never have I visited
my second husband's grave
This guilt too thin
to cast a shadow

Not like my failure
in Colorado Springs
the War's first year
when I chose not to buy
thumbsize water buffalo
in the jeweler's window

Small perfect-curving horns
laid back along his withers
seed-shaped eye
that watched me walk away

ELIZABETH CALLAWAY

Wallflower

oh, she's here all right

but not among line dancers in
cowboy boots under the
glitter globe that
spatters leopard spots on
shoulders, faces, walls

she's here
(she's always here)
a panting panther
crouched behind tall grass
in nightmares

she won't insist you stay
she *won't* —
(no longer than a song)

so tonight
it's all right
ask her to dance

MARY-LANE KAMBERG

The Fool is the Hanged Man

Not knowing that Saint Lucifer's nickname
was ignorance Neil married a Russian
woman with a deck of torn playing cards
and a crazy crushed velvet flowered hat.

Some said he must have been just plain nuts not
to know that a woman with a pencil
is never the queen of hearts when she deals
out letters on Sunday's kitchen table.

But Neil didn't notice what didn't tug
at the end of his fishing line. He thought
she was the fat cat card and didn't care
that his queen of spades wasn't in season.

STEPHANIE A. MARCELLUS

My Mother in the Suit that Holds All Colors

Thirty years after he'd snapped her
giggling in the white swimsuit,
the guy she'd known in high school
showed my father he still carried
her curves and long legs in his wallet.
She kept that figure longer than her less
slender girlfriends could forgive.

But mostly, she still owned the laughing
heart that, along with several margaritas,
had fueled her famous flamenco across
the hotel lobby in Majorca, Dad grinning
at his wild girl, still staccatoing her heels at forty.

Now Dad's heart is silent as the tiles
of that lobby after he'd guided her,
suddenly dizzy, up to bed.
She covers her body in gray and black,
looks in mirrors when she has to,
calls herself too skinny.

Is it too late to bring back the blazing
colors of that country? Or to revisit
the one trip she took without him?
When the taxi let them off in Mazatlan,
her mom and sister checked in
while she swept down to the beach,
heart drumming a rumba
against the white shore of her blouse.

Slipping off her sandals like an eager bride,
she nestled her toes into hot sand,
so held by waves plunging toward her,
she didn't see the man approaching.

He must have spied the girl in the white maillot,
the woman seized by the rhythm of an evening.
He asked her name, then said, *Roberta,*
let's hold hands and run into that water.

Did she smile that he'd spotted her thoughts
as though they were bright fishes
darting through clear water?
When she demurred, he shook his head:
You used to be a lot more fun, Roberta.

May she one day find her way
back to that shore, feel again the fire
in her feet. And, if he asks her,
may she reconsider.

JUDITH SORNBERGER

Changing

men may read this
and young women

Unlike
adolescence—
this Change
is a secret.
The blood that will not stop
wise blood
not contained
but flooding out
hidden.

The hair on the face
waxed away
in private.

The rush of heat
red face
sweat running between the breasts—
perhaps, sparing embarrassment,
it will come
only at night—

helpful books
advise leaving the toes
out from under the covers,
to cool off,

but I, in astonishment
at this changing body, lie
naked
over the air conditioner vent
laughing
alone.

ANNE L. HAEHL

She Forgot to Ask,
"Where the Hell is Broadwater?"

She was sittin' in the blue
bench bar seat drinkin' Pabst
Blue Ribbon Lite in the dusky dark
of Rock-n-Horse Lounge

when he opened the door
slow and sure, kicked cow
shit off his Tony Lamas,
straightened his neckerchief,
stepped on in.

She sucked down her beer
as his Wrangler western cut
covered bowlegs headed her way.
"Are you married, Ma'am?"

"Yes," she said.
He straddled the Naugahyde
chair like a bronc, slid
it closer to her booth,

smiled a tobacco-stained
gap-toothed grin.
"I'm from Broadwater."
They drove Highway 26
in his new Dodge Ram truck.
Patsy Cline sang, "Send Me
the Pillow that You Dream On."

MARY JACKSON KRAUTER

Belonging

Funny — how one thing
or another gets left or lost
or thrown away
Like the little bracelet
Lisa found in the sandy
dooryard of the old homestead
then lost an hour later
As if that thing had to stay
on the prairie

I head back to a class reunion
to say hello to people
I haven't seen in thirty years
to trade hugs and stories
smiles and kisses
To find that some part
of us has clung
to the prairie
Has waited
to welcome us back

GINNY ODENBACH

After India

After India took my notebook

After the laundry in Srinigar ruined my blue dress with scorch marks

After we spent all our money on shopping and tips

After we fell in love with the kids

After we woke every day at 4 a.m. to Call to Prayer and our sleeping was
screwed up with the time change and we were so tired we had to nap in
the afternoons

After dahl and curry, mutton and roast chicken, spinach, panere (cheese), flat
bread roasted over the fire with strawberry preserves, omelets every
morning, the endless stream of vendors on their chicharas to the house-
boats — "Excuse me, Sir, Madam, would you like to buy flowers, post-
cards, jewelry, linens, "I am a tailor"

After floating through lotus pads and buds opening into huge pink flowers,
Habid, 70 years old rowing four adults and their luggage

After streets with small Indian taxis, scooters, bicycles, a cow meandering
across at the light

After dripping wet even our underwear, 115 degrees in Delhi

After soldiers, machine guns, bunkers, and patted down body searches

After leis of marigolds in Delhi, leis of bachelor buttons in Srinigar

After packing, repacking, eye-identifying luggage — sure it gets in the taxi, on
the bus, checked in at the plane

After the Baste, worse ghetto in Delhi, little kids with puffed bellies standing
in line with their cans for milk at the Hope Project

After Carmen tours us through the Hope Project, showing us charts for milk
and how much weight each child gains

After Suzanne holds the babies, their young mothers come for classes on
nutrition and how to stay well, learning not to drink the water out of
ditches

After the pool of sewage in front of Murshid's tomb

After the Paradise inside Inayat Khan's tomb, floors of marble, tree growing
through the roof, Bliss radiating from his gold-covered casket

After Christ's Tomb — who's in here? — two bodies? huge footprint in
cement, Baba prays outloud

After kids follow us wherever we go, gleeful and curious, wanting "one pen"
— we give a couple, create a riot with kids hanging on the side of the
taxi

After our teacher refuses to go in the mosque because the women cannot go
and Baba, the Turkish sherif, mugs with the children, Bob teaches them
the word "awesome"

After coke which must be drunk right there so bottle can go back in the
wooden carton

After winding walled streets of Srinigar, sewage running in etched cement
    channels

After chai and biscuits

After our houseboy names Bob, Baba, and walks into our bedroom at night
    to put things in the cabinet

After fields of purple flowers in Gulmarg in the Himalayas

After trekking to the top of the mountain, panting at 14,000 feet in my clogs,
    jamming my toes into my shoes on the way down, slowing everyone else

After Debra tries to help me and I fall in the mud

After the horsemen follow us thinking we will get tired

After a coke in base camp halfway up, we meet the others who rode horses,
    guides hanging onto their tails

After cheese, water, bagels on the top

After dancing, praying, chanting for Peace Peace Peace for this land and the
    horsemen saying, "You came all this way to pray for peace. It isn't even
    your country."

After a fire in our stove in our mountain room

After burnt birthday cake and singing "Forever Young" on guitars in the
    Highlands Park Lobby

After walking with Abdul the guide we don't need but he needs the money

After pictures with the Hindu family at the sweet red temple

After leaving my son and his girlfriend's picture on the temple bell at the
    Shiva Temple

After having a red dot put on my forehead in the steamy temple inside, a
    flower-decorated lingam in the center

After I leave two American dollars and get half a bag of prasad (sweet blessed
    popcorn)

After Bob leaves his hat and Sabina leaps like a mountain goat up the 150
    steps to retrieve it

After I tell almost everyone's fortune in rhyming poems

After moonrise from behind the Himalayas, Call to Prayer floating over the
    water, on top of our houseboat in Srinigar

After Bill Elliot tries to explain the conflict — Kashmir sees the Indian army
    as an army of occupation

After buying a vajra, bronze mask, statue of Sita in Ladekh shop

After taking off my metal bracelet the last morning — knowing this part of
    my life finished that I must leave it behind in India, giving the bracelet
    to Carmen for her daughter

After diarrhea the last morning

After Bob vomits on the way to the airport

Security check through all our baggage

Women soldiers looking at all my sketches and giggling

Bob giving away two cigarettes, two candy bars, a peppermint to get his medicine through the checkpoint

After roses all over Murshid's tomb in the dargah, Shahabuddin's sweet singing, my pens exploding, Shahabuddin reading the ink on my hands

After missing out on the henna at the wedding

After all dressed up we sit in a room with the bride in red and gold splendor, rings and bangles on her fingers and arms, women singing and drumming, "Soon your husband will come and you will be so happy," the senile grandmother sticks out her tongue and lays her head on my shoulder

After we eat in groups of four: huge platter of rice, the cook adds morsels one at a time on top from his huge kettle — mutton, meatballs, cheese, intestines, we eat with our fingers, they videotape us and interview us — "How do you like Kashmir? Have you ever eaten food like this before? Do you like this food?'

After Asalem brings Bob a beer at the wedding — "They won't know what it is"

After the houseboat keeps moving even though it isn't when I've taken my malaria pills

After Shahabuddin tells me there's lots of dark forces here my anger isn't personal

After our "family" meals — Suzanne and Karl, Nancy and Casey, me and Bob around the embroidered tablecloth table in our houseboat — beans, cauliflower, squash, chicken, fish, boiled potatoes with parsley, Basir asking if we want more

We take turns leading grace

After Nancy asks if we've changed a lot since Bali — she had a different impression of us then

After Nancy's nose piercing and infection

After dark Corey beautiful in her flowered dress at ancient Mogul gardens, old roses dating from the time of Akbar

After Zia weeps at musicians in the dargah, reaches for money in his gold vest pocket, touches it to the tomb and shuffles it trembling and bowing to the musicians over and over

After fried eggs on white bread in the Hope Project, dripping wet and devastated from the poverty, Shahabuddin and I split the last sandwich

After lunch back at the $400 a night Imperial Hotel, marble floors, 12 foot ceilings, antique carved furniture, "Sir'ed " and "Madam'ed" down the hall

After drinking beer in the lounge with Karl and Suzanne, band playing old Beatles songs, trying to explain to 19 year old Nathan Beatles coming to India and meeting the Maharishi

After lunch in opulence after the Baste, weeping at Unchained Melody on
grand piano in the dining room, the dichotomy of delicious food we can-
not finish

After Baba's sweet round face and hand over his heart, he doesn't speak
English

After praying in empty canopied space at the wedding with Baba, "The
Americans are praying!" Shahabuddin quips

After buying papier mache boxes, scarves, shawls

After guys on the street try to buy Bob's binoculars

After a beggar girl follows us on the street for blocks and won't go way

After the merchants in boats try to sells us jewelry, papier mache, tonkas as
we sail to the gardens

After I get left behind for shopping, Shafee tells us to go sit in the front of the
boat and relax, doesn't want us to wait in the back for the taxi or buy
from other merchants where he doesn't get a cut, he wants us to look at
his rugs, "I'm not buying rugs," I say, "I don't need any."

After I yell at Asalam about being left behind

After we order cotton outfits in white like Shafee's and they come the last day
in blue polyester

After the blister on my toe from climbing the Himalayas in my clogs

After zikir and prayer and dinner and song

After Jesse's What-Color? eyes

After Amber's popeyed stare

After Gary works polarity on my migraine

After Sabina's songs

After buses with no air-conditioning and fans that don't work

After flowers in our houseboats

After Nathan playing soccer with the Indian kids

After kids splashing and swimming to us in the water

After the women in their new blue dresses and shawls

After the taxi drivers say they haven't had a fare for two weeks

After I know I had my notebook all the way to Amsterdam and now it's just
missing

After the prayer wheel flies out of my hand and bams two dents into my cof-
fee table at home

After all this

After all this sitting up in bed, we watch 4th of July fireworks explode over
our heads — grand finale a mile away at the lake — and dream of wars
while firecrackers crack across Nebraska night

BARBARA SCHMITZ

Cat Revelation

for Caitlin

I know a thing or two about cats,
and that scrawny black skeleton with dirty socks
curled in the empty geranium pot on the porch
was one fine haven for bugs and stink.
Ball of running sores, why cling to our yard
for a two weeks under threat of animal control,
then vanish? Then three days into my blissful relief
and a new potted geranium, the neighbor's daughter,
best friend of our own, knocked at the door
cradling that sack of cat piss, child weeping,
cat dripping and reeking of gasoline:
"My mom's at work and my dad's in the shower,
and I thought you'd know what to do,"

And I thought, oh you lucky man in the shower at this
of all times—me with a house full of children
and a known oversized bathtub at the top of the stairs.
I have resisted moments of truth in my life—
sled rides on thin ice, candy from strangers,
raw oysters from New Jersey—and I know how
to say no to destiny, but I said,
"Give me the cat and we'll wash it."

Kneeling by the tub where a tall woman
could stretch out and enjoy a good soak,
I reddened my hands through twenty sloshing
shampoos, the last six with laundry detergent,
Five visiting children and two of my own
leaned over me shouting advice, falling onto
my aching shoulders or into the tub.
Fumes watered my eyes, as I kneaded
that paltry body that never mewed
scrambled, scratched nor bit, but stood
in the frothing waves and took whatever I sent
her way—head above water, eyes heavenward.

There's nothing more certain than this:
no one can wash a cat twenty times in front of children,
dry it, and watch it eat a can of tuna intended
for dinner under a patch of warm late sun angling through

the kitchen door, reflecting gold in the cat's left eye,
without something turning over in the soul,
without the cat revealing its true name.

DRU WALL

August 1990

The '64 Plymouth was
brown or maybe purple once.
When Dad brought it home
we all got in and went for a ride
in the country.
The previous owner left it in her garage
for over twenty years.
We found a newspaper
in the glove compartment,
date, April 27, 1967.
The Plymouth had an AM radio
and we listened to oldies
and we drove through the dusty hills,
singing.
Then we came to the road
where one night after a long fight
my mom had shouted,
"Let me the fuck out of this car."
And Dad had left her there
in the middle of nowhere.
But that was another car.
We went past that place
so fast it was almost like we
were never there.
We drove to a hill overlooking
our whole valley.
The stars were like an army
advancing from the sky.
The valley was dark except for a light
here and there from a farm.
Mom, Dad, my sister and I sat
on the hood of the Plymouth
and talked about people we knew,
and our days,
and those rampaging stars,
and especially this new old car,
that we loved so much,
that we depended on so much already,
even though we knew
in some inner valley
that this car, like the last,

would become more and more us.
And behind us on the strong back
of the hill were the other cars
we'd loved,
watching us like sad abandoned angels,
and I knew without turning
you were there,
even those of you we never owned
or even touched.
Some we visited on the lot
and wanted and lusted for
and some that were just dreams
or glimpses of another life
we could have had.

ELIZABETH CLARK

⮜ Wild Columbine ⮞

A delicate but hardy perennial widely distributed in the wild or in the garden, columbine adapts to a variety of conditions. It does best in light shade but will tolerate full sun if daytime temperatures are not too high. In early times, the seeds were pulverized and rubbed on the hands as a love charm. Columbines are difficult to arrange as cut flowers. When a truly exquisite effect is desired, cut a single bloom and place it in a vase by itself.

September, Getting Married Again

In the night of the long day
On which we have driven five hours
To find your father,
Who has prodded and measured us,
And we, afraid,
Have said this one to the gold bar

In miniature, for the rings,
And he has promised to make them;
At midnight, on that night,
Cold and afraid, wakeful,
I come to the kitchen.

In the midst of a welter of china
My children have dirtied in the course
Of their bodies' nurture—
In my absence, yellows and reds
Crusting the sides of dishes—
Is the cardboard box
Your mother has filled
For our pleasure:

A butternut squash in the shape
Of our body; onions
So rich a purple they are royal;
Their papery brothers;
The orbs of fall tomatoes,
Scarlet, rimmed with gold
And capped by a green star;
And dull green apples
Round beyond compass measure,
Pure white at their center,
A perfect fullness of flesh
That taken hold of and opened,   .
Will make our eyes water.

HILDA RAZ

My Dream, Your Dream

In half-light salt
crusted in my eye
corners but I haven't
been weeping, only
traveling in a country
where you come careening
around a corner on your bicycle, wind a wall
you've smashed into,
far side of your face
gone flat on the bone.
I reach to wake you up
to me but you say no
and turn into a half-light
of your own, hair a crest
on the pillow and you're
heading into blue rain
rising fast over the windy
crescent of some western hill.

HILDA RAZ

The Garden

I don't remember the accident.
I only remember the garden,
ripe strawberries, their juice,
carrots, moist earth clinging,
the taste of grit in my mouth,
my favorites, fresh peas,
two luscious rows to search through,
looking for the largest,
snapping each from the vine,
opening the shell,
raising pod to lips,
tipping my head back,
eyes dazzled by sunlight,
tongue probing to release
tiny membranes,
and joy of devouring
sweetness.

My mother and I work in the garden.
Chuck, our hired hand, strides past.
Hoe in hand, I follow him.
My first love, fourteen years my senior,
a tall lanky youth of sixteen,
brown hair, warm eyes,
quick to smile, quick to laugh,
Chuck loves to tickle, tease me,
and I endure his schoolboy torments
for I know they are given in love.

In church,
all eyes to the front except mine,
I stand on my mother's lap,
encircled by her arms,
twisting to look over her shoulder,
waiting for my young god.
Late,
Chuck slides into the back pew,
a grin and a wink, my reward.

Chuck doesn't see me leave the garden.
I am behind the farmtruck as he

backs out of the garage.
My hoe catches the truck's axle,
pulls me under its wheels.
My mother's screams stop. In the hospital,
thirty miles away, a doctor
looks at my legs,
shakes his head,
Only time will tell how soon I will walk again,
Meantime, I need to be carried
everywhere,
or left behind.
A red wagon, new, painted,
a child's toy,
becomes my temporary legs.
My parents pull me,
taking turns,
around the yard, corrals, and garden.

Looking back,
Maybe, I was supposed to learn the lesson
you fall in love, you get run over by a truck,
the equation that love is pain and a red wagon,
and yet,
this is not what I remember,
I remember peas, strawberries, carrots, earth,
I remember the garden.

BETH TORGERSON

At a Window Facing West

Waiting again at the kitchen table
she watches the light
through the Roman shade;
yellow, gold, grey, gone.
His faint knock—twice, perhaps
three times in quick succession—
makes her smile. Lifting the shade
she sees him grinning at her
his breath a white veil
between them.

Opening the door, she unwinds
the muffler from his neck, tugs
at the collar of his coat as he shrugs
out of it and, as he bends
toward her, takes his cap
wet with snow, from his thick hair.

Two chairs scrape against
the brick floor, the sound abrupt
and surprising in the silence
of this November evening
that they begin by reading
to each other, shyly at first,
voices breathy and tentative:
  I'm Nobody! Who are you?
  Are You—Nobody—Too?
  Then there's a pair of us?
  Don't tell!

At the staircase, as she gains
the first step, he pulls her around
to face him, kisses her delicately, slowly.
Taking his hand, she leads him
past the window locked against the cold
to her bed, dark wood
warmed by yellow moon.
His body is sweet, hot summer;
the touch of his gold ring
on her back burns like ice.

As she sleeps, he steals
a look at the glowing face
of his watch. The pale light
of the clerestory window defines him
as he gathers his clothing
dresses quickly and eases
the door closed behind him, cold wind cheating
up the stairs. She moves
into the empty space
he has left behind.

PAT HEMPHILL EMILE

Drill Bits

Is it spring again?
Yes, creek-bed willows
have kindled their fires.

Beside our frosty driveway
daffodils are trusting
tender buds to the cold.
Lowly crocuses burgeon from snow
in rich purples and golds.

In the warmth of our kitchen
two forsythia cuttings are venturing
with clear yellow blossoms.

I go to our garage looking for nails
and come upon a box of drill bits
meticulously arranged by size.
I miss you then
as never before.

IRENE ROSE GRAY

Meteor Shower

Lying by your side in the convent orchard,
in the unmown midnight lawn,
I turned to tell you that I felt the dew
settling on my face and folded hands,
smelled sweet pears and apples
each time the breeze stilled,
their bouquet covering us like rain.
I could have been a stone
resting on a murky lake bottom,
then our child rolled like a minnow
beneath my skin like a sudden silent galaxy.
Streaks of light sparkled
behind broken cloud;
there, and there.
Together our hands floated—
white moths among the branches—
while somewhere around us
a soul stood in awe of itself,
waiting to be found.
As we walked home
our pockets filled with purple plums,
small yellow pears and apples.
We didn't know she would be slow to talk,
but one day say "A is for avalanche"
and almost never stop. We didn't know
she would chant "My daddy
is a hexagon, my momma is a diamond"
as she mounted the stairs to nap.
We saw only the light from our kitchen window,
the cat sitting by the table,
the bowl waiting for fruit.

DIANE HUETER

Aubade

I wake at five to stainless light:
We've rocked the dark away,
Our breath, our bodies all
That warm the winter room.

Your heart knocks its mooring.
Going is a destination:
In this pale hour between two snows,
Only small birds must move.

JEANNETTE BARNES

Sonnets

...so my love, I knew that I was wounded,
and no one spoke there except the shadows,
the wandering night, the kiss of rain.
                                    Pablo Neruda

Left to
struggle with the absence of air,
like the way we screamed "Dog pile!" and
tumbled into each other, tangling our bodies, hoping
to end up anywhere but the bottom.
Get off, a tiny voice would whine or gasp,
suddenly really afraid,
the game serious as it gets.
Each time Mercy came.
We peeled away layer by layer,
to the one spared.
Off Pacific Street in
a bookstore with the
comfort of a fireplace,
hot coffee of the day, Cherry Mash flavor,
sleet moving in from the south earlier than expected,
I warm my hands with a pink book, the
sonnets of Neruda.
He was so good, so bold,
as sentimental as he wished,
telling his love
what love is
or is not,
in the sweet pain of breathing.

SHELLY CLARK

Sunday Lunch in Ponder, Texas

All the waitresses who knew us had gone.
The owner glared at television
where grainy players rushed from end to end.
The fan stirred grease smoke and dust.

Cotton-candy meringue on dark chocolate,
hamburgers searing on the grill—
the cook was the same
but portions were smaller.
Still plenty.

We ate in the car with windows down,
watched the rambles of sky.
On the radio, the hop and squeak of a country fiddle.
Scissortails glided between barbs and thorns.

A striped butterfly settled on his hand,
fanned the meat smell. He let it stay
as long as it wanted.
I remembered
once I pointed to a butterfly
and it laid the soft trust of its body-weight on my skin.
He said it was a blessing.

I placed my fingertips lightly on his thigh
for the ride home.

MARTHA ELIZABETH

Blue Marker Landscape

From our Sunday bed by the window
I watch the neighbor's black motorcycle
creak its weight against dry boards
on a spindle rail porch.
In the flashing wind, last apples
flip from their homey branch,
splitting against the roof
for the pleasure of crazy wasps.
Beyond the piney border of our street,
fields toss their stubbled dregs
to the swaying meadows
where a black dog tags a gold man
through the high and shifting grass,
And crows annoy the fence posts,
calling for rain.

Turning over, I study your curls,
redolent in the sun.
From under your side I pull
Caitlin's blue marker
left in bed last night.
She drew flowers on my back
and wrote, "My brother is a stupid head."
I could write on you, you're so asleep:
"Kick me" in century schoolbook,
"My love is like . . ." in palatino.
Your spine makes a better shaft of wheat.
Curve another six across your left.
Blue sheaves demand a high horizon,
farmhouse with a spindle porch—
careful, no tickles—
water tower leaning into shoulder space.
No time for dogs, people, motorcycles.

Wind kicking up, moaning.
Look out, Dorothy, it's a twister.
Horizon smears, turning and throwing
the lower forty over me.
Wires blow down.
Blue wheat burning.
Marker lost.

DRU WALL

Pulling Up Beside My Husband at the Stoplight

We are going to the same place
but we take two cars. Sunday morning
and there's not much traffic
so I pull up beside him at the light.
The sun is shining on the road.
Here he is in his car

beside my car,
the curve of his shoulder
through the glass, his face
fresh from a shave, his hair
against the brown of his neck.
He turns and blows me a kiss.
I watch it float on by. I ask
for another. I think of him
coming into the dark bedroom

in the mornings,
the sound of his workboots
across the carpet,
the scent of his face
when he finds me in the covers,
pulls the blanket away and
kisses my eyebrow,
the corner of my mouth,
tells me the weather report
and the precise time of day.
I roll down the window,

whistle in my throat,
pull my glasses crooked on my face,
do my best baboon snorting,
pound the horn
as if it were bread dough.
There's only the lady in the white Taurus
but he is embarrassed, glad to see the green.
I'm stepping on the gas,
catching up, wondering
what I can do at 56th and Calvert.

MARJORIE SAISER

I love you most in the mornings

I love you most in the mornings.
When you turn over and say "Go run"
after my snooze has been hit for half an hour.
When I leave the bed after holding you
and you sprawl across to compensate.
When I'm deciding what clothes to wear
and you squirm when I sit on the edge of the bed,
undressing and dressing in front of you,
your mouth in an upturn like you can see.
When I kiss you goodbye and, without
opening your eyes, you reach for my hand.

HEATHER MCSHANE

Girls Who Will Never Marry

We howl. Dance snaky.
Faces red under a pumpkin moon
Our arms fly, release
Milkweed threads into alfalfa-scented air.

Possum play possum under loblolly pines
Cicadas have long shut up
We are choke cherry starving for love
Below a sky wired with stars.

Barn doors are never locked and we
Want to lay with teenage boys
Who smell like quarter horses, feel
Hands and knees wedge our thighs apart.

Fingertips still stinking of saddlesoap
Will find a way to make us scream
Tempt us with a sweet deal
Make us sing songs of invented sin.

Come morning, our hair spiky with hay
We hear the devil-tap of hooves
Watch the boys fade away, vanish, merge
Into an otherwise slow wooing of life.

DEBORAH BYRNE

Yin-Yang
Lincoln, Nebraska, USA

I would like to be on top of the food chain,
but I know I am only a bat, blind with only radar
to bounce off objects, trees, walls,
get entangled in your hair, like a lover's fingers
making you wild with passion,
become wet there where it matters.
I am a child of such love, adulterous, but real —
speaking for itself, without reason behind it:
why do we need a reason to be whole, to be happy?
Please tell me, why, when I am here on this earth
a Piscean, swimming in opposite directions,
a double, a reflection of another, a you?
I draw trees with branches everywhere, fingers,
black on white paper touching, but only slightly, bat-like —
and one day I will make my medallion of jewels;
I paint it in watercolors, red, yellow, black —
wanting that special artist, a Lakota Sioux to create it,
so I can wear it proudly on my chest, richly set,
the only one of its kind, on top, a circle divided
into halves, multicolored like me, of two worlds,
the old and this New one, a *conquistador* of the prairie,
both full of fire, mystic, surreal, cock-like,
crying out at dawn, making the sleepy-heads wake,
ready to change the pastures, find new ground,
feed the chickens with new knowledge, with wisdom!
I know I'm not the deer we saw crossing the back road
at midnight, behind Pioneer's Park, antlerless, unprotected,
running away from our lights, afraid to be touched.

BILJANA D. OBRADOVIC

Cardinal: Dark to Deep or Vivid Red

I can understand, dear, that
you wonder if I know what I am doing,
marrying this man I've known
one winter plus a year.

Isn't this a little fast, Mom?
Are you definitely in love?
I've seen people in love before
and you don't seem to act like that.

Well, the neighbor's fake cardinal
showed up that winter after Christmas,
appearing on the clothesline in the back,
then gone, then hanging on the ash tree
out in front, J. P. and I amused. But when

we read a poem together
—*cardinals in the tops of trees,*
whistling for love—I began to see

how much this man would mean to me.
He said in all his years of farming,
he saw a cardinal act like that just once,
hunched forward on a low branch of a cedar,
head hung down. Not singing.

J.P. figured the bird had lost his mate,
that he was waiting there to die.
Last summer, right before he cut his wheat,
he showed me around his farm for the first time.

I'm remembering the way he walked
over his own ground. Solid. Eager.
The handshake of boot and earth.
I hadn't thought of that before.

LYNN OVERHOLT WAKE

Six Minute Blizzard

In the quiet morning I move from room
to room, walking off the blur of sleep.

One pass by the front window — bright
blue sky, bluster of clouds, the wind tries
the panes with its fingers — showing off.

Bathrobe. Coffee. Kitchen window —
somehow, a blizzard kicks up
and visibility's near zero. Snow blasts by,
blows itself into cyclones in the backyard.
Across the street, a wreath is ripped
from a front door, goes rolling
into the distance. I watch it go.
Snow begins to show itself on lawns.

But I turn to put on socks.
I turn to get another quick sip
of still-hot coffee. Not more than minutes,
but when I turn back to the picture window
the past has been erased. The wind
still blows, but sun blares its blue sky certainty —
not a snowflake in sight.

It does this all day. For minutes, a blizzard,
then none, the skies screeching to a halt.
All told, we don't get more than a dusting.

I remember when we blew up balloons
for some party — made each other laugh
till the ones we held deflated. Hours like this.
Gave ourselves headaches, finally, and only
for a few balloons.

I think I loved you once. For six minutes,
somewhere, it was that simple. That
surprising. But I turned away — just
for a moment — and how easily all of it was swept
away, like weather on the prairie,
like the wind that knocks off the wreath —
one unbelievable gust — and is gone.

LIZ AHL

Too Much Give

In yard goods, there's a yardstick nailed down
on the cutting counter, scissors on a string.
Every Ben Franklin is the same, even here
in Two Harbors, a tourist town. The maple floors slant
and give as you walk around, scanning
bolts of material lined up, piled up, some askew.
Beautiful colors, neon cottons, watery silks, pastel
jerseys. Today I find black velvet, gorgeous
for a crazy quilt, feather stitched with
lavender and gold. Now I'm fingering some blue cotton stars—
I'll know from the feel if there's too much give
to be of use. I dig through the remnant bin, scraps
for baby things, 37 cents. It's automatic, this bargain
hunting, goes back to the days over a dozen years now,
when I walked to town three times a week
with the baby in the stroller,
my life predictable as a clock.

Morning walks, afternoon naps.
5:00, the first glass of French Columbard.
In the spring, bouquets of lilies from the yard.
6:00, cooking dinner. Baby down,
time for quilts, and books, stacks of books.
Time to wonder if he'll come home, if he'll
want dinner, if he'll be pissed
because dinner wasn't what
he wanted, *because*... I never got beyond the
because when he started hitting, my fear
held down by the brandy under the sink.
Nothing was better than being a mother.
That's what I said then. I got up every morning
on time, happy to see my baby. The baby
didn't know anything was wrong. That's what I said then.
I ran on schedule, so different from my college
stance—I laughed when I read Ben Franklin's diary, how
he agonized over his daily schedule! Now I
was the one walking to the Ben Franklin
making a schedule work.

That was a long time ago, and here I am
in the Two Harbors Ben Franklin, making an

unscheduled stop. The kids are intently picking out
embroidery thread—purple, kelly green, and red.
They're weaving bracelets while riding
in the car. In fact, that's why we stopped,
they ran out of red. I look
across the cottons, see a young woman
holding her baby on her left hip, holding up,
with her right arm, a swatch of cloth with huge red
and white sailboats—red is the best color for
baby quilts—red is the first color they can see.
She's gazing off, imagining a new design.

Everything that happens is supposed to happen:
I'm here today to forgive that girl,
to forgive her for sewing instead of writing,
for staying home when she should've run,
for drinking when she should've
dialed 911. I'm here to forgive her
for making a life of
remnants, for living a life with too much
give. She looks so frail and lonely
over there, the chunky baby laughing on her hip.

ROSEANN LLOYD

County Mental Health Clinic, 1976

So, the therapist said, turning to face
him in the padded easy chair, where he sprawled

in his inimitable fashion, arms relaxed on the arm rests,
legs open, stretched out into the center of the room

where he took up more of the available space than the other
two—the therapist and me. *So*, the therapist said again,

she says she's ashamed of herself because she didn't leave you
after you repeatedly battered her.

But now that she's said this, here, to a third party,
you can be assured

that if you touch her again, she will
leave you for good. What I want you to do now is take off

your glasses and let her hit you in the face.
Hit you anywhere she wants. Hit you as hard as she can.

I couldn't tell if the therapist was serious.
But I could see my husband

could no more let me hit him
than he could admit that his beatings of me were wrong.

Nobody touches me, he said. He looked shocked
that another man would betray him in this manner.

I couldn't bear to look at his astounded face.
The muscles in my face tightened, set.

I was getting ready to walk away, take the baby, go.
I turned, looked out the window.

Watched a small bird fly from one bare gray tree
to another, the clouds and river and sky all flat gray

behind them. The soul of our marriage
has flown out of me, I thought. There it goes—

with a body, soft gray feathers, and wings—
and nothing I can do will bring it back.

When I looked back at the room,
the men were blurry through the steamy window.

I could see their mouths opening, closing,
but I couldn't follow the conversation any more.

ROSEANN LLOYD

Traveling Directions

Put lipstick on.
Lift up a section of your hair,
comb down it,
repeat.

Use plenty of hairspray—
Revlon is best).
Put on a hat (preferably with flowers).

Put on your white shoes
Cuban heels—Mom won't allow higher).

Wipe lipstick off
so when your father says,
"Are you wearing lipstick?"
you can say,

"No, Daddy, honest—see?
Put on your white gloves
with the lace at the wrist
but be sure to take one off
for communion).

Look in the mirror.
Pick up the white purse.
Go downstairs.

Listen to your father yelling,
"Fran, get that kid ready, or we're
not going."

Listen to your brother cry.

Get in the car.

Sit on the seat, sideways, then
swing your legs up—be sure
never to show
your panties
or your slip.

Fasten your seatbelt.
Listen to your father say, "Dammit,
fasten Jerry's seatbelt, do I have to tell you
everything?"

Reach over.
Scream as your brother pulls off your hat
and pulls your hair all straggly.

Wait while your mother
puts your brother in front
and sits in back.

Die inside because of your messy hair.

Get out of the car when it stops.

Go up the stairs,
into the church,
where no one can yell.

ANNE L. HAEHL

Mattress

I'm reading the Norfolk Daily News want ads
looking for...stuff,
because I don't have much.
>   Good mattress. Not used much.
>   Moving, must sell.
>   Inquire at Skinny's.
I've been sleeping on the floor
of my apartment for two months.
I go to the store downtown that sells
CD's, T-shirts, sex toys.
There's a redheaded woman behind the counter
smoking a cigarette. I ask about
the quality of her mattress. How much?

She says it sleeps great,
the brand is great.
Great at $100.00 She exhales.

Outside, she helps me
        load it onto the
            roof of my
                '85 Escort.
                Her
            tiny body
        is crammed
    into a smaller
    vinyl black skirt.

She climbs onto my already dented car
like an erect, flashy hood ornament,
but on the roof instead of the hood.
I'm hoping the rest of Norfolk will not notice
two women wrestling with the rectangular box.
But she screams like a woman
who has just turned into Medusa—
She is moving out of his dirty life,
moving to a dirty jail,
selling his dirty stuff.

She throws down a thin rope
to secure the sleeping box.

I'm trying to figure out what to tie it to,
when I notice—
Stab marks made with obvious force.
I believe I can smell the rusty crimson stains
that even the police are interested in.
Never mind the cigarette burns.

"So what happened with you two?"
I am quiet. She is not.
I'm hoping she will get off my car,
but again she backfires.
"I tried to kill him."

Every night I remember.
It's all I can afford.

MELISSA BEERY

Girl Talk (Coffee/China)

Told me handpicked by Juan Valdez 'n
yes Columbian coffee gets the morning
out of bed 'n into the springtime shower
puts me safe on the streets with a full belly
all this good life paradise stuff
but can't help seein' Juan moonlightin'
in coke fields his wife 'n kids not knowin'
how famous on TV his name his fingers

'n there's this woman at her knittin' machine
somewhere in China puttin' together 'n
on my very back this white cotton sweater
wonderin' what she'd be
had she been so lucky
t've been made in the USA.

NANCY MCCLEERY

Girl Talk (High/Bird)

Told me had a friend so high-strung
if she'd let go his hand at a concert
he'd rise to the rafters, a helium balloon.

A dancer, she said, he seemed to lift off
en pointe tap skylarking or waltzing
one of those boys light on his feet

everything in the highest register
no one could match his obligato his steps
'n laugh that fella could laugh at anything
the announcement I'd been practicin' yoga
on 'n off for twenty years had him snortin'
as if it were a mantra however he couldn't sit
couldn't meditate but he could concentrate

never saw a fella so reluctant to give up
on a good joke even when it was on him
even when not really a joke but a slur
like someone callin' out hey you faggot
he'd treat it as if it were a jest

even when in the last stages of the plague
he never lost his *joie de vivre*

went out of state to die like an old
sparrow crawled off to hide in the shade
of some low spirea or currant branches
his wings his feet finally stilled although
something remained suspended floating

and I've asked homophobics, she said,
what if he'd been a son or a brother
how could anyone be against anyone

so giving so high-spirited so full of malarky
blue mud the old blarney.

NANCY MCCLEERY

My Daughter Brings Me
Garbage Flowers

digs them out of the floral shop
trash at the end of her work day,
an evening job arranging flowers,
lifting her spirits after teaching
Special Education. Blown roses,
mostly. Last week thirteen of them.
I don't stop smiling for days.
Deep red. Last month three lavender.
Sometimes pale yellow, pink, white.

Occasionally a mixed bouquet,
spring flowers. Flowers that don't
and won't sell. Too fully opened.
Wilting a bit. Old. Older.
We cherish, we salvage what we can.
Mirrors, these companions. Old friends.

Most want the virgin rose buds.
She knows I prefer the blatant,
immodest, blowzy, open blossoms.
Brings them wrapped in pastel tissue papers
holding them in her arms the way
I carried her before she walked.

Memorial Day week, the shop floor
covered with buckets of blue and white
hydrangeas, blue flags, freesias, carnations,
pots of green and yellow philodendron,
geraniums, petunias, lobelia. And peonies,
the beauty of pink and white and fuchsia
blooms. A backdrop for dreams in color.
Pale, still bodies of war dead. These tributes.

And there behind the counter, a knife
in her right hand, my daughter,
cutting thorns from stems. Smiling.

NANCY MCCLEERY

Sunday Afternoons
My Son Bakes Bread

makes it from scratch. Salt-free yeast bread,
whole wheat, plain white, and today,
Babka, my favorite. His wife prepares
two pans with a crumbled mix of butter,
sugar and spices; then cuts the citron,
lemon and lime, for the dough

which has risen once, been punched down.
I make only fast breads. Irish Soda Bread, banana,
peanut butter, bourbon-pecan, Poor Poet's Bread.
All without yeast. Requiring no kneading.

Lost to the rest of us, his face down, smiling,
he becomes, though he'd frown at my saying it,
the boy I raised, focusing completely,
concentrating as he's done since a toddler, now

the six foot four and half inch frame
bent over the floured board, working the dough,
palms shaping it, turning it around and around,
making two small loaves.

While they rise, we tell what's new,
as they bake, we swap stories.

Some call for a shot of rum over them
while cooling. He ignores this for now,
sends a loaf home with me. This treat.
This nurturing. Returning the favor.

NANCY MCCLEERY

ER Euphemism

Be brave, I say, do not move
I am sorry to hurt you.

She is limp, tiny, too quiet.
The ER's a flame of activity and
there's no nurse's note.

The young mother weeps
wrings her hands
the knot of her curls over her child
in the curtained space.

I cup my hand under the child's head
the size of a small cantaloupe
the same woody skin with
pliable, doughy, interior.

It's hard to remove the tangle of her
from her mother's limbs.

It's dark, Mommy.
Mommy? Where are you?

Touch the occipital curve and
the child's face
becomes a wrinkled map
pain, fear, compliance.

There is a strong family resemblance
the lift of the eyes, the set of the mouths
only the child is so much thinner
her cheeks mold in.

She asks again for light.

The nurse appears now
sterile gauze to the wound
under pressure
something congeals on the scalp
something knots behind my eyes.

Suspect NAT, the nurse whispers
small as conspiracy
Non Accidental Trauma.

I strap her to the gurney
swab her elbow hollow
fresh alcohol careens through
Saturday night's arena.

The IV runs in   a lullaby leaks
from my lips   and I tell her
What,
what can I possibly say.

GAIL WALDSTEIN, M.D.

My Brother

Home from boot camp,
he rolls back the living room rug
to teach me the Texas jitterbug.
I'm twelve, can't recall his touching
me before except to shove or hit.

Jerry Lee Lewis sings
Great Balls of Fire as Gary's arm,
newly tattooed with a cobra,
circles my waist,
and hip to hip we move backward,
past the coat closet — where I used to
hide, afraid of his after school moods —
past the picture of Jesus, kneeling
in doubt on the Mount of Olives.

He twirls me out, reels me,
sends me spinning again, but I
keep my balance: lock my eyes on his.
I'm a good dancer. I can read his wrists.
When he praises me for catching on so fast,
the small dog in me wags, changes its mind,
shows its tartered teeth.

SONDRA UPHAM

Mother Believes

My father, in heaven, watches us,
still wears his blue and gray uniform,
corporal's badge,
leather holster, gun, his tall brown boots.
Even when he's reading the news
or fishing, he's listening for our voices,
in case we call to him.
That's what she says.

I'd like to see him
stand up on the bandmaster's stage
in Memorial Park, on John C. Fremont Day,
when the whole town is gathered,
frown his great black brows
and proclaim: *This is my daughter. I named her.*
Whoever harms her, answers to me.

SONDRA UPHAM

untold tyrants

the day you
wounded me with
rocks shot from your
BB gun then swore it was a
harmless deed

the night you were
all liquored up and
running amok and you
yanked on my long
dark hair

times you
nailed me to the
hard ground your
adolescent spit hanging
over my face

the night you
sneaked out the
back door and
appeared in the window the
boogeyman himself

nights I would go up the
stairs under protest then
inspect beneath my
unmade bed for
evidence you were there

nights I watched the
trees outside the
window dancing in the
wind sure it
was you

the night I left the
kitchen window unlatched
doors bolted then sensing a
presence awoke to see you
standing over me

the night I hid
curled up in the
corner of my bedroom
when you came for
your little girl

the midnight I hid like an
escapee behind the
wintry bush on Hammond
Street when you returned to
take back your possessions

nights you
chased me in my
dreams forever trying to
kill me until I took your
weapons away and
found my own

HAZEL SMITH HUTCHINSON

when the four o'clock whistle blows

rhubarb stalk in hand
I run out from behind
the falling down barn
to see him

not expecting
a hug
only a look
into his black metal dinner pail
just in case
there's anything left

HAZEL SMITH HUTCHINSON

Take Cover

My father's silence
Twists the cottonwoods off their moorings
Spews plate glass shards on our dishes.
Crack a window
Hide in the stairwell
Eat VanCamp's cold from the can
My father's silence
Could scare even Mister Kennedy
Threatens to end the world
Hold your breath
Plan a route
Pack one bag.
My father's silence
Bursts his eardrum
Leaves deafening scars.
Speak up.
Shut down.
He hurts.

RITA SHELLEY

Such a Sky We Had

Last June bright stars and a field
of fireflies, more

of both than either
of us had ever seen. You
stopped the car; I walked

down the road, you up,
and we walked just as if we
were still together

forever, as if our light
had not gone cold already

many summers back.

MAUREEN HALLIGAN TOBIN

South Dakota

We're riding in a car
just like when we were married
only now we're on the divorce road.
I didn't want to be on the divorce road
but you dragged me into the car,
and ridiculed me every time I said, "I love you."
We have children.
You ranted and threatened and went faster and faster
until I accepted.
I said, "OK, we'll go to South Dakota."
"I want to go to Wisconsin," you'd say occasionally.
"But we're on the divorce road to South Dakota.
We need to stop and look at the map."
"This is the way I want to go," you said, speeding
weaving faster into the sunset.
I see that we're going to South Dakota.
Why can't you see that we're going to South Dakota?
I tried to throw myself from the car, but the children stopped me.
I don't want to go to South Dakota.
The plains become higher, dryer.
The lakes and trees, the blue and green of Minnesota lie behind.
The lake place, the country home, the children's college
...gone to the lawyers.
We sit in the therapist's office, the Badlands between us,
the threats of murder, destruction, violence, rage.
"We should be friends. We should get along.
For the sake of the children.
My rights," you say. "We should be in Wisconsin."
"But we drove on the divorce road to South Dakota."
Both male heads turn toward me. I'm just a crazy woman.
"We drove to South Dakota. We're not in Wisconsin.
You wouldn't stop. You wouldn't listen.
You didn't leave us friendship."
"You should be in Wisconsin," the therapist says.
"I couldn't stop him."
The hate — how long did you hate me?
The threats, the violence, the destruction, the fear, the pain
drove us to South Dakota.
"Forget the past. You like to be a victim. You deserved it. You made me."
But this is the path you chose for us. Your manhood took us to South
    Dakota.

I can't pretend we're in Wisconsin.
That would be crazy. I can't help it if I see we're in another land.
For the children, for myself, for you,
I can't tell you we're in Wisconsin
when we drove to South Dakota.

REBECCA WEST

Grandma Ellen Tells it Like it Was

Back then
there was no Crisis Line,
no Friendship Home to take you in.
You had made your bed, and there you would lie.
So you acquired the proper downward glance,
learned just the right brush strokes
to keep the picture pretty.
And when his heel came down
you did what you must
and kneaded your rage
into a hard round ball.
It was poison,
but it was yours.
You kept it tight inside.
There is no disgrace
in sleeping with the enemy.
You did it for the children.
You did it to survive.
And more often than not
he would die
first.

LUCY ADKINS

Gorilla Warfare

Without knocking
my son bursts
into my bedroom.
"Mommy, what's guerilla warfare?"
I stumble over a definition
so, rolling on my side,
I lean over the edge of my water bed
to retrieve my tattered gray dictionary.

Due to fatigue, my son's pronunciation, or
my stupidity,
I look up g-o-r-i-l-l-a
and to my chagrin
the term "gorilla warfare" is not defined.
However
I note
that the word gorilla
is derived
from the Greek *gorillai*
believed to be the name of
"an alleged tribe of hairy African women."

"What's guerilla warfare?"
my son insists.
"It's the kind of war
black women
wage every day,"
I reply.

ANNETTE L. MURRELL

Dry Seasons

My heart lies fallow
season after season.
Untended land
aching to be tilled,

sown and reaped.
Hope withers beneath
a scorching sun
and desolate days

with no scent of rain.
My soil has become
hard, cracked,
bitter with drought,

barren under harvest moons.
Of what value is land
if it sustains no inhabitants
or bears no sweet fruit?

ANNETTE L. MURRELL

I wanna be a bad woman

I've stayed in the front yard all my life.
I want a peek at the back
Where it's rough and untended and hungry weeds grow. A girl
gets sick of a rose.

Gwendolyn Brooks
"A Street in Brownsville"

I wanna be a bad woman:
the kind of woman my grandmother, georgia mae,
rolled her eyes at and hissed a tsk tsk with her sanctified tongue,
pronouncing as we passed, "that hussy's on the road to perdition!"

I wanna be a bad woman:
loud, loose, hard drinking and hot for sex,
who spends afternoons drinking colt 45 on her front porch, legs parted wide
   like the red sea,
cussing out anyone foolish enough to suggest they be crossed.

I wanna be a bad woman:
a woman whose men must pay her rent, car note and utilities before they
   climb into her bed,
who looks grocery clerks dead in the eyeball as she counts out her food
   stamps,
who speaks only black english and refers to the president as "that horny peck-
   erwood."

I wanna be a bad woman:
like miss ethel who stood in her front yard every morning toothless and with
   no brassiere,
sipping a water glass of beef eaters while waving at me and slurring, "keep
   smiling baby,"
as I passed her house on the way to school, trembling with fear and envy.

ANNETTE L. MURRELL

Early Childhood Education

Inside her eyes
she sees the veins of her eyelids,
the yellow dots the world is made of,

and then there is Dad
holding the light bulb sun,
softball earth, ping-pong moon.

Now watch the girl
with the gap in her teeth
and the guileless grin.

Who is that girl?
Bored, not knowing better,
in third grade.

Syllabication.
You could look that stuff up
in the dictionary.

The clock
     never
         to   move again.

Mrs. Breitfelder plodding between rows.
Who could complain?
Easier to climb into fog.

She came home and read books
about the solar system. Wrote
an entire planet book during spelling.

PAM HERBERT BARGER

When I am Old

I will not go gently.
I mean to go less gently.
I'll learn not to hold my tongue.

When they knock, I'll tell those
black-suit salvation salesmen
how full of it I think they are.
I'll world peace *them*.

I'll keep getting fatter
and I'll listen to Aretha Franklin
loud and I'll have more flowers
and fewer vegetables.

I'll sit out back sweating
while the sun deepens my wrinkles.
Pull a weed,
tease the cat,
pull a weed,
tease the cat.

PAM HERBERT BARGER

Withers to Woman

Throwing bare legs over sorrel back
a girl mounting gradually to woman
on withers backbone
in soybeans and tasseled corn
running muscles
below strong thighs
the stars invisible to their rhythm

She would ride
wind in hair
chest exposed and flat in the
thick sun scented breeze
field rows passing like prairie pedestrians
freedom in these hooves
bare feet clinging and nudging
along the trail of laid pipes

A bound midwest river would burst
  overhead
    unconfined
      pivoting arms
whirling
      wetness cool
onto July nakedness
    a liquid rainbow
            colliding
        spinning
    dancing
  hooves toes
withers woman

AMY PLETTNER-LIND

Since I saw you last

Since I saw you last,
I abandoned the poem about leaving,
I said "no" to the last infidelity.
I said "no" to those whom I knew
wouldn't last.
I left my plants and sticks in Maryland.
I left Maryland.

Since I saw you last,
I've moved as far from an ocean
as one can in this country.
I've let my mind stretch and roll
into the prairie sky, and from here
I've remembered you differently.
That our passion for each other
was in proportion to the pain
in the rest of our lives,
and that that, after all, isn't passion.

Since I saw you last,
I've retrieved myself from all of the places
I've been with you. And with others.
The island, the lighthouse, the comforting fog.
I released the poem about cycles.
It is out in the world now,
in the wild. Unsupervised.

KIM TEDROW

Climate

"The poetry here is in the changing"
Joe Ruggeri

An endless horizon of snow
flat against a blunted sky.
Sun far south — a shelf of light
— not that hot bath of sun
we knew that first
September weekend.
Not anything less than
your large and lively water,
the plains in winter are covered
by the same element
in a slow, orderly form.
Do you forget that we
come from the same stream?
That the current that saves you
is also the current
that howled through each
of my first thirty-two years?
The difference in climate,
my love, is that the poetry there
was in the waiting.

KIM TEDROW

Big Sky Blue

CHAUNA CRAIG

My mother wouldn't let me wear white. She had her suspicions, and how could I argue when I knew my guilt? We told the rest of the family that the apple green silk went best with my coloring and only my mother and I knew about the worm in the apple. The others might have suspected something, rushed plans and all, and I figured I'd have to tell them once I started showing, but all of us — Mother, Tom, and me — wanted the wedding to be tasteful and free of nasty gossip.

And while they privately fretted over how an airman's salary could support a wife and child, I worried over another possibility, that we'd all be transferred to another air base. I knew that my intended didn't much like Great Falls, but there were worse places, I assured him. He usually agreed with me, citing high school buddies who'd ended up in North Dakota, but when the winds blew fifty miles an hour in freezing temperatures and he had to run drills out in the field, Tom cursed this place.

He wanted to be closer to his family in Texas. I knew that. He was just two years out of high school and lonely for the desert and his friends and his mama's barbecued chicken. He cried once to me, drunk on whiskey, about all these things, and I almost believed that the force of his sadness could bend the military to his wishes. He'd whisk me away to unknown territory, a land of scorpions, separating me from my parents, my younger sister, Edith, who I adored, and all the scattered cousins and relatives in Butte and Helena. I'd only known Tom for five months, and most girls in my position were looking for exactly what I feared: a ticket out of Great Falls, Montana. That's why my high school friends flirted with the air force men they'd see at the Woolworth's lunch counter or Tracy's downtown. The thrill of travel, the security of government benefits, they wanted these things. But I was only eighteen and, despite my excitement at all the change on the horizon, afraid.

"A married woman!" Edith whispered, her bright eyes flashing as she french-braided my hair the morning of the wedding. "My sister will be a married woman. That's practically the same as being old." She pulled my hair a little harder when I tried to punch her, and I glared at her, though secretly I loved the attention. Edith was only fifteen, not even old enough to date by our family's rules, so everything I did with a boy was as thrilling to her as Peyton Place. She was always asking me what a kiss with tongue felt like, and she'd tease that I should show her how to do it right.

My obvious choice for maid of honor, she was taking the role seriously. The wedding shower was small but splendid. Edith had borrowed recipes from her home-economics teachers and made sugar mints and beef briquette for my friends and aunts. She'd bought the ingredients with her money from working in the church nursery. I knew she'd been saving it for something special like a prom dress, and then she chose to spend it on me. She'd flat refused to play the silly kitchen appliance games suggested to her by my cousin Rhonda. Edith had style. She checked out books on home decorating and cooking from the public library. She fingered the expensive silks at the fabric store and tried not to seem disappointed in the cheap dress I bought her. Mother warned her not to put on airs, but she said she was going to be somebody. Mother told her she already was somebody, but that only made my sister laugh, scornful at such a young age. Sometimes I'm surprised that Edith didn't marry military, but she wouldn't have been satisfied with anything less than an officer, and those were hard to come by.

"Do you think things will change with us when I'm married?" I asked, suckling my pinky where I'd worried the skin with my teeth until it bled. It was a horrible habit, one I only indulged when I was especially anxious. Edith slapped at my hand and held a tissue to the tiny cut.

"No," she said. "Except we'll probably stop fighting over space in the bedroom." I needed to hear that, because all the evening before I'd moped about moving to the apartments on base. Tom had reserved a two-bedroom duplex apartment for us. I'd only seen it from the outside because he said he wanted to surprise me.

"There. You look beautiful." She finished tying the green ribbon at the end of my short braid, and we looked at ourselves in the dresser mirror we'd cracked three years earlier while trying to juggle bottles of nail polish we'd stolen from the five and dime.

"Mirror, mirror on the wall..." I began.

"Who's the fairest of them all?" Edith finished in a nasal voice that always made me laugh. We stared at each other, half-smiles on our faces until Edith grumbled. "Oh, I'll give it to you this time. You're the bride after all." I pretended to gratefully accept the crown, though we both knew I would have won on any day. I had what my aunts called a "country rose" look: light brown, wavy hair, eyes the color of cornflowers, pale skin with roses on my cheeks and little white teeth as delicate and even as a doll's. Edith, with a gap between her front teeth, envied me my smile.

"All the makings of a desirable wife," my Aunt Ceci concluded whenever she saw me at holiday. "And so strong," she added when I carried the food platters to the table. She, like my mother, thought Edith put on airs that belonged anywhere but Montana, but they all agreed that of the two of us, Edith had talent. I didn't mind because I was content to be thought pretty, and I could see plain as anyone how talented my sister was, how she could make something beautiful of the thinnest air.

"It's a work of art," I announced, fingering the pin curls around my face, admiring what I could see of the small, pink blossoms she'd woven into my braid.

"Thank you, Mrs. Berrian," she teased, tasting my new name in her mouth. I groaned and told her to go get ready. After she'd gathered her pink dress and bustled into the bathroom, I posed in front of the mirror, applying ice pink lipstick and mouthing my name. Hello, I'm Francine Berrian. Mrs. Berrian? That's me. I'm Mrs. Tom Berrian. Mrs.Thomas Berrian. Thomas and Francine Berrian. I might have run through the possibilities all morning if my mother hadn't stopped me.

"Enough of that foolishness," she snapped. "We're going to be late if your father doesn't find a car soon." She was wearing a cream-colored suit with matching pillbox hat that she'd borrowed from one of the church ladies. Mother was on the larger side, and I thought she looked like a lump of dough. Before I could find a kind way to suggest she go with her usual red church dress, I realized what she'd said.

"What do you mean find a car?" We had a car, a battered Chevy Bel-Air that my father had bought from one of his co-workers at the smelting plant. The guy had run it off the road while drunk, and because he didn't want to get his insurance cancelled, he'd sold it quick and cheap.

Mother sniffed and adjusted the button straining at her bosom. "It wouldn't start this morning. We were going to get donuts for breakfast, and it wouldn't start." She shrugged and added that my father was visiting the neighbors to find someone who would help out. In those days just about anyone would lend a hand, so I stopped worrying and started hoping my father would scrounge up a shiny Thunderbird or something just as flashy. I'd heard of people who rented limousines to go to their weddings, but I wanted something with real roar.

"You were going to get donuts?"

My mother always said she didn't believe in bakery products that weren't homemade. She said the sugar used by stores was bad for us, though we all knew the real issue was expense. "You've got a sweet tooth," she shrugged. "It's your wedding day."

Then she told me to hurry and finish dressing. I gladly obliged, because I was eager to get to the chapel and catch an early glimpse of the man whose name I was soon to take.

My parents were disappointed that we'd selected the air force base chapel instead of my home church to be married in. But we had to marry quickly, and because it was early summer, the church was already booked for many weekends to come. I was a bit disappointed myself, but I didn't let on around Tom or my mother. Pastor Redding had baptized me when I was a baby. He'd given me a white bible at my first communion and his pocket was always full of butterscotch candies. It seemed only right that he marry me, but he was committed to the wedding of Sally Holmes and Allen Pettit, both remarrying after years of widowhood. Fortunately, most of the church members were coming to my wedding, including Pastor's wife. And they'd got Pastor's new assistant, Jonathan McEwen, to do the ceremony. It was his first wedding ever, but I wasn't worried. What could he screw up when everything was written down in a slender black book?

Edith helped me with the blue garter she'd given me, and after one last check in the mirror, we scurried to the kitchen to find our parents arguing. My father had a donut in his mouth. Powdered sugar snowed onto his suit jacket as he grunted in response to my mother's shrill chastisement.

"How could you forget to put gas in the car? Your own daughter's wedding. Were we all supposed to walk to the base?" She kept repeating the same questions as if she expected answers. My father shrugged and rolled his eyes at Dave Kaplan, the neighbor who had apparently diagnosed the car's problem and taken my father for those donuts and a gallon of gasoline. I was relieved that the problem was solved and it wasn't me she was picking at, so I sneaked a chocolate-glazed donut from the white bakery box.

"Francine!" My mother shrieked. "You can't have chocolate. It'll make your face break out."

"In an hour's time?" I looked up at the kitchen clock, a German-made cuckoo clock that had belonged to my great-grandmother. It was nearly ten, and the wedding was set for eleven o'clock. Years later my own children would drive me crazy by shouting "I'm cuckoo for Cocoa Puffs!" every time it marked the hour, but then I liked the tinny ding and hollow "cuckoo!" that followed.

My mother had kept the clock hidden during the war because she was a patriot. After the war, when patriotism was confirmed through the accumulation of material goods, she'd brought it out again, our only really valuable possession. It still worked beautifully, and as the eldest daughter, I was to inherit it when I married. I thought to remind my mother of that, but there wasn't much time left before the ceremony, and I felt nervous. The donuts didn't seem appetizing to my tightened stomach anymore. Edith snatched the chocolate one from my hand and darted out onto the front step before anyone could complain.

My mother returned to snipping at my father, and I surprised myself by calmly announcing, "There's no time for quibbling now. We need to get going." It sounded so adult, and my parents both stopped and considered me like I was a priestess delivering an oracle.

"Yes, Fred," my mother repeated, as though she were the one to pronounce our departure. "We need to get going."

He looked at Dave who shrugged and finished his cream-filled long john. My father looked like a gentleman in his Sunday suit, but I could tell from his expression that he wanted to impress his buddy and shock my mother by saying something slightly nasty. He glanced at me then, and his whole face seemed to open to absorb the image of his daughter as bride.

"But I don't want to get rid of her so soon." He mumbled that, then smiled shyly like he'd been forced into a confession. I was tickled. My father was usually more gruff with his children than my no-nonsense mother, more out of exhaustion than anything else. He worked long shifts at the Anaconda Copper Company up in Black Eagle, and when he came home, his idea of relaxation was reorganizing his tools or, in winter, he preferred to take a hot bath and read Popular Mechanics. He mostly just didn't want to be bothered.

I leaned in to hug him, but that was more than he could take in front of Dave and my mother, so he patted my shoulder awkwardly and repeated that we'd best be going now that the Bel Air was "fixed."

We lived near downtown, and the fastest way to Malmstrom Air Force Base was also the scenic route that wrapped inside the river and gave a view of the hydroelectric dams, the huge smokestack at the Anaconda Copper Company, and the rolling plains beyond. The sky was bright and alive with blue that morning as my family sat silently in the car, awed by the importance of this event and all the changes it would bring. The only clouds were manmade, vapor trails from the airmen's jets that broke up and drifted into nothingness even as I watched.

I sometimes wished Tom were a flyboy instead of a missile technician. It seemed more glamorous to me, although my father, who liked Tom a great deal, defended him, saying that missiles would save us all from the communists. October's mess with the Cubans had us all scared, especially because Tom liked to brag that the Great Falls base would be one of Russia's first targets. "Don't worry," he said as he stroked the back of my neck. "We'll go up in a fiery kaboom. No suffering in bomb shelters. Not in this part of the country."

I'd met him at a dance club and bar. This is not the story I told my parents, both of whom believe we met when my friend, Sandy, and I were eating ice cream at Gibson Park. I said we'd been eating and swapping gossip, and just as we started to crunch our cones, two handsome men had walked up and offered handkerchiefs for us to blot our sticky mouths. One was Sandy's boyfriend, Syl, and the other had been my Tom. My mother loved this story, I could tell. She got a moony look in her eye whenever I told it, then she'd ask my father why he didn't carry a handkerchief. This always got laughs, because none of us could imagine Fred Linton with a handkerchief. He was a short, balding man with deep laugh lines around his eyes and permanent grease stains in the calluses of his hands. He might offer you a stick of gum, but never a handkerchief.

I didn't have the heart to tell my mother that no one carried handkerchiefs anymore and certainly not in Montana. It was just a detail I added because it sounded romantic, and I'd seen it in picture shows. Once, when Tom had been over for dinner, my mother had just finished slicing onions for the meatloaf, and she came into the living room with a thin stream of tears on her cheek. She kept looking at Tom, repeating that she could use something to wipe her tears away. He was baffled, having never heard my detailed version of our supposed park encounter. When he pointed to her apron and suggested she use that, my mother whirled around in a huff and at dinner she made him hint around and finally ask for second helpings.

Edith made fun of my handkerchief story, especially because she knew the real version. I'd been tipsy with beer at a bar and had literally fallen into Tom's lap. He and Syl were new to Great Falls, and Sandy and I recognized them as airmen right away from their flat tops and formalities. We'd driven around the city for an hour or so, then we'd gone to make out on Airport Hill. Edith hated the handkerchief version because she said it was disgusting. "Eating ice cream cones and having two men, standing over you, give you something to wipe your creamy mouths with? Come on, Francie!" she squealed. Only my sister was allowed to call me "Francie." There was a popular toy doll by that name, and I thought my full name was more sophisticated anyway. "Don't be vulgar," I'd told her, unsure of what exactly she was implying. Edith had a way with innuendo. Everything seemed sordid the way she said it. With my parents she was more careful, merely smart and sassy. With me, she opened a world where every word passed between men and women seemed X-rated.

We were waved in without registering at the base gates because there was an air show open to the public that day. The poster shouted in capital letters: "ONE, TWO, THE BIG SKY BLUE: Watch 'em perform amazing air feats!!" My mother asked about the noise, and the MP assured us the show didn't start until noon, half an hour after the ceremony was to end. We drove on to the chapel where a few cars waited in the parking lot. I recognized the family car of Sandy who'd said she and Syl would arrive early to help out, and I recognized also the car of the organist, Mrs. Howe. My stomach was hurting more from nerves, or maybe the baby. I wasn't sure because my morning sickness came in the afternoons. At any rate, it hurt more when my mother announced that Tom's car was nowhere to be seen.

"He's not supposed to be here yet, Mother," I said through tight lips. "It's bad luck to see the bride before the wedding, remember?" She'd told me that when he called the day before to see if I could meet him for hamburgers. I'd turned him down, even though he said he really needed to see me. Edith said it would just build his anticipation anyway. "Same as holding out sex," she'd whispered. "He'll want you that much more."

"That doesn't mean he can't be here at a decent time," Mother snapped back. My father shot her a look that I didn't quite catch, but she turned and apologized. "He's a good boy. He'll be here soon, so we better get you inside." Edith rolled her eyes and held the car door open for me. I stepped out into a gust of wind that whipped my dress against my legs. Great Falls and all its wind. It's why we'd decided to braid my hair. A set would have gotten all tangled like my mother's. She took her hat off so the wind could-n't, and immediately her curls tangled and frizzed.

"She forgot her kerchief," Edith giggled, making lip-smacking sounds. "Maybe Tom will have one for her." I slugged her, and we ran to the chapel, swinging the door open and startling Jonathan McEwen, who was scanning his prayer book. Others called him "Pastor," but I couldn't think of him that way. He seemed too young, so Edith and I referred to him as Jonathan, though never to his face. He'd only been with the Presbyterian church for three months, so we'd never had to talk to him before.

"Hi, Pastor," Edith greeted.

"Good morning," he replied, adopting a pastor's rich and theatrical tone of voice. Jonathan was six feet tall and skinny with a wild tangle of brown hair that he kept close-cropped to keep it under control. He had small, dark eyes, horn-rimmed glasses, and a long sloping nose that made him look scholarly. I knew he'd just graduated from a bible college somewhere back East. "It's a great day to be married," he offered, still looking at Edith.

It was the first time he'd met us. In those days people didn't do rehearsals and rehearsal dinners and all that. Edith was wearing light yellow, an increasingly popular color for brides who spat on tradition or, like myself, weren't allowed to wear white. So I can see why the young pastor thought she was the bride, but it still insulted me. Didn't I have the glow of new life on me?

Edith pointed to me, and he repeated his statement about what a nice day it was. It seemed less and less nice to me as I began to get nervous in the formal-feeling chapel. Today I would meet my in-laws for the first time. They were flying in from Dallas so Mr. Berrian could stand as best man for his only son. I began to fret that his mother wouldn't like me, and of course it would be too late. I'd be stuck with people who hated me for the rest of my life. But then I thought of Tom and the gentle way he had of stroking my hair and making me feel better, and I figured I could handle that for the rest of my life.

"I'd better get back to the little room before the guests arrive," I said. "Could you show us where it is?"

Jonathan walked us to a conference-style room with a full-length mirror on the door and said he'd come get us when the time came. Edith thanked him, and when he was gone, she whispered, "He's cute, don't you think?" I giggled, trying to picture Edith with a pastor. I never imagined myself in that role, not then I didn't.

We waited in the room together, making little jokes and enduring my mother's constant checks. My father was seating guests, and my mother complained that he walked stiff as Frankenstein. Sandy reported on who was there and who wasn't. At ten minutes to the ceremony, Tom and his family were in the "wasn't" category.

"Maybe they got held up at the airport," my mother suggested. "What time was he going to pick his folks up?"

"I don't know." I could hear my voice in my head, and it sounded robotic. I was scared and I didn't know why, except that I had a feeling I would never see Tom again. I imagined him driving too fast in his excitement to get all the way back to the base. He'd probably taken 10th Avenue South, the busiest street in Great Falls, and he'd run a red light or rear-ended a farm pickup. And that was it.

"What do you mean you don't know?" My mother sounded irritated, but I recognized a sliver of panic in her tone.

"You wouldn't let me talk to him yesterday!" It was the first and last time I ever screamed at my mother, and for effect I stamped my foot in childish tantrum. The heel snapped off my right shoe. They were old shoes, so I didn't feel guilty, just mortified that I'd be married in stocking feet, barefoot and pregnant in a holy sanctuary.

At that point, my father opened the door to the little waiting room, ready to take my arm and walk me down the chapel aisle. He seemed confused at first, but that quickly changed to anger.

"You don't raise your voice to your mother!" he bellowed, his own voice elevating in volume with every word. My mother suddenly switched allegiances and told him it was okay, I was just worried that Tom hadn't arrived. My father looked at his watch and seemed surprised that it really was eleven o'clock. He repeated that it was never okay to talk that way to a parent, but his voice was lower, and he too sounded worried.

Sometime in all this exchange my sister had slipped out. It was just the three of us in the waiting area: my parents and myself, dressed up again for a big event. The last one had been my high school graduation, only a week earlier. It seemed much, much longer since I'd stood with other nervous seniors in a blue graduation gown borrowed from a neighbor's older son, straining to see my family and my almost-husband in the crowd. Neither of my parents had graduated high school, and they'd wanted to throw a party, but I asked them to save the celebration for my wedding, which was all that was on my mind as the class officers spoke of the future. No thoughts of the baby. Not then. I couldn't feel it or see it yet, and eighteen-year-olds need tangible evidence to believe. I think that's why they make lousy Christians. Tom was real and solid under my fingers. I couldn't build a future on the absence of monthly blood and an occasional wave of nausea.

At two minutes past eleven, there was a brisk knock on the door, a knock that sounded a lot like Tom's. I jumped from my chair to answer and then insisted my mother do it. It still seemed bad luck to let him see me. My mother cracked the door. Then, with a sigh, she swung it open to reveal Pastor Jonathan.

"Time to start," he said gently. "Where's the groom?"

My mother was quick thinking on her feet. "Just running a little late. Could you let the guests know?" Jonathan surveyed our faces, and we all gave him reassuring smiles that broke off as soon as he turned his back to do my mother's bidding. My father excused himself to the bathroom, leaving my mother and me to fidget in the waiting room.

"I never said you couldn't call him," she defended herself. Her borrowed hat had slipped its bobby pins. It sat cocked on her hair like a synthetic nest among brambles of hair.

"You did," I replied. My voice was flat and lifeless, and I could feel a thickness in my muscles like I could fall over and sleep a hundred years. Like Rip Van Winkle, I'd wake and my mother would lay silent in her grave, no longer irritating me. My sister would be married with a host of adoring children and grandchildren crowning her golden years. My father? Well, he must have still been in the bathroom, because I didn't have a place for him in my fantasy. Then there was me. Old and confused at 118, they'd find a bed in a nursing home, and they'd ask me to just go back to sleep. But after a hundred years' rest, I'd have insomnia. I'd probably die of it.

My father returned, disappointed that the situation hadn't changed. He stood awkwardly in his Sunday best, trying to smile at me. Shortly after, Edith showed up, her face red and her eyes narrowed in what I quickly identified as barely restrained fury.

"Tell her," she demanded, stepping aside to reveal Syl, whose face was as red as Edith's. His head hung low. Sandy stood behind him, looking as confused as I felt. "Tell her!" My sister gave him a sharp push and he stumbled into the waiting room. We all stared expectantly, hungry for an end to the waiting that seemed twice as long after eleven o'clock as it had before.

"He's gone," Syl explained, though it was no explanation.

"Gone where?" My mother and I asked at the same time, but he turned to me.

"Texas, I guess. I didn't think he'd really do it, Francine. I thought he was joking." Edith stood glaring at him, like Syl was the fugitive groom. The rest of us were still unclear on what was happening. I felt like I was in a dream with everything moving almost too slow to understand.

Edith hastened our understanding. "Tom went to Texas to be with his girlfriend there. His family wasn't coming up here, because they didn't know anything about you."

My father made a sound like a growl, and my mother put her hand tentatively and awkwardly on my shoulder. I had to struggle not to fall in her arms and bawl like a baby.

"He had another girl? And you never told us?" Sandy lit into Syl. Later they would break up over my failed wedding, and that night at the bar with the flyboys would be as if it had never happened. Just another pipe dream.

Sandy said she couldn't trust him after that, and she kept imagining a farm girl back in Wisconsin, pining for him to come home.

My father was the one who cleaned up. He went and spoke to the guests, sending each home with whatever they'd brought and an apology. He took down the plastic flower wreaths that Edith had arranged for the chapel, and he called the grocer who'd made a small wedding cake and said we didn't need it. It was pre-paid though, so he picked it up the next morning and took it to church for social time after the service. I didn't mind. I never wanted to see, smell or taste it. Edith told me later that it was too sweet.

I think my mother was in shock. She spoke very little and kept trying to touch me, her way of commiserating and apologizing for all the bickering the wedding had caused between us. She told me to stay home from church the next day, to rest my eyes, which by then would be sorely puffed from crying. Finally, standing in the waiting room, no longer waiting, I asked her to give me time alone, and she disappeared without a peep, probably to talk to my Aunt Cecilia who'd taken a bus from Butte to get here.

In my stocking feet, I slipped out the back door because I wasn't ready for the sympathy pats and the pitying looks. Let my sister handle that—she'd rip into Tom Berrian until they'd be afraid to mention his name at all. The pavement was cool and solid under my feet. The wind had trickled to a light breeze, unusually warm for early summer in Montana. It played with the curls around my cheeks, and when I closed my eyes, I imagined it was Tom's breath the first night he made love to me. I'm still ashamed that I yielded so easy, but it was so sweet, despite my fear that Tom's dormitory mate would walk in, despite the strange sensation of pressure in places I'd never felt before.

A year later, Edith called me, crying and convinced she was bleeding to death. I could hear a man's voice in the background repeating "Oh Jesus" in high, frightened tones. I'd nearly hung up to call the police when I realized it was only her hymen that had broken. Explaining that, I saw how she knew much less than I'd thought.

So my first experience, even if the very doing of it convinced me to marry or burn in hell, was a good one. I was standing in back of that chapel remembering the best of my former husband-to-be, not the fact that he'd gone AWOL from me and from his career. I never did hear what happened to him. I suspect a court martial, but even then I wasn't interested in the end of his story. I was remembering Tom leaning over me, the radio playing the Four Seasons, my body shivering from fear and a new sensation that felt like heaven. Eyes closed against the increasing wind, I started humming "Big Girls Don't Cry" and was startled by a hand on my shoulder.

In a fairy tale, the hand would belong to Tom Berrian. He would have realized his cowardice and hurried back to marry me. But it was Pastor Jonathan who stood at my side. I braced myself for his sympathy, or worse, the lecture I would later come to accept about this all being a part of God's plan. Right then I needed only to remain in Tom's ghostly embrace. But Jonathan snapped the spell. He dropped his hand and pointed over my left shoulder.

"Look," he said. "The air show." Sure enough, six jets were storming to heaven in close formation. I had been so lost in my dreams I had barely noticed the racket they made. The jets splintered out of formation and began to loop in and out of each other's paths. The choreography was amazing, the danger thrilling. The thunder of the jet engines overhead drowned out every-thing—the crowd's roar of applause at each stunt, the whine of the wind, Jonathan's small talk about how he'd loved airplanes since he was a little kid.

I made him repeat himself when the jets strayed far enough out to make conversation possible. He said, "I wanted to be a flyboy, but I found safer ways to be near God." He grinned, and I could see the little boy he'd been, the eager child who'd held toy planes in his outstretched hands and dreamed of flying. I grinned back, my way of assuring him that his dream was great, its loss no more than what was to be expected. I ignored the sting of tears at the back of my throat, grinning as wide and carefree as I could.

"Safer ways," I repeated, watching the jets shredding the air, their wingtips almost seeming to touch.

That Christmas, after the baby that was never much of a baby slipped away in a clot of blood, after four months of working the phones at the oil refinery and suffering the slaps and pinches of grungy workers, I quit my job and I married my pastor. My mother said nothing about my lily-white dress.

Six years later, well-versed in Jonathan's faith and pregnant with my second child, I watched Neil Armstrong take his magical step. My small son, sitting on his father's lap, clapped his hands wildly and, like most mothers that year, I imagined him becoming an astronaut.

As I watched Neil bounce so lightly on the surface of that pitted moon, I felt my child kick. The movement sent a small, deep shiver through me, and I thought of Tom for the first time in a long while. My body's memory flashed sharp. Sensations I'd never known with Jonathan soared through my muscles in a long, hard ache. Tears tickled my eyelashes, and when my hus-band saw my face, he smiled. "Amazing, isn't it?"

I nodded.

I couldn't sleep that night, so I got up and wandered into my son's room, bumping my head on the little mobile above him: circus animals wearing funny hats. I brushed a sweaty strand of hair from his brow and put my lips close to his ear.

"Fly," I whispered. "Fly, fly, fly."

Sex

AMY KNOX BROWN

Riding back to Lincoln, all the windows down, air tossing and heaving through the car, Elise looks in the mirror of her compact and sees a mark on her neck, redder than blood, the size of a quarter. Lips dry with dust, salt of sweat, shorts damp between her legs, the muscles of her thighs tight and stiff as though she's been running. July, Nebraska, everything turned to dust.

Elise lights a cigarette and glances through her sunglasses at Shawn. She imagines if she had x-ray vision, if she could see through his shirt, there'd be a thin film of dust on his skin, dust smeared by the prints of her fingers, longer strips cleared by her tongue. He looks over at her. "Hey," he says.

"Hey," Elise says back. They're both exhausted and it's too hot to talk. Elise thinks of the cool shower she plans to take when she gets home, what shirt she can wear to hide the mark on her neck. She shuts her eyes and feels Shawn's fingers touch her hand where it lies on the seat between them.

How they've spent the summer: every afternoon they drive Shawn's '40 Chevy out to Homer's Auto Parts, a huge field of wrecked and rotting cars several miles outside of town. Shawn's always looking for something for his car—new hubs, a hood ornament, the dream of perfect authentic seats; his Chevy's a project he can spend his whole life working on.

And the Chevy's a perfect excuse for the project Elise and Shawn work on together. First they talk to Homer and gather lore on one of the cars. That Caddy, Homer says, pointing his cigarette at a '62 Fleetwood—Homer could be anywhere from fifty to seventy, his skin wrinkled from summers of sun, grease etched in permanent lines under his nails—I bought from a couple kids back in '71. Running away to Las Vegas to get married, blew the engine out on Cornhusker Highway. Towed it here and it's sat in that same spot since. Wonder what happened to the kids. Elise and Shawn make noises of agreement—Hmm. Elise imagines the couple, waiting for Homer, staring at each other over the smoking hood of the Cadillac, in the middle of their first shared disaster.

Shawn tells Homer what he'd like to find, his goal for the day, and Homer waves them off toward the cars. Help yourself. Happy hunting. Elise and Shawn wander down haphazard rows, far from Homer's office, until an old Cadillac, Ford, a wrecked ambulance, catches their attention. Shawn opens one of the heavy doors and slides into the back seat behind Elise, where, in hot, cobwebby air, they shrug out of their clothes and have sex.

Today they found a '58 Calais clear at the back of the lot, its body faded to grey, thistles growing up from the floorboards in the front. Sitting on Shawn, facing him, Elise listened to mice scrabbling somewhere nearby—everything wants out—until that moment she'd come to expect when any sensation outside her own body ceased to matter. No one told her sex would be like this, that there'd be a point—naked, sweat streaming down her back, eyes clenched shut, all her energy focused on the spot between her legs where she feels him moving like a piston pushing into cylinder walls—when who he is makes no difference. In that moment, all she thinks of is herself, her own pleasure, and if she'd open her eyes to see Shawn transformed into someone else, someone she doesn't know or like, it won't matter: she knows she'd be unable to stop moving or pull away until after she's come, once, twice, each convulsion of the muscles inside her riveting and distinct as a punch in the stomach.

But of course she's been told that who you are with, how you feel about the boy, love, respect, make some difference. "It's better with someone you love." Who's told her this? Opening her eyes to look at Shawn as he drives, Elise thinks the statement can't possibly be true. Love has no bearing on her afternoons with Shawn, though she might be a little in love with different parts of him, the things he does to her: his hands, his teeth scraping into her skin right at the point where her neck and shoulder meet. It must not hurt—though the marks he leaves look painful and raw—because she never thinks at the time that she wants him to stop.

***

The raised buildings of the city poke up ahead of them, and she thinks of all the miles they've traveled this summer, from Lincoln to Homer's and back, all the car seats they've left stained with sweat, dented with impressions of their bodies. Afterwards, every time, Elise opens her eyes to sunlight shattering against the windshield, sounds from the field surrounding them—insects, the scratchy noise of grass rubbing against one of the cars—gradually filtering into her consciousness while she lies, listening to her heart pound, wondering what other girls have stretched out on this seat, how many may have sat here on their way to church.

Stop, Then Go

AMY STUBER

The woman in the bus seat next to Alice tuts and chants, some new-age meditative key word string. Healer, fortune teller, Alice might have presumed had this woman looked more the part, less Iowa. But this woman's mumbling, Alice realizes, is not encoded. She's right off the farm: mind wind-rattled, round, chapped face, eyes blown wide, hair in a similar state of shock which some once a week beautician has attempted to tame into a tight cap of dried out white. White white, colorless really.

Nine childless years married to a farmer and Alice is acquainted with this look, hands so raw the skin peels from the fingers—not a snake sort of shedding, replenishing—but a gradual wearing away; each day there, waking up with Joe in the hand-me-down iron bed, washing dishes in the nicked porcelain sink, Alice expected to see bone emerging from beneath too-thin skin. In bed, Alice's husband, Joe, used those dry leaf hands, those fingers, that machine arm technique, to drag her breasts up from their slipping down points under her arms, up onto her chest and rub hard, the sort of pressure Alice imagined a movie gangster intended when he whispered about rubbing someone out.

Then mornings, sun pointing out the dust, Alice cooked biscuits and sliced ham under the broiler, eggs with the yolks upright, almost stiff, farm things. At first, she didn't know. Of course you'll be expected to cook, her mother had said at the bridal shower, presenting Alice with a red and white checkerboard cookbook.

Those first weeks, she pulled the book from the shelf above the sink, all those studio kitchen photos, decorative meat, multilayered cakes with frosting shaped into garden flowers. She imagined it takes fifty minutes to solve television murders for those error-free blank-aproned studio chefs as she warmed a soup can of yesterday's grease over a gas flame, poured it into a pan and readied her plastic spatula.

When the bus hits a pothole, the old woman beside Alice, full house of playing cards in hand, bumps up from her seat and lurches toward Alice's forearm, toward the metal arm rest that divides them. Alice has seen people falling into gravel or concrete, shooting their hands out in front to break the impact. But this woman doesn't worry about protecting her face. She's more concerned with keeping her cards equidistant, as Alice envisions a career black jack dealer might handle his table on a cruise ship in rough waters.

The old woman wants Alice to play, motioning to her with a nod and a suggestive upshift of her hand. Alice points to her headphones, newly acquired for the trip, shakes her head a little to indicate a distracting beat, a lie really since she forgot to buy a tape to slide inside and, with the bus crossing county lines, state lines, she can't pick up any station for long.

The woman, disappointed, lets her mouth slack and then shapes her lips into a series of repercussive kisses. For some reason, Alice finds herself imagining her lips fused to the lips of this woman, the years of old air that might roll out in sighs from this woman's body into hers, preparing her for crows feet and further loosening of the skin on her elbows and an unwanted low-level comfort that comes from years-old desire long gone dull and a slight hobble that evokes pity from strangers. This, she imagines the woman's breath telling her, is also your future.

At the bus terminal entrance, Alice's brother, Leo, stands with his hands spread wide, his eyes turned up, expectant, eyeing the first exiting passengers. Alice can see him through the tinted window as she waits for the people in the middle rows to file out. Leo, a silver-dollar size wooden cross on a chain jutting out from the spot on his neck where the collarbones meet. The old woman nudges Alice as they move toward the front. She points to Leo, points back to Alice, perhaps meaning she sees a resemblance. My brother, Alice says to the woman who shakes her head up and down, yes.

When their feet touch the ground, the woman turns away, checks the shape of her hair with both hands and crouches into the back seat of a waiting station wagon.

As she gets closer, Alice notices Leo's head, almost entirely bald now, and half-hidden under the baseball cap he keeps lifting on and off.

Leo works as a youth minister, taking kids on weekend retreats, building houses for the homeless, eating pizza and drinking warm soda in plastic party cups in the church basement on Sunday nights while the ninth graders eye the door. The lack of hair, Alice knows, only exaggerates the generation gap. Alice nods to him and Leo emits a slight roar, his trademark greeting, the way their mother used to wake him in his morning bed as a child, a generous fairy tale grumble, much like a vocal bear hug, a gesture that did nothing to prepare him for real life.

Anyway, Leo doesn't really hug. Instead, he clutches forearms, clings to hands like a politician. Leo, at her wedding, Alice remembers, touched every person in the place. Guests started to form a wide circle around him, all those farm people, clean, recently scrubbed for the occasion, good in a plain way, and afraid of contact.

Leo had always believed in eliminating boundaries. "We could learn a thing or two from the Europeans," she can remember him saying, meaning that he had seen French actors kissing both cheeks in television movies and liked the idea.

She remembers Leo at their mother's burial, holding onto the foot of her coffin like his touch was enough to keep her there.

Leo's church-funded apartment, the bottom floor of a house diagonal to the church building, holds more table games than furniture. Upstairs, Leo tells Alice, the church secretaries type the once-a-month newsletter and address announcements to members, organize canned food collections, pen thank-you notes to stand-out donors who give beyond their ten percent.

It's dark by the time they get inside Leo's apartment, but all the windows stand open, some without screens. Alice can see gum wrappers on the carpeting, pieces of leaves, mud in clumps.

A cracked full-length mirror leans against the wall by the blocked staircase, and Alice wonders if Leo ever looks in it and really sees, a man near middle age sitting cross-legged in a circle of teenagers singing. She knows she is rarely this honest with herself, although she will admit to anyone interested that she was lured into marriage by the promise of a solid-sounding last name.

Singleton, Joe. The fourth mouth Alice really kissed, the second body Alice felt naked, the one she married after the other one moved to the city, the first person she bruised by punching in the jaw in a rare display of anger, the tenth or eleventh cursive name to be surrounded by stars in her early high school diary, the only one outside of her family with whom she'd raised her voice to a scream, the person who ate a large breakfast every morning because it was supposed to be the best thing for you, the one who drove her around, up and back all the two lane roads after her mother's burial, the first person she'd showered with, the only person she'd ever known to follow a strict shower routine, right arm, left arm, right leg, left leg, back, face, hair, out, the person who sat out on the porch with her to watch the town families in square cars, three kids lined up in the back out to see the changing leaves, the person who shared her fear of the city slap that stung any time she drove up the ramp onto the highway, the only one to whom she cried after talking to the doctor about her two incomplete pregnancies, the person who woke, worked, slept without thinking while Alice went three nights in a row staring out the bedroom window at the land that spread out around the house like an unending mote, the one who'd once held her face in both of his hands, the person who had tried to show her what it was like to be still, quiet, slow, unconcerned, the man whose every careful move and word, whose silent presence had started to, in Alice, spark a slight but noticeable current of irritation that led to her core.

At Leo's, Alice sleeps underneath the pool table in what should have been a dining room, uninterested in the offer of Leo's bare mattress. He gives her a couch cushion for a pillow and pulls a child-sized sleeping bag over her legs, turning the blinds with a swift twist.

"So you just left?" he asks her, crossing his legs and leaning his forehead into the fake wood side of the table. This, Alice thinks, is what he lives for, gaining the subtly elicited confession after posing a series of well-orchestrated questions. This is his walking on water.

Alice looks at her feet poking out from the sleeping bag, the way the toes curl over each other.

"I left a note," Alice tells Leo and turns her back to him, imagining Joe waking without her, middle of the night, looking in the bathroom, expecting to find her there, rubbing her eyes, looking in the mirror but not really at herself.

Leo sighs, lowers his hand over her back and just barely grazes the skin, a mock-pat, and walks into his room. She can hear his body shifting on the mattress, settling.

Maybe, Alice thinks, Joe walked through all the rooms of the house, cold floor on bare feet, checked outside, the barn and all the other outbuildings, maybe expecting Alice to jump out from behind a tree, half-hiding, laughing a little. Sometimes they played games like this.

Back in the bedroom, he found Alice's note, short, not the explanation she knew he deserved, but all she could commit to paper at the time in the weak forty watt bathroom light, leaning up against the tile to write: "Leo's," "a few weeks, maybe," "don't know." She struggled with the letter, even that short; years since she had really put pen to paper, written anything other than lists of things to buy in town.

Now, she imagines him wondering what he did wrong. It is like him, Alice thinks, to want all the blame.

It wasn't any one thing, Alice would tell Joe if he were here, if he were the type to track her down at Leo's, the determined soap opera type who would pound on the door and scream her name until she answered, pick her up with a sweep and take her straight home, the type who can cover distances in seconds and erase years of blank stares with a few well-charted words.

But the only person who shows up at Leo's door in the middle of her first night is a fifteen year old short term runaway boy wearing black boots that end just below his knees and knife cut army shorts. He walks right in and spots Alice's open eyes under the table, stares for a minute until he can focus, then nods. "From a distance," the boy tells her, "I thought you were Leo." I'm a full foot shorter, Alice thinks to herself, and not bald. The boy picks up a tennis ball and throws it against Leo's bedroom door. First thing, Leo, slightly agitated, Alice can tell by the way he shuffles his fingers at his sides, but trying to play his part, puts his hat on, pulls the rope around his robe tighter, slips into his unlaced hightop tennis shoes and takes the boy and his backpack and his loud boots out onto the front step.

From inside, Alice listens to the way Leo's voice rises up and then subsides. Alice remembers the last letter she received from Leo, almost two years ago, a full year after their mother's funeral, a confession, really, in which Leo described a night when he pushed, physically shoved, a fourteen year old boy in his group, one night that they spent in a high school gymnasium in another, much larger nearby city, a three day trip involving reconstruction of abandoned buildings, that night when three of his boys kept the entire gym awake with dirty jokes until Leo singled out the offenders and started threatening, knocked one of them over, forgetting the size difference, forgetting everything. Leo, standing there in only his underwear and a t-shirt, his feet slipping over the rows of nylon sleeping bags until he also, almost fell.

Okay, there was one thing, though. Alice could tell Joe this:

"Last summer, early summer, I remember arguing during the day, remember, I was checking the vegetables and you were planting marigolds around the border to keep the bugs away, and that dog that we'd never seen before ran right past us and around to the front of the house.

"That day, I was talking about what to do with the tomatoes, the early ones that we'd started inside in the basement and then moved out, spaghetti sauce, salsa, some kind of soup, the ones we didn't can right away. And you weren't listening at all. You were thinking about how the ground felt under your fingernails or looking for white worms in the soil, or not thinking about anything at all, just working.

"Of course it was trivial, like most fights, the kind of thing that happens a million times a marriage. But, for some reason, that day, I thought about dropping everything, walking all the way into town, staying away to scare you, maybe ordering Manhattans in the one bar by the store, a drink I'd always wanted to try, thinking about the look that might cross your face if you really had to wonder.

"But the bartender there wouldn't know what a Manhattan was, I remember thinking, knowing instead, that I would end up drinking warm tap beer with a circle of ruined farmers, huddled around pocked tables, the farmers avoiding their wives and the bank men.

"So I didn't move except to keep pulling tomatoes and dropping them into the already half full cardboard box. What scared me the most was how much I could conceal, hide from you, what you might hide from me, how shaky and slight the rope of connection onto which I had been hanging everything that mattered.

"And even before it did, I knew how the fight would end. You would look down at the weeds in the ground like they were the source of trouble. And I would walk out to the north edge of our property, through all the trees and out again, eventually back to the house. Before any of it happened, I knew how the day and night would progress, how we would eventually come together, with a sigh or a look, an acceptance that this was our life and it was sometimes good."

When Leo brings the boy back inside, they are telling jokes about amputees, armless and legless men called Bob or Matt or Art. Alice is half-asleep enough to find them funny. Outside, it's beginning to get light. Leo picks up the phone that hangs on the wall leading to the kitchen, asks the boy for his home number, and dials. Alice notices a sticker of a superhero she doesn't recognize on the outside of the receiver. When Leo moves closer, pulling the cord tighter, waiting for a response at the other end, she sees that the face of the figure resembles all those Sunday school pictures of Jesus, beard, wide eyes, thick long hair. But this Jesus is wearing a cape that looks like the sky, blue with clouds billowing out behind him, and holding a shield covered with angels. Leo picks at the edges of the sticker as he speaks. Their mother wasn't religious, and Alice has always felt that a God might be nice, but who really knows.

When Leo begins to talk, his phone voice sure and plotted as a salesman's, he turns his back toward the living area, peers into the kitchen. The boy, now sitting on the couch, rolls his eyes and puts his feet up onto the ripped arm of the sofa.

Alice attempts a staring contest with him and wins. He smiles, big grayish almost buck teeth, when he blinks. To him, she still hasn't said a word.

Before Alice married, she worked as a receptionist in a dental office. Still, sometimes, she notices teeth first.

She can remember Joe coming into the office, kicking the carpet around with his work boots, shaking chips of mud loose from his shoes, half-smiling at a stack of magazines. Alice hadn't seen him in the year and a half since high school, had heard that he was married, maybe even a child, but she noticed, that day, no ring.

Alice remembers being impressed by his teeth from the start, bottom row wide and thick, packed a little too close together, but clean, flossed, strong. They married soon after that, only four months of dating, car drives, a few movies, one night in a hotel in the city, and then they had the house and Joe took out a bank loan to pay the mortgage and buy the ring.

When Alice wakes again, it is morning. The boot boy is gone, home with his parents, Leo explains. Alice stands up to stretch, rub away the imprint the couch cushion has left on one side of her face, and she sees a woman pressing her face up close to the side window, pushing her lips into the glass as she speaks, creating a circle of mist with a red "O" at the center that Alice thinks looks slightly sexual.

"Laura," Leo explains, waving, "one of the upstairs secretaries. Remember, I told you, they work upstairs," he says and moves closer to the window. Alice imagines Leo and this woman in bed, her red lipstick leaving stains on his uncovered mattress, the concise movements they would employ in order to convince themselves of the purity of their actions, their mechanical gestures proof of their ability to manage desire.

At the window, Laura, more made up than Alice imagines anyone employed by a religious organization would be, tells Leo that the repair man is coming today to fix or replace the leg of the pool table, broken or cracked during last week's outdoor-turned-indoor, seventh grade, touch-turned-tackle football game.

"Five o'clock," the secretary says, her voice rising as she climbs, her words merging with the scratch scratch of her skin-colored panty hose rubbing together at the tops of her thighs as she goes.

Alice inspects the table, sees the crack she didn't notice last night, sees the way table top balances, shakes a little even when Leo walks around the room. Alice wants to punch him for letting her spend the night there. Leo just shrugs and says one word: "faith." And then he laughs like a person who wants to believe but can't, as if to say, as much as she is trying, he is too, and walks out of the room.

"Aren't you supposed to wait a year before doing this?" Alice asked when Leo suggested he set Alice up with his friend, Frank, an acquaintance really, the only male teller at Leo's bank.

When he made the offer, Alice had spent only one week with Leo, not quite two weeks away from Joe. Her one phone conversation with Joe had been brief, the few quick words you might hear couples offering each other before boarding different morning trains. Her departure, clearly, in Joe's opinion, equaled a vacation, an interlude, nothing final.

But Leo had plans for Alice, a meeting with Frank, a "blind date" Leo called it, even though Alice hadn't used the word date in that sense since high school, when, in a town that small, none of her dates could have been blind, unknown to her before the actual meeting.

"Anyway," Alice asked him in between gulps of orange juice, "Aren't you supposed to wait a certain amount of time before dating?"

"That's for death," he responded. "Death insists upon a certain reverence. Leaving your husband. Rules don't apply."

When Frank pulls up in front of a bar a few streets over from Leo's, he makes Alice promise she won't tell Leo he took her to this place. Inside, Alice notices, the place is decorated with Old West memorabilia, wanted signs, wooden stocks, rusted handcuffs, bullet hole baseboards, antiquated looking framed pictures of Jesse James.

Frank orders drinks for both of them, vodka tonics made with lemon flavored vodka. "Something new," he tells her as he swallows in one gulp and she watches his Adam's apple shift and then pop back into place.

He's not so bad, Alice tells herself, nice hair, not receding, good smile, then pinches her own wrist under the table for thinking of him this way. She listens to him as he talks for a while about the new tires he put on his car, about the good Leo is doing for the community, nodding periodically to keep up her end of the conversation, until Frank goes to the bathroom to, she assumes, check his hair, poke over his teeth with a finger, making sure fragments of lemon haven't gotten stuck in between.

Without really thinking, Alice gets up from the table, grabs her purse, walks toward the door.

Outside of the bar, the sun is still up a little. Alice checks her watch, one hour later than it really is, still set for her time zone.

She wonders about Joe, about where he is in the house, about the irreplaceability of years, about how life is a mix of moving forward and back, even though the calendar doesn't reflect it, realizes really for the first time that Joe has probably slept straight through every night since early childhood.

If Joe were here, Alice thinks, he would point out the sick trees, the bark peeling away from trunks, the flowers planted too close together in the narrow beds that circle the apartment houses, how if you stared for a few seconds without averting your eyes, the buildings started to look like they were folding in like cartoon walls closing in fast. Or he would say nothing, just stare, and her eyes would follow his. Even here, Alice realizes, she can think of herself only in relation to him, how far he is from her or how close. And then Frank grabs her elbow and the feel of his fingers stops her. He is winded, exhaling hard like someone at the end of a distance run, his eyes still blurry, adjusting to the outdoor light.

"I assumed you'd forgotten something at Leo's," he tells her, "that maybe you needed some air." He stops to breathe, pushes loose strands of hair back from his eyes, and she decides to follow him, wherever he suggests they go.

As a child, Alice remembers waking early at her mother's house, rolling out of her single bed and tearing outside in just her nightgown, racing Leo up and down, through the rows of corn.

When they saw their mother coming, slippers slapping down the back steps, screen door springing back, their mother half awake in that blue quilted bathrobe she wore every year of Alice's childhood, when they saw her, they hid down behind the corn, the amount they had to crouch dependent upon the month. June, July, August. By the end of the season, they could stand and flap their arms, even jump, without being spotted. Their mother would come to the edge, as if approaching a sea. and call to them: Leo, Alice, where are you?

Talking to herself: I don't know. Maybe the soil's swallowed them up. Maybe the scarecrow stole them.

Then Leo first, then Alice, stumbled up to their mother's shins, hunched over like two mushrooms poking up from the ground, all three of them laughing a little. My little babies, their mother would say, even though they weren't so little. And she would drop down over them, arms like wings, like shelter, and they could lean into her and close their eyes.

Frank's apartment resembles a hotel room: cold comfort, unforgiving squared-off sofa, bed in the same room with a comforter thin as a sheet and stretched tight. Alice cannot believe he's lived here long, in this one room, no trinkets, no matchbooks, no keepsakes, no photos, just two framed prints of fast-moving water.

"Four years here," he tells Alice and starts kissing her neck in a way she cannot remember having been kissed, although she's sure this is something Joe must have done in the beginning.

She loses track and then he's moved onto her face, lips over her eyelids, down to her mouth, leaving a slight liquidy trail as he goes, like a slug crossing concrete. She wonders if she's now glowing a pattern of silver. While Frank moves her over to the sofa, Alice tries to think of herself in a ruffled apron and lace-up shoes walking to a restaurant job each day or sweeping the halls of a grade school after hours, of getting a small apartment and looking down at the people passing in the street, killing time at the end of her shift, putting her feet out on an iron balcony and drinking cold tap water out of a plastic bottle stored in the refrigerator, falling asleep with her arms and legs stretched out over the bed, her hands and feet hanging down toward the floor.

Frank puts his hands through her hair, his fingers snagging on the knots. She feigns a moan, a quickness of breath, resignation, a response she thinks is appropriate. This, she tells herself, is what people do.

"What do you want?" Frank asks her as he pushes a bra strap out from under her short sleeved shirt, his voice slow like he's talking through water. She looks at the framed waterfall photos, thinks about the way her tongue feels on Frank's sharp-edged teeth, looks at shallow lines on his closed eyelids.

Alice tries to remember when she was last asked that question. What does she want: Suspension of disbelief, she thinks, cessation of thought, air in the lungs, the moment before the kiss, right before the unfamiliar hand touches skin. Stop me there, she wants to say to him.

But she says nothing like that, instead pushes him onto the bed, causing the taut elasticized sheet to snap off two corners. She laughs a little, but he doesn't notice. Frank, she says in a voice lower than her usual voice, amusing herself, playing the role of soap star, film star, romantic lead. She remembers her grade school teacher with hair piled high who tested them all for e.s.p, seated them across from each other, one row of senders, one row of receivers, lined up at those low wooden tables. Imagine, the teacher told them, her voice lilting up at word's end, imagine only blue sky, nothing else. Clear your mind, she told the receivers, Alice included, prepare it for the message that will come.

And Alice, with Frank, tries to do just that: concentrate on her grade school teacher's blue sky, the blank slate, lie on Frank's half bare mattress, kiss him without thinking and just keep going.

Leaving

KATE FLAHERTY

Driving gives her hives, but Sarah's determined to leave Nebraska. She's highlighted the map, Triple A style, and she won't turn around. She's driving seven miles over the speed limit with the windows down and the radio up, a cooler of Cokes in the back. She's got all these ideas in her head about women who stand in front of juke boxes and jut the hip, just so, then dance alone, beer in one hand, cigarette the other. Yes. This is romance. And why shouldn't it happen for Sarah.

Of course with romance comes fear. Reverend Bob, who likes to sack groceries for Sarah because she's not so fast as those high school girls who work afternoons, tells her the horror stories of I-80, as he casually places egg cartons sideways and bananas on the bottom. The cars are always '70s models, rusted-out Rivieras or Bonnevilles, and they'll follow you for miles before running you off the road. Reverend Bob's stories end there, with him pointing a box of spaghetti in Sarah's face as an extra warning that he could go on but he won't. "Young ladies do not run around all by themselves." Reverend Bob is a man skilled at discussing what one should fear, with little sympathy for romantic notions.

"To hell with Reverend Bob," Sarah says, pushing in the cigarette lighter, instantly feeling guilty for saying that to the old man who can't possibly hear her. As if she needs Reverend Bob to remind her the world is evil. As if she didn't learn that over Christmas when Hal came back from the University saying, "I couldn't help myself, Hon, I was like a kid in the candy store," meaning he'd slept with pretty much any girl who agreed to go out with the dumb old side of beef that he is. Of course he told her this at the Chinese Palace in Lexington, knowing she wouldn't get up and walk out being twenty miles from home, and knowing she wouldn't throw either a fit or her chicken lo mein because Sarah never did those kinds of things in public. She just said, "Shut up, Hal. Bring me home," and they rode back to Cozad in stony silence with the exception of Hal's yelp when Sarah bent back the fingers of a hand roving toward her knees.

"To hell with Hal," Sarah says, crossing her eyes to get the lighter to meet with her cigarette. She's not too smooth at this yet, having only started smoking after Christmas, when she began running around with Jenny, the girl in the bakery, down to Joe's on Friday nights. Tacos and beers 25 cents. They drink with the guys from the meat department who always give Sarah a scare because they're all missing a finger or two. It makes Sarah's mother sad, seeing her go off to Joe's on Fridays, coming back late smelling like smoke and beer and red hot pepper, and hanging out with Jenny. Jenny was a few years ahead of Sarah in high school but dropped out because she had a little baby boy, whose father went to college the next year and never came back. But Sarah likes Jenny and she's sorry she never talked to her before, except to ask for price checks.

She rolls the window up halfway so ashes don't blow back at her, and sighs out a cloud of smoke. "You need to get out of this town, Sarah," Jenny said to her last Friday night at Joe's. "Then you'll see how much better off you are, and lucky you're not waiting around four more years just so you can clean the dirt out of old Hal's boots every night. Count your blessings girl," Jenny said taking a last swig of beer and gingerly putting her clear plastic cup down on the table. "Stick around too long and you'll get stuck. Like me."

"Aw Jen," Sarah said carefully, because this conversation, which they'd had before, often led to tears on both sides. "It's not so bad here, not really." She stared down into her plastic cup of beer, the fizz all but gone. She knew it was terrible for Jenny, who seemed to live only for her little boy Stan, now in first grade and playing pee-wee soccer. Otherwise Jenny had resigned herself to living with her parents and working at the Hinky Dinky for the rest of her life, probably going to Joe's every Friday for the rest of her life too. And when Jenny cried about it, Sarah cried too, thinking how easily she'd begun to slip into the same kind of thing.

But now she's leaving, determined, and she just doesn't know if she plans on coming back. She has the week off. Sarah and Hal planned before Christmas to go away for his spring break to somewhere warm, because they'd never done anything except save their money. Everything was in the future. Hal saving to go to the Ag College in Lincoln, as if his dad hadn't taught him all he needed to know already. Sarah saving because Hal saved, too stupid to realize he was only going to the University to get his last kicks before coming back to Cozad to farm for the rest of his life, too stupid to come up with something better to do with her money. So here she is, 22, in a 1981 green Chevy Celebrity inherited from her grandmother, with $800 in travelers checks hidden away in the glove compartment and a week off to do whatever she damn well pleases.

"I guess I'm entitled to my kicks too," Sarah says, learning on the gas a little harder, and looking into the rearview to see what her French inhales looks like before lapsing into a coughing fit

I-80 goes all the way to San Francisco, and that's where she plans to end up—not the warmest place she could go for spring break, but she has no visions of guys on tropical islands buying her fancy drinks laced with grain alcohol. This trip isn't for pleasure, it's to escape to the end of the world, and San Francisco fits the bill if all you've got is a used Chevy Celebrity. Sarah's grandmother would have wanted her to take her car to San Francisco. She was always pushing her to get out and see what was what in all those movies they rented the last years of her life and watched in her living room. To have a scandalous excursion, Elizabeth Taylor-style, tragic and scarring, or to take cities by storm in an Audrey Hepburn escapade. Because Elizabeth Taylor always seemed too tortured, Sarah and her grandmother generally agreed with Audrey Hepburn was the way to go. Although Sarah had to admit she'd never seen an Audrey Hepburn movie involving a solo drive to San Francisco, she could imagine the scene. A convertible of course, Audrey wearing large black sunglasses and a long filmy scarf the color of melons, whose ends ripple in the breeze behind her, because the wind always blows the right way in movies. She's smoking through her long cigarette holder and smiling her Audrey smile, because she's free as a bird and the trunk is full of champagne.

Sarah knows her grandmother would not have wanted her to spend the last four years driving a bigger and bigger rut between her folks' house in Cozad and the Hinky Dinky in Lexington, spending every weekend renting movies to watch on Hal's parents' VCR, throwing her back out for a little loving in Hal's truck when they made a stop on the way back to her folks' house after dropping the movie at the video store. Not that her grandmother had anything against Cozad, where she'd lived her whole life. Her grandmother was just strongly against what she called "stagnation." "Keep an eye on yourself girl," she'd say to Sarah. "Make sure every day you're where you want to be. If not, then you'd best get a move on." Sarah had known, as her grandmother said these things, that she wanted Sarah to move on, but invisible threads seemed to hold Sarah fast to Cozad, and for these three years following her grandmother's death.

Sarah admits that unless she's actually able not only to drive out of Nebraska, but also get out of the car and talk to people, touch and see things, the windshield of her Chevy Celebrity will turn out to be just another TV screen, but she hopes she's got enough steam worked up to at least get to San Francisco. Or Nevada. Or Wyoming. Just anywhere she can stand in front of a juke box and pump her money in and make her selections, and dance and drink all by herself, looking so powerful and mean that all those guys on the barstools jingling keys in their pockets that go to rusted out Rivieras in the parking lot won't even try to tell her what for.

Hal sure tried to talk her out of going, thinking he could still get her to go to Florida with him and make up. He cornered her at the Hinky Dinky where she couldn't leave her post, helping Reverend Bob sack groceries at her check stand. Reverend Bob joined forces with Hal, because he'd never believe Hal was a lying cheat (Hal had been born into his church—Reverend Bob's other part-time job), also because of his conviction that I-80 would be Sarah's certain road to ruin, but mostly because he could just stand there and take a breather while Hal would sack everything that came his way.

"Sarah, honey, you know I can't do without you," Hal said, and Sarah thought how much he sounded like the sappy singers on the Muzak she listened to all day. "I just went a little crazy is all. You were so far away. What could I do? Come on, Sarah, let's just go to Florida." And just like the Muzak, Hal sang the same song every time he drove out to Lexington from Lincoln. Although she was impressed with Hal's persistence, she was angry and wanted to remind him he'd never come home this much before they broke up.

"What could you do?" she finally said. Sarah had a mind to tell him honestly, tell him that he should have had the balls to break up with her before he started screwing around, but with Reverend Bob right there, she held herself back. "What could you do? I can't say I know, since I've never been faced with the overwhelming social opportunities you're telling me about, but I'd sure find a more decent way to work it out than waiting until you drag your sorry self back home, thinking I'll be so happy to see you I'll forget where and who you've been with while I've been here, working every day, coming home to nothing better than a rental movie with my mom and dad and a bag of microwave popcorn." Sarah was a little shocked at herself, and Mrs. Svoboda, who had the misfortune of having her groceries sacked by Hal at that particular moment, looked even more disturbed.

"Sarah, you can't just throw five years away and pretend it never happened, can you?" Hal's face had gone red with anxiety, but despite his sincerity, Sarah couldn't help feeling like a plucked turkey, her feelings and the ugly betrayal she felt splayed naked there on her Hinky Dinky check stand. But she was also afraid that she really didn't care all that much about what Hal had done, but just maybe wished she'd thought of it herself.

"Hal, stop that right now and put the detergent in a separate sack. You want Mrs. Svoboda's milk to taste like Tide?" Sarah said. She'd even managed to make Reverend Bob a little abashed; he said nothing and wouldn't look up as he handed Hal the extra bag for the soap.

Sarah didn't give in, but she did miss their late night truck rides and pit stops, missed the talk about the future—so many things to talk about, and despite how ugly it seemed to her now, she had to admit she didn't know what she'd do without Hal. It's true that when they went out in high school, deciding then and there what their life would be, waiting for Hal saved Sarah from having to deal with a folder full of college applications and cut-out ads for secretarial and travel schools. Then there was her grandmother filling her with frightening ideas of success and choosing careers. Sarah's grandmother had been alone since her grandfather died of an aneurysm at 41. She went back to work as a nurse, raised four kids, Sarah's father included, and never remarried. While she never pushed her into making any decisions, Sarah knew her grandmother hoped that her simple survival would show Sarah the need for independence. When Sarah was seventeen, she wanted to wait for Hal; it was the only thing she could think of.

Now she realizes how little she's done, how much she's opted out of.

She doesn't know how to stop being a supermarket cashier; it seems to get harder, as the days keep passing, to change the course that she's set. It kills her to be away from Hal, but also scares her to think he's the only man she's ever slept with, though the prospect of anyone else is unimaginable. And it scares her that the whole time she yelled at him that last day in the market, all she really wanted to do was cry and punch him in the chest until he wrapped his arms tight enough around her so she'd stop, and he'd say "Sarah, Sarah," and everything would be all right.

Sarah rolls the window up until there's just a little crack for her to push her cigarette butt out. Her ashtray is filled with gum wrappers in case her mother ever rides with her and asks about the acrid smell. She has a terrible fear of pushing a flaming butt out the window, watching it bounce along the side of the car, afraid it will somehow get sucked back in and smolder in the back seat or get tangled in her hair, and her parents will discover she smokes by reading about it in the police blotter of the Cozad Weekly Bee when she's the cause of a horrible accident. Sarah looks in her rearview, hoping to see the glowing butt rolling away on the asphalt but there's nothing. "Shit," she says, "Shit, shit, shit." She rolls the window the rest of the way up, so oxygen can't feed the fire, and sniffs the air for smoke, but she can't tell what's real and what's her imagination, already heightened by the nervous anxiety of a solitary road trip and too many Cokes. Sarah sees the off-ramp for a rest area and flips on her blinker.

Reverend Bob warned Sarah against stopping alone at rest areas, but she's not up to searching for her cigarette on the side of I-80 where the wake of passing semis would shake her car from side to side. She pulls in to park and leans over the back to stick her hands into the seat crevices and feel around on the floor, but she doesn't find anything. She decides to use the bathroom and then check the car again once she's out, convincing herself if it's not a raging fire by then, it never will be.

Having also heard Reverend Bob's horror stories about rest area bathrooms, Sarah cautiously peeks under the stalls when she walks in, but no one is there. She slams the door shut, sliding the lock over and once she sits down, makes a lot of noise pulling off toilet paper just to avoid sitting in silence. She sighs loudly. She doesn't even remember if she had to go anymore, but if she can concentrate, it will keep her from having to stop again soon. Every time she stops she'll have to consider whether or not she wants to keep going or turn around. She knows this rest area is just outside of North Platte. The time zone hasn't even changed yet; she could be home for dinner if she wanted.

Sarah zips up her jeans and comes out of the stall to look at her face, blurry in the warped bathroom mirror. "In case of emergency, break glass," is scrawled in lipstick across her image. Sarah leans closer to the mirror, touching her nose to its slimy surface, wishing desperately for it to come into focus. She is absolutely certain now she is going crazy. She has felt at times she might be going crazy, standing in front of her register, trying to scan a carton of ice cream over and over and over, even though she knows the bar code is smudged, ready to burst into tears but refusing to punch the numbers in until Reverend Bob gently takes it out of her hands and reads them to her. She felt she was going crazy in Joe's every Friday, when one of the meat department guys would casually caress her knee with his big paw, wink at her when she blushed, and pull her up to dance. She even felt she was going crazy in Hal's truck, her head always precariously close to the arm rest and the knob for the window, and she'd peek out at the windshield full of sky, wondering if her grandmother still knew who she was and cared.

Now, leaning into that rest area bathroom mirror, quietly starting to cry, barely two hours from a home she couldn't go back to and any number of hours from any number of places she's not sure she wants to be either, Sarah is sure she's gone crazy. As if, Sarah thinks to herself, as if you'd get one foot into a bar without running. As if you could dance alone without looking at the floor or hiding in the corner behind a crush of people. "As if," Sarah says, lightly banging her head against the mirror, "As if."

With a shock, Sarah remembers her car, and runs out of the bathroom to see if it's in flames, but it's sitting there quietly waiting, not caring which direction she chooses to go, as long as she's moving. No, no, no, Sarah thought, I will not be Elizabeth Taylor. She isn't quite sure how her mind has moved to this, but it seems logical now that she's crazy. She wipes her eyes on the sleeves of her shirt and finds a napkin the glove compartment to blow her nose. "Oh well," she says, "well, shit." She has barely gotten two hours away from home and has already had a nervous breakdown, but somehow everything seems a little better. She gets a Coke from the cooler and leans against the car to take a swing. Despite Reverend Bob's horror stories, this rest area hasn't been too bad, Sarah even feels kind of rested. She looks up at the sky, wondering if her grandmother can see her, wondering if maybe Audrey Hepburn can see her too. She knows she's got to get back into the car, turn the key, and leave. She's got to decide before the next exit, which way to head. She thinks about Cozad and San Francisco, she thinks about Lexington and Lincoln and New York City. She thinks she should just drive her can to the North Platte Greyhound station, call her parents to come pick it up when she's gone, and take a bus so she won't have to think anymore. Finally Sarah thinks of all those highway lines on her map that she didn't highlight, and how she'd just chosen the one that was easiest to spot—it was the widest, safest looking one of all. And she wonders how many of those other lines also lead away, how many of them lead her back to Hal, and how many of them will just stop her dead in her tracks, unfinished roadwork, broken bridges, faulty detours.

Sarah drinks the last of her coke and puts the can on the sidewalk. She puts one foot on the can and stands on it with all her weight, using the other foot to kick the smallest dent in it, bringing her down and smashing the can flat. Then she fishes the other three empties from the car and smashes them all the same way, then picking them up and shooting them one by one into the trash, almost wishing someone had been there to watch. With nothing else to keep her, Sarah opens the door and slides behind the wheel, props the road atlas up in front of the steering wheel, pulls the ashtray out and dumps all her gum wrappers on the floor. She's going to be on the road a long time, any way she figures it, and she doesn't want to pull over like this again.

Size

JONIS AGEE

Shirley Jo Hallum was in love with the midget down the street who had taught her son to ride a bicycle. His was a family of midgets, with one tall brother who dated every tall girl he could find. Shirley Jo at five-four-and-a-half was too in-between to catch his interest. It didn't matter. Martin, the oldest of the midget brothers, was the man she had her eye and heart set on—whether it was the way his sturdy legs pistoned along the ground beside her son teetering on his blue bike down the pavement until it turned into dirt, then on until they were merely a pale dust trail, or the way he nightly stood at the edge of the pavement in the fading light after supper in the summer and in the late afternoon before supper in winter, and tossed the ten-pound shot put from one small hand to the other, absent-mindedly catching it as if it were a tennis ball while he sighted in on the spot he would heave at down the road. He was trying to build upper body strength: bulging arms, bulky shoulders to match the short thick neck, the large head with the kind brown eyes.

How could she thank him for taking on the father to her son and teaching the inept eight-year-old to ride a bike, his one childhood dream after he saw a bike racing movie on cable last winter? She was too busy working at the dry cleaner and the cafe doing their books and payroll and filling in at the counter when it got crazy at the little strip that passed for a mall on the outskirts of Spartus. On her feet, she was as klutzy as her son. She'd proved that the first day of bike riding by collapsing both of them into the ditch. Her son had looked up through his tear-filling eyes with the kind of reproach the dog gives when you kick it.

It was Martin, coming out for his nightly practice in the early summer cool, who dug them out of the deep grassy ditch and set the son right again. Martin who ran alongside, steadying the boy like a monkey perched dangerously on the back of a galloping pony. Or so it seemed to Shirley Jo Hallum who promptly set the compass of her imagination on love. She believed in the circus and Martin's black pony tail jogging in the middle of his back down the road to disappearance in the dust and evening fog rising out of the pastures just beyond the last house, which of course, was the midget family's.

Painted cobalt blue by the previous owners, it was the kind of house you expected things from, and it hardly ever failed the neighborhood. A grazing pet goat was staked in the backyard. A dog the size of a Shetland pony pulled a cart around and around the house on hot days to the whoops of midget brothers who some reported as Siamese twins since they were never seen apart and hadn't started school though everyone believed their ages to be ten or eleven, but no one wanted to swear for sure. They had big huge banging parties for no reason, singing and laughing and spilling out onto the lawn after dark for fireworks three midget boys set off across the empty pastures to the multiple *oohs* and *aahs* of the family, heard all the way up the block, pulling children from their beds to the windows with a mixture of envy and delight at the wet bursts of colored light.

It was hard to say how many children there actually were. Some said seven, others ten, plus the giant, who was only a regular sized twenty-year-old enlarged in the company of midgets. Were they dwarves? guests always asked when the family piled into their bronze van and moved at a stately pace down the street as if they were in a church processional. Dinner discussions in a lull always came back to the midgets. Sightings up town, skewed courtships, sometimes the drunken antics of father or son, too hard to tell apart, the neighbors said.

Shirley Jo didn't have any trouble telling them apart. When a person looked, there was a world of difference. *Really*, she insisted to her friend, who did her hair almost for nothing every Friday at the end of the day so she'd look weekend nice until Tuesday or Wednesday. Wendi with an *i* not a *y* stared at her in the mirror, shrugged, and crisped another curl with the iron, then shrouded them both in a cloud of sticky spray to set the 'do with smoke from the cigarette she kept burning like incense in the ashtray. The beauty parlor in the walk-out basement of her house at the head of their block always had that stale, ladies restroom smell of smoke, toilets, and cosmetics that made Shirley Jo hold her breath. Well, not the whole time, but she tried breathing through her mouth enough that Wendi asked her if she was having allergies.

Those dwarves get sick a lot, asthma, lung weakness, blood clots, phlebitis, that's a real problem, Wendi said as she popped two Buds for them and took a long drag off the cigarette she rarely bothered to smoke. This was the Friday wind-down, and both women propped their feet on the green plastic-seated chairs opposite and wiggled their toes in their tennies as if that were the one thing they hadn't been allowed to do all day, wiggle their toes.

"You ever seen their feet?" Wendi asked, watching the tall brother walking back from town through the abandoned pasture that divided their street from the next. "Club toes, I heard, sometimes they're webbed. That's why they can't walk good. Waddle around. You ever see the mother over there? I can't remember if I ever saw the mother. She must be a midget or whatever, dwarf, I don't know. After my first husband Darwin confessed one time he got drunk and slept with a midget woman, I couldn't never let him touch me again."

She squashed the cigarette on the sole of her shoe, drained her beer, and dropped the butt in the can. "Whew, I'd take that tall one. He looks regular, cute as a pie on a plate. I'd like a slice of that." She pushed back the strands of dried yellow hair she'd kept in a permanent curl so long it looked like it never had any texture or shine at all.

Shirley Jo just listened. She wasn't about to tell Wendi that lately Martin had taken to teaching her son how to play catch and bat a ball and run. And that lately she'd taken to asking him in when it got too dark to play anymore and her son was in the tub soaping off the sweat and dirt, almost a real boy now. Martin didn't drink, but it wasn't something she cared about, so she gave him ice tea with dark green mint so fresh from her backyard it tasted like the sun and dew, in addition to the bite and rub of leafy texture on her lips and tongue she wished was Martin's in her mouth.

Once, the tall brother came to fetch him, and she'd noticed how awkward he'd seemed next to Martin's compactness, as if the tall brother's limbs had hit a bump in the growing road and gone sprawling out of control. They needed pruning when seen in the neat proportions of Martin's body. It made her breath stop, then come feathering out like a slow leak in a tire. She fought to save it, stumbling all over herself in that too big clumsy way that made her understand the sympathy in Martin's eyes as he left.

Right at the end of summer when the county fairgrounds opened their gates for a week, Martin asked Shirley Jo if she'd like to go out sometime. This was after she'd had him to an official Sunday dinner in the after church time, though she didn't go to church anymore since the minister started calling the house to yell at her for running her husband off before he'd had a chance to marry her. That'd been so long ago she hadn't actually missed going to church until the Sunday she invited Martin because it seemed weird to have a big roast chicken dinner at one when you hadn't done anything official all morning except read the funnies and mow your lawn. The whole thing was off-kilter, she knew, but like she told the minister that last time, she just had a white trash soul when it came to love, and she couldn't bring herself to marry a man she didn't love or trust to put gas in her car, and she couldn't bring herself to go to a church that wouldn't understand a thing like that. That had pretty much put love and god on hold. Neither one had inquired after her health for so long she figured she'd gotten over religion and romance in one fell swoop, until she saw Martin trotting beside her son on his bike.

The 4-H kids sprawled tiredly on the bales of hay and straw banking the pens of sheep and cows and pigs weren't much bigger, some of them, than Martin, but they still recognized his difference and sniggered when Shirley Jo and the midget strolled past. Martin's face got blank as paper and Shirley

Jo's got red. She tried to think of something to say or do, but Martin's fingers tightened on hers and pulled her past the moment. Out on the midway, she knew people were staring, maybe thinking he was one of the carnival men, not the man down the block who was bringing her son into boyhood at last, the man who showed her how to use the weed wacker without cutting her ankles to shreds, the man who just tonight had leaned over in the car she'd given him the keys to drive, with the seat pulled all the way up so he could toe the pedals, and kissed her mouth with his soft full lips minty from toothpaste and mouthwash, the exact same kind she used, she wanted to say and did as soon as his hand left the back of her head, where it had held her safely, firmly in place for as long as it lasted. The mouth wash was just her nervousness. What she really wanted to say was, *here, take my heart and drive it to the Half Moon Motel.*

They were at the Ferris Wheel, not the towering double they had at the state fair, just the regular size that still stepped you up notch by notch as each chair filled, until you stood at the top of the world, gazing down at the tops of people's heads and the tents and buildings and farther away the tops of trees squat as bushes and houses whose roofs could be peeled back with a fingernail. All that magic in store for them, the ticket man, a tattooed old carny, tilted his head and in a hoarse whisper from his ruined throat, said, "You mean one child, one adult, don't ya?"

"Let's go," Shirley Jo said.

"No — give me the tickets —" Martin's jaw was set in cement she could scratch her initials on.

"No, I don't want to ride anymore—" She panicked at the idea of their being trapped in that little bucket hoisted up inch by inch so everyone could see them.

"Come on. I've got the tickets, come on —" He dragged on her hand but she twisted loose. Martin turned away as if he'd been shot in the face and disappeared into the crowd that had been growing with the evening. It was impossible to see where he went among the press of larger bodies that urged her the opposite direction toward the freak tents and snake exhibits.

"Martin, Martin," she called, shouldering her way against the other bodies wanting in, not out of the midway.

She waited for two hours by the car until the drunken men began to stagger in her direction with offers for any number of services except the one Martin could provide. Finally, she climbed in, pushed the seat back, and drove out of the parking lot, down the dark road toward home. By the side of the road gold and green eyes stared out from the underbrush at her. Figures appeared she was sure were Martin, only to dissolve into shadows as she drove by them.

Parking in her driveway instead of putting the car in the detached garage because she was too tired, too discouraged to lift an arm toward her future at that moment, she stopped and stared at the cobalt blue house down the block lit up and pulsing with color and music as if the entire fair had followed the midget family home. She took a step toward the house, then a step back. What if he didn't want her, what if it had all been a mistake on her part, this business she'd started with him? Maybe she shouldn't have changed her hair, taken the spray out so it hung freely and now limply on her shoulders. Maybe in the morning she should just make Wendi give her a perm so it sprang in harsh tight brown waves from her head. Forget the new silky feel it had. It was too thin, too useless for anything like tonight.

She heard herself talking and it wasn't necessarily her voice. It sounded like the minister from the church without love, it sounded like Wendi up the street wanting to make sure she knew about midget feet. Well she was wrong. Shirley Jo knew for a fact that Martin's toes were five single beautiful digits, as pale and individual as uncooked links of sausage, so pure and sweet she panicked that she'd never get to taste them, never feel his strong body holding her beneath his, making her get grace again, the way she had that one light moment in the car when she could trust his hands and arms to make them both perfect and regular for love. Inside the house a boy slept, waiting for her to find a father and friend for him. Down the block the house clanged and charged the night with joy, waiting for just about anyone who dared to join in. "Well, I've come this far," she whispered as she turned toward the street.

Contributors' Notes

Lucy Adkins (100, 181, 305) attended the University of Nebraska-Lincoln and received her BS at Auburn University in Alabama. She has taught high school English and experienced many other kinds of jobs. Her poetry has been published in the *Nebraska Poets' Calendar*, the *Owen Wister Review, Nebraska Territory, Woven on the Wind*, among others. Adkins is a songwriter, collaborating with her husband, Tom. She is currently working on a novel.

Jonis Agee (343) is the author of nine books, including four novels: *Sweet Eyes, Strange Angels, South of Resurrection*, and *The Weight of Dreams*. She is Professor of English and Creative Writing at The University of Nebraska-Lincoln. Among her awards are an NEA grant in fiction and a Loft-McKnight Award of Distinction. Three of her books were named Notable Books of the Year by The New York Times. Her newest books are a collection of short stories, *Taking the Wall* (Coffeehouse), and the novel *The Weight of Dreams*, which won the Nebraska Book Award for 2000.

Liz Ahl (49, 53, 54, 281) was educated at Emerson College, the University of Pittsburgh, and the University of Nebraska-Lincoln, where she received the Academy of American Poets prize. Her poems have appeared in *Sundog, Southern Poetry Review, the American Voice, Crab Orchard Review*, and others. A member of NGWG, she teaches creative writing and literature at Plymouth State College in New Hampshire.

Mary Andersen (65) was a Kinkaid Homestead child, living in a sod house, traveling in a covered wagon, and growing up in the sandhills of Nebraska. She has taught in rural schools, small towns, and at University of Nebraska — Lincoln. Her BA and MA are from University of Nebraska — Lincoln, with additional graduate work at Columbia. Her poetry is published in *A Flowering: A Festival, Celebrate, Lifelines*, and *NCB Quarterly*, among others.

Kaye Bache-Snyder (63, 91) is a former correspondent for the Denver Post. Her PhD is from the University of Wisconsin. She has published prize-winning poems, short stories, and essays, and recently completed a novel. Bache-Snyder lives in Longmont, CO, and leads workshops at the Arvada Center for the Arts and Humanities.

Jamie Bacon (125) is the pen name of a writer/physician who lived in Nebraska for 12 years. Bacon has presented seminars on poetry in medicine. She has published essays, poems and book reviews in *The Pharos, Nebraska Psychiatrist* and *Psychiatric Times*, and before medical school, she worked as a correspondent for the *New Haven Register* in Connecticut.

Denise Banker (45, 46) earned her bachelors degree from the University of Nebraska-Lincoln and her masters from Concordia University in Seward. Her work has been published by the National Council of Teachers of English. She has been a teacher and a florist, and is currently teaching at Concordia University and working on a PhD in Creative Writing at the University of Nebraska — Lincoln.

Ann Bardens (80) received the PhD in English at the University of Nebraska — Lincoln. Her book of poetry and art is *Stone and Water* (Canoe Press, 1992). She teaches at Central Michigan University, freelances, and has published in journals and anthologies.

Jeanette Barnes (272) took her B.A. in English from the University of West Florida and her Master's in Library Information Studies from the University of Alabama. Winner of the 1975 Bridges Prize in Verse, the Nebraska Award in Poetry for 2000, finalist for the Nimrod/Hardman Prize, and recipient of a Pushcart Prize in 2002, she has published in *Shenandoah, Nimrod International, Kalliope, Wind, Greensboro Review, Nebraska Review, Potomac Review, Cumberland Poetry Review* and many others.

Monica Barron (144) has published in *Indiana Review, Telescope, Ploughshares, Cincinnati Poetry Review, Chariton Review*, and *Women's Review of Books*, among others. Her creative non-fiction has appeared in the anthology Exposures. She is a member of the editorial collective of Feminist Teacher magazine and an associate professor of English at Truman State University.

Grace Bauer's (23, 24, 50) poetry collections include: *Field Guide to the Ineffable: Poems on Marcel DuChamp* (Snail's Pace Press), *The Women at the Well* (Portals Press), *Where You'll See Her* (Pennywhistle Press) and *The House Where I've Never Lived* (Anabiosis Press). She teaches at the University of Nebraska — Lincoln where she is coordinator of Creative Writing.

Melissa F. Beery (70, 288) is attending the University of Nebraska — Kearney as an undergraduate with a double major in English (writing emphasis) and Biology (environmental health emphasis). She plans to do graduate work in creative writing. Beery received the Award for Best Work by an undergraduate from *Plains Song Review* in 2002.

Miriam Ben-Yaacov (61, 148), a native of South Africa, is a graduate of University of Nebraska at Omaha Writers' Workshop. During her late teens and early twenties she lived in Israel. She and her husband have lived in Omaha for the last twenty years. Ben-Yaacov has published both fiction and poetry, and works with the Iowa and Nebraska Arts Councils as an Artist in the Schools.

Artis Bernard (152) grew up in Hot Springs, SD, and graduated from MacMurray College in Illinois. After a year on a Fulbright Scholarship at the University of Munich, she worked in New York City, and now lives in Houston, TX. She is a graduate of the University of Houston Creative Program. Her poetry will appear in *Paris Review*.

Diane-Marie Blinn (203), originally of New York City, has lived in Norfolk, Nebraska, since the 1980's. She received her PhD from the University of Chicago and has been an educator as well as a Rubenfeld Synergy intern. She has studied with Julie Cameron, Natalie Goldberg, and Barbara Schmitz, and has published poetry in *Nebraska Life*.

Imogene Bolls (172) grew up in Kansas, the source of many poems in her three books and more than 600 poems in national journals and anthologies. She was a professor and poet-in-residence at Wittenberg University, Springfield, OH, and currently lives in Taos, NM.

Denise Brady (150) hand-produces literary first editions of poetry from her Omaha-based press. Authors published by Bradypress include Jonis Agee, Marilyn Hacker, Hayden Carruth, Michael Skau, Nancy McCleery, and Greg Kosmicki. Brady is an MFA student in the art department at University of Nebraska — Lincoln and active with the Nebraska Book Arts Center which she helped found at University of Nebraska at Omaha. Her freelance work includes the design of *The Nebraska Review* as well as *Curious Rooms*, edited by Christine Japely in Norwalk, Connecticut.

Judith Brodnicki (36, 37) is a graphic artist, musician, and writer whose poetry has appeared in *The Cape Rock, The Nebraska Review*, and others. She holds bachelor's degrees in writing and in music history. She lives in Omaha and is active in Delta Theta Chi, a sorority that promotes literacy and life-long education.

Constance Brown (195) has been an editor and writer for most of her life, publishing in National Geographic books, as well as magazines such as *Smithsonian, National Wildlife* and *Travel & Leisure*. She holds an MA in English and taught writing at the University of Colorado before moving to a ranch along the Hat Creek Breaks in Wyoming.

Deborah Byrne (278) has received many awards, including the Grolier Poetry Prize and the Edgar Allen Poe award. Her poems have been published in numerous journals, including *Calyx, Wisconsin Review*, and *Many Mountains Moving*. Many of her poems have appeared in anthologies. She presently lives in Columbus, Ohio.

Kathleen Cain (183) is the author of *Luna: Myth and Mystery* (Johnson Books, 1991), a nonfiction work about the folklore and mythology of the moon. She is a contributing editor for *The Bloomsbury Review*. Her creative nonfiction was included in *In Brief: Short Takes on the Personal* (Norton, 1999). A graduate of the University of Nebraska — Lincoln, she lives in Colorado.

Elizabeth Callaway (101, 246) retired in 1987, after working 25 years as Tech Illustrator for the U.S. Navy in California's Mojave Desert. She received a BFA from University of Nebraska — Lincoln in 1940, and an MA in creative writing there in 1994, also minoring in photography. She spent the first half of her life in a farming community on the Kansas-Nebraska line.

Lu Carter (243) is a registered nurse whose poems have been published by the *National League for Nurses, the Western Journal of Medicine, the Vermillion Literary Project, Nebraska Life*, and Papier Mache Press. She is a northeast Nebraska native living on a half-section of farmland in Wayne County.

Pamela Carter Joern (1, 214) grew up in the panhandle of Nebraska and now lives in Minneapolis. She has written five plays produced in the Twin Cities area. Co-editor of *Re-membering and Re-Imagining* (Pilgrim Press), she has published in *Water-Stone, Minnesota Monthly*, and *Feminist Studies*. Her current work is a collection of short stories. A graduate of the MFA program at Hamline University, she teaches classes at the Loft Literary Center in Minneapolis.

Ardiss Cederholm (177) was born in northwestern Iowa and lives in Lincoln, Nebraska. She is a retired teacher and member of Chaparral Poets. Her book of poetry is *Seasons of the Heartland*. Cederholm's work has been published in *Midwest Poetry Review, Poetalk, Plain Songs Review, Celebrations iv*, and *Nebraska Life*.

Nicole Church (133) won the Vreeland Award for Creative Writing at the University of Nebraska-Lincoln in 1996 and the Wilbur Gaffney Award for Expository Writing in 1997. Her work has appeared in *Laurus, the Lincoln Journal-Star*, and *Fine Lines*. She is working on a collection of essays about living in North Africa as a child.

Elizabeth Clark (85, 261) grew up in Imperial, Nebraska. She is a senior at Sarah Lawrence College in Bronxville, NY. Her work has appeared in the *Nebraska English Journal* and *Fine Lines*, and has received recognition in national student contests such as The Scholastic Art & Writing Awards, River of Words sponsored by the Library of Congress, and Emerson College's student writing competition.

Shelly Clark (69, 161, 273) taught English for fifteen years at Chase County High School in western Nebraska and journalism for two years at Midland Lutheran College in Fremont. Her poems have appeared in *Plains Song Review, Nebraska English Journal, Nebraska Territory,* and *The Caravan.* She is currently co-editing a book of interviews with Nebraska writers.

Chauna Craig's (314) fiction has appeared in a dozen journals including *Prairie Schooner, South Dakota Review, Quarterly West* and *Ascent.* Born and raised in Great Falls, Montana, she earned her PhD at the University of Nebraska and currently teaches creative writing at Indiana University of Pennsylvania.

Tricia (Patricia) Currans-Sheehan (114) holds a BA from Briar Cliff College and both MA and PhD from the University of South Dakota. She teaches at Briar Cliff, where she founded *The Briar Cliff Review.* She won first and third prize in the 1997 Iowa Literary Contest, was a finalist in the Marguerite De Angeli Contest, the New Millennium's fiction contest and *Potpourri's* fiction contest. Twice nominated for a Pushcart Prize, she has published in *Connecticut Review, Calyx, Virgina Quarterly Review, Puerto del Sol, Wisconsin Review, South Dakota Review, Kalliope,* and others. Her collection of short stories, *The Egg Lady and Other Neighbors,* won the 2000 Heartland Literary Competition.

Amber Dahlin (78, 182) is a freelance writer living in Idaho Springs, Colorado. She received a PhD in Composition and Literature from the University of New Hampshire and has published a memoir, *Blowin' Smoke,* as well as many poems, articles, and a screenplay. Currently she teaches memoir writing, hosts writing retreats, makes handmade books, and specializes in writing family histories for clients.

Kathleen Davis (59) graduated in piano performance from Oberlin Conservatory in Ohio and recently retired from a thirty-five year career in piano teaching and performance in Colorado. Davis's poetry and prose has been published in *Buffalo Bones* and in two anthologies of Evergreen Poets and Writers.

Marilyn Dorf (107, 184) grew up on a farm near Albion, Nebraska. Her work has appeared in *Nebraska Life, Grassroots Nebraska, Whole Notes, Kansas Quarterly, Northeast, Plainsongs,* and other journals. Her chapbooks are *Windmills Walk the Night* and *Of Hoopoes and Hummingbirds.* Her third chapbook is from Juniper Press (2002), *This Red Hill.*

Eileen Durgin-Clinchard (173) earned her PhD from the University of Nebraska-Lincoln. She is an activist, celebrating her ACLU membership. She participated in the Ft. Kearney Summer Workshop and has studied with William Kloefkorn at the Nebraska Wesleyan University. Her poetry has appeared in *Flintlock.*

Martha Elizabeth (66, 274) is a writer and artist, earning a B.A. in drama at the University of Virginia, an MA in interdisciplinary studies at University of North Texas, and an MFA in creative writing at the University of Montana. She has won a Dobie-Paisano Fellowship for poetry. Her poetry collections are *The Return of Pleasure* (Confluence Press, 1996), which won the Montana Arts Council First Book Award, and *Considering Manon* (Pudding House Publications, 2000).

A.B. Emrys (10) has been an editor for *Black Maria*, and *Sun Dog*, and guest editor for Platte Valley Review's issue on pop culture. She teaches writing and general studies at the University of Nebraska-Kearney. A poet, journalist, and scholar, she has published in *The Journal of Popular Culture* and *Popular Culture Review*, as well as in the anthology *Sacred Ground: Writing About Home* (Milkweed Editions, 1997), the editors nominating her for a Pushcart. She is the 1997 winner of the Mary Roberts Rinehart Award and co-director of the Fort Kearney Summer Writers' Conference.

TigerLily Ernst (154) is a native of western Illinois and a current resident of Vermont. She has studied creative writing at the University of Nebraska and will complete her degree in Iowa. Her work has appeared in *Plains Song Review, Poetry Motel*, and *Wavelength*.

Sarah Fairchild (97) has published in *Plainsongs, Whole Notes, Dragonfly, St. Judith's Light, The Lyric*, and other publications. She is the editor of Black Star Press which publishes books of poetry and the Nebraska Poets Calendar. She has taught writing and literature courses at Southeast Community College in Lincoln. Her awards include a $2500 second prize in a national bicentennial competition.

Karen Fields (170) died in 2000. She was a reviewer of music, particularly jazz, and an oncology nurse, as well as a student at the University of Nebraska at Omaha.

Kate Flaherty (336) is a Contributing Editor at Prairie Schooner and editor, with Hilda Raz, of *Best of Prairie Schooner: Personal Essays*, published by the University of Nebraska Press. Her essays and stories have appeared in *Rosebud, Connecticut Review, Pennsylvania English, Fourth Genre, Short Story*, and others.

Gaynell Gavin's (130) essay, "Fall," is from her work-in-progress, *What I Did Not Say*, a memoir of her years practicing law. Her work has appeared in such journals as *The Comstock Review, Kansas Quarterly, Natural Bridge*, and *Tulane Review*. She is an editorial assistant at *Prairie Schooner*.

Jamey Genna (223) has published short stories in *Hard Roe to How* and in *Ignatian Literary Magazine*. She is a high school English teacher in the Bay Area, receiving a Master's in Writing from the University of San Francisco.

Susanne George-Bloomfield (200) is a professor of English at the University of Nebraska at Kearney, specializing in literature of the American West. Her work includes *The Adventures of The Woman Homesteader: The Life and Letters of Elinore Pruitt Stewart* and *Kate M. Cleary: A Literary Biography with Selected Works*, both from University of Nebraska Press. Most recent is *An Uncommon Woman: Elia Peattie, Frontier Journalist*. She edits the *Platte Valley Review* and writes literary criticism as well as book reviews, essays, poetry, and short stories. She has served as the national President of the Western Literature Association.

Karen Gettert Shoemaker (8, 166) received her PhD in Creative Writing from the University of Nebraska — Lincoln in 1997, where she also taught literature and writing classes for several years. Her first collection of fiction, *Night Sounds and Other Stories*, is published by Dufour Editions (2002).

Irene Rose Gray (103, 270) was educated at Wayne State College, Denver University, and University of Nebraska — Lincoln, teaching Latin and Greek in the Classics Department at the latter until her retirement in 1970. Her poetry is published in *Season Sampler, Nebraska Chaparral Poets, The Blessing of the Animals* (with Marilyn Dorf, 1996), and *Nebraska Poets Calendar*. "Blue Hill Blues" is her musical composition.

Anne Haehl (252, 286) earned an MA in English and a doctorate in Speech Communication at the University of Kansas. Her work has been published in *Chiron Review, Studio, Potpourri, Coal City Review, Midday Moon, Christian Poet, Sensitive Poet* (on-line), and the poetry anthology, *Prisms of the Soul*, among others.

Mareen Halligan Tobin (93, 167, 302) opened a bookcafe in Kimballton, Iowa, in 1998. She teaches GED and adult basic literacy classes part-time and is bi-residential, living half the year in Manhattan, half in Iowa. Her poems and stories have appeared in *Poems Niederngasse, Eclectica, Mefisto, American Tanka*, and *Snow Monkey*.

Twyla Hansen (25, 89, 176, 185) received her BS from the University of Nebraska and was employed as a horticulturist for twenty-five years. Her poems have been published in many periodicals including *Crab Orchard Review* and *Prairie Schooner*, and in several anthologies, including *Woven on the Wind* and *Leaning into the Wind* (Houghton Mifflin). Her books of poetry are *How To Live in the Heartland* and *In Our Very Bones*, with her latest, *Sanctuary Near Salt Creek*, from Lone Willow Press (2001).

Pat Hemphill Emile (67, 236, 268) graduated from the University of Nebraska — Lincoln, spent several years in western Nebraska, and returned to Lincoln, where she managed the Lincoln Symphony Orchestra for nine years. In 2000, she received the PhD in English from University of Nebraska — Lincoln and is currently a lecturer in that department. Her poems have appeared in *Hedge Apple*.

Pam Herbert Barger (28, 309, 310) teaches Suzuki piano, develops land, and sings and plays keyboard with the FabTones, a dance band. She received her Bachelor of Music degree with high distinction from the University of Nebraska — Lincoln, and has published in *West Branch, Sistersong, Weber Studies, Platte Valley Review, Nebraska Territory, the Nebraska Poets Calendar*, and the *American Suzuki Journal*.

Joan Hoffman (52) lives on the Lazy Horseshoe Ranch west of Clearwater, Nebraska. She has lived in Nebraska most of her 78 years and loves it. Her work can be found in anthologies such as *Leaning into the Wind* and in her chapbook, *Call Me By My Real Name*.

Diane Hueter (241, 271) lives in Lubbock, Texas. A chapbook of her poems, *Kansas: Just Before Sleep*, was published by Cottonwood Review Press in 1978. Recently, her work has appeared in *Clackamas Literary Review, Borderlands: Texas Poetry Review*, and *The Texas Review*. She has read her work in Washington state, Kansas, New Mexico, and Texas.

Mary Jackson Krauter (56, 253) is a Social Worker employed in Scottsbluff, Nebraska, where she works with people who have chronic and persistent mental illness. Her work has been published by Papier-Mache Press, the eleventh muse, *Pudding House Magazine*, International Writing Program at the University of Iowa, and in *Emerging Voices* and *California State Poetry Quarterly*.

Josephine Jones (94, 95, 175) was recently awarded a Literary Fellowship by the Idaho Commission on the Arts. A nationally published writer of articles, reviews, and poetry, Jones conducts creative writing workshops with children and adults and lectures in western women's history. She performs her work solo, with the multimedia Tungsten Trio's projections and live music, and in the poetry duet Couplet.

Mary-Lane Kamberg (248) has a bachelor's degree in journalism from the University of Kansas. In 1999, her poetry won honorable mention in the Council on National Literatures and the Potpourri national poetry competitions. Her poems have appeared in *A Celebration of Women, Cicada, Kansas City Parent, Late Knocking, The Mid-America Poetry Review, The Mythic Circle, 100 Words, Potpourri*, and *Sunflower Petals* among others, as well as in three anthologies from Whispering Prairie Press. She is co-leader of the Kansas City Writers Group.

Monica Kershner (109, 111), a Nebraska native, recently moved to Denver, Colorado. She received both her Bachelor's and Master's degrees from the University of Nebraska at Omaha. Founder of the Omaha Poetry Slam, Ms. Kershner reads in public as often as possible and has had her poems published in several small press magazines and in chapbooks by Morpo Press.

Peggy Kirwan Dinkel (40) was educated in Denver, and also attended the University of Beirut in Lebanon. Before retirement she worked in politics, the construction industry, and banking. Her work has been published in several small presses, and she is an active member of Voices of Women, a women's writers group.

Amy Knox Brown (325) holds a J.D. from Nebraska's College of Law and a PhD in English/Creative Writing from University of Nebraska — Lincoln, where she received the Vreelands Award and the Mari Sandoz/Prairie Schooner Prize for fiction. Her fiction has appeared in *Missouri Review, Witness, Shenandoah*, and other literary magazines. She is currently working on a novel called *Terms*, which is set in Lincoln in 1983 during the filming of *Terms of Endearment*.

Mel Krutz (108) writes children's literature, as well as writing of cognition and literary development, reading, learning and teaching styles, and censorship issues. Her work has been published in *Plainsongs, Fine Lines, The English Counselor, Plain Song Review, Rural Voices*, and other Nebraska, Ohio, Illinois, New Jersey, and Montana publications. She received her PhD from University of Nebraska — Lincoln and is the author of *Our Common Space: Preface and Poetry*.

Marilyn Krysl (186) has published seven books of poetry and two of fiction, including *How to Accommodate Men* (Coffee House Press). Her poems and stories have appeared in the Pushcart Prize Anthology and O. Henry Prize Stories. She won the 1994 Negative Capability award for fiction, the 1995 Spoon River Poetry Review award, the 1996 Cleveland State Poetry Center Prize, and is the recipient of two NEA grants, a residency at Yaddo, and grants from the Colorado Council on the Arts and Earthwatch. She is director of the Creative Writing Program at the University of Colorado at Boulder and contributing editor of Many Mountains Moving.

Kyle Laws (39, 145) was nominated for a Pushcart Prize in 1999 and has been a featured reader at poetry festivals in Kansas and Florida. Her work has appeared regularly in little magazines. Laws' first collection of poems, *Apricot Wounds Straddling the Sky*, was published by Poetry Motel's Suburban Wilderness Press. In 1997, Kings Estate Press published a collection of her work, *Tango*.

Samantha Lines (81) currently resides in Kearney, Nebraska. She holds an MFA from Bowling Green State University in Ohio and has published poetry in such magazines as *Beacon Street Review, Midwest Poetry Review, Cold Mountain Review, The Brownstone Review* and *Whole Notes*.

Karen List Wingett (74) has taught English and Creative Writing at Norfolk High School, Norfolk, NE, for twenty-four years. Her poems have appeared in *Poetry Motel, the Mid-American Poetry Review, Nebraska Life*, and in the anthology *Mothers' Words*. She holds a Bachelor's degree in English from Yankton College and a Master's in English from the University of South Dakota.

Roseann Lloyd (282, 284) is a translator, editor, and poet. Her book, *War Baby Express* (Holy Cow! Press, 1996), received the Minnesota Book Award. The anthology she and Deborah Keenan edited, *Looking for Home: Women Writing about Exile*, received the American Book Award. Her new book is *Because of the Light* (Holy Cow! Press, 2002). Lloyd is a recipient of a Bush Foundation Fellowship and a community activist, one of the founding members of the Silent Witness Exhibit, a traveling memorial to women murdered by their partners.

Denise Low (208) teaches at Haskell Indian Nations University. Her books include *New and Selected Poems: 1970-1999* (Penthe 2000); *Kansas Poems of William Stafford*, ed. (Woodley 1990); *Touching the Sky: Essays* (Penthe 1995); and others. She has recent essays and poems in *North American Review, Arts & Letters, Connecticut Review, Chariton Review*, and *Potpourri*.

Carol MacDaniels (1949-2001) (165) graduated from North Bend (Nebraska) High School before moving to New York where she received her BA from Dowling College. She returned to Nebraska sixteen years later to become a teacher of middle school and to teach composition at Peru State College. A mainstay in the Nebraska Writing Project and the School at the Center, she co-authored *Guide To Nebraska Authors* (1998), and *All Roads Lead Home* (2001).

Kelly Madigan Erlandson (75, 178) received the John M. Reikes Creative Writing Scholarship at the University of Nebraska. Her work has appeared in *Iowa Woman, Caney River Reader,* and *Plains Song Review*. Her essay "This Covers Him, This Crosses Him" was a finalist in the *Missouri Review* essay contest for 2000.

Stephanie Marcellus (249) teaches Writing at Colorado State University as she works towards her MFA degree. Her first book, *All That I Thought Was Light*, was published in 1998 by Black Star Press. Her work has appeared in *The Logan House Anthology of 21st Century American Poetry, Platte Valley Review, Nebraska Territory, The Reynolds's Review*, and elsewhere. She is working on a collection of poetry entitled *We Did Not Stop To Know*.

Joanne McCarthy (140) grew up in eastern Montana. Her father's family had homesteaded in South Dakota. McCarthy's poems have been published in *Calyx, Green Fuse, Kalliope*, and other literary magazines, as well as in anthologies such as *At Our Core: Women Writing About Power* (Papier Mache Press, 1996).

Nancy McCleery (290, 291, 292, 293) has lived and taught in Nebraska, Florida, New Jersey, New York, Alaska, and Missouri. She holds an MA in Creative Writing from the University of Nebraska. McCleery has four collaborative works and five poetry collections including *Staying the Winter*, Cummington Press, 1987; *Blown Roses*, bradypress, 2001; and *Girl Talk*, forthcoming from The Backwaters Press, 2002.

Jazmyn McDonald (77) lives in Lander, Wyoming. Her work has been published in the *Owen Wister Review*, and several WyoPoets chapbooks.

Deborah McGinn (79) is a teacher of creative writing at Lincoln High School in Lincoln, Nebraska. She earned a Bachelor's Degree and a Master's in English with a creative thesis at University of Nebraska — Lincoln. Her work has been published in *Plains Song Review, Fine Lines, Free Focus, Whole Notes*, and *Poetic Voices*.

Katherine McKeown Roush (1946-1999) (42, 43) was a poet and conservationist who served on the original board of the Montana Nature Conservancy. She studied French at Stanford University and creative writing at the University of Montana. Her ranch in Florence, Montana, was a sanctuary for wildlife.

Heather McShane (277) spent her formative years in Omaha, Nebraska. She holds a Bachelor's degree in German and English from Doane College in Crete, Nebraska, and has had poetry and artwork published in *Xanadu*, Doane's literary magazine. She currently resides in Chicago.

Jean Miller (35) is a woman of the plains, drawn to the land, moving from a life in Omaha to an old farmstead in rural Blair, Nebraska.

Judith Minty (31, 32, 33, 34) is the author of eight books of poetry, most recently *Walking With The Bear: Selected And New Poems*. Her first book received the United States Award of the International Poetry Forum. Minty is a teacher of writing and a long-time student of the migration patterns of birds. She presently lives in Michigan.

Annette L. Murrell (306, 307, 308), a professional singer for twenty years, performs jazz, blues, and gospel in nightclubs, churches, and schools throughout the country. She has recorded an album called "My Shining Hour." She received her PhD in English and Creative Writing at the University of Nebraska — Lincoln and is presently an assistant professor of English at Nebraska Wesleyan University. A recent essay is forthcoming in the journal *a/b: Auto/Biography Studies*.

Charlene Neely (146) has lived in Lincoln, Nebraska, and several small towns in Nebraska and Iowa. Her poetry has been published in *Plains Song Review, Songs For The Granddaughters, Dreams For Our Daughters*, and other magazines and anthologies. A favorite project is creating poetry with the grade schools in Utica, NE.

Sheryl L. Nelms (38, 84) has taught writing and poetry workshops in Arizona, Oklahoma, South Dakota, and Texas. She has edited Oakwood, and served as contributing editor to Byline and Streets. She is currently the essay editor of *The Pen Woman Magazine*. Many of her poems, articles, and short stories have been published in magazines and anthologies. Nelms has seven collections of poetry.

Biljana D. Obradovic (88, 156, 279), originally from Yugoslavia, has a BA from Belgrade University, an MFA in Creative Writing, Poetry from Virginia Commonwealth University, and a PhD in English from the University of Nebraska, Lincoln. Her first collection, *Frozen Embraces*, a bilingual edition, won the Rastko Petrovic Award. Her work has appeared in *Poetry East, Bloomsbury Review, Prairie Schooner* and others. She received the Masaryk Academy of Arts Medal for Artistic Achievements and is a member of the Association of Writers of Serbia and Assistant Professor of English at Xavier University of Louisiana.

Ginny Odenbach (254) is the author of five chapbooks of poetry, *Before Turtle Island, The Wildflower Farm, Pleasures, The Footprints of Shadows*, and *Equinox*. With a coauthor she has written three books for young readers, *Sunblade, Feather*, and *Badger*. Odenbach lives in McCook, Nebraska.

Lynn Overholt Wake (280) graduated from the University of Nebraska — Lincoln, earned an MLS from Simmons College in Boston, and is currently writing about children's literature and ecocriticism, working toward a PhD in English at University of Nebraska — Lincoln. *Flight and Resurrection* is her self-published chapbook of poems. An essay is forthcoming in *Wild Things*.

Stephanie Painter (157) lives in Casper, Wyoming. Her Bachelor's and Master's in visual art are from the University of Wyoming, and her MFA in Creative Writing/Poetry from Vermont College. As a member of WordBand, a trio performing choral poetry of the spoken word, she participates in grant-funded projects throughout Wyoming. Her poetry has appeared in *Woven in the Wind* and other anthologies, as well as *Rhino, Worcester Review*, and *Contemporary Review*.

Pat Pike (48), a University of Nebraska — Lincoln journalism graduate, served as an editor for 30 years, including rural editor of the *LincolnLand Sun*, and editor of *Norden News*. Her chapbooks are *Prairie Almanac* and *Small Packages*. She has recently published a children's book, *When Chloe Comes to Tea*. Her poems have been published in *Plain Songs Review, Celebrate, Humor in Poetry*, and *Prairie Voices*. She is a member of the Lincoln Chaparral Poets.

Mary Pipher (122) is a clinical psychologist and author of *Reviving Ophelia* (Putnam), *The Shelter of Each Other, Another Country*, and, most recently, *The Middle Of Everywhere: The World's Refugees Move to Our Town* (Harcourt).

Amy Plettner-Lind (311) received a BS in Human Development from the University of Nebraska — Lincoln. Her first real publication appears in this book. She lives near Garland, Nebraska.

Hilda Raz (163, 235, 264, 265) is a poet, critic and Professor of English at the University of Nebraska — Lincoln, where she is also Editor-in-Chief of the literary quarterly *Prairie Schooner*. Her books of poetry are *The Bone Dish* (State Street Press, 1989), *What Is Good* (Thorntree Press, 1988), *Divine Honors* (Wesleyan University Press, 1997), and *Trans* (Wesleyan University Press, 2001).

Susan Richardson (113) earned a BA from Colorado State University and attended graduate school at University of Montana. She has published over 100 poems, stories and essays in various magazines and anthologies. She grew up in Denver and has lived in Kansas and Wyoming, recently moving to Idaho.

CarolAnn Russell (86, 158, 239, 240) is a poet and professor of Creative Writing in the English Department at Bemidji State University. Her books include *The Red Envelope* (University of Florida Press), *Feast* (Loonfeather Press), and *Silver Dollar* (West End Press), as well as two chapbooks *The Tao Of Woman* and *Without Reservation*. Her work has won awards from the Academy of American Poets and the Poetry Society of America.

Marjorie Saiser's (160, 276) books are *Bones Of A Very Fine Hand*, which won the Nebraska Book Award, and *Lost In Seward County*, both from The Backwaters Press. She received the Nebraska Literary Heritage Award and a fellowship from the Nebraska Arts Council. Her poems have been published in *Prairie Schooner, Georgia Review*, and other journals. A book of poems is forthcoming from Lone Willow Press.

Barbara Sanders (83, 141) has worked as an executive in advertising and public relations and as a hospice caregiver. She was recently poet-in-residence at a hospice in North Carolina and currently lives in Madison, Wisconsin. Her poetry has appeared in *Calyx, Crazyhorse, Lullwater Review, Mudfish, The MacGuffin,* and is upcoming in The *South Carolina Review*.

Terry Schifferns (143) lives in a cabin on the Platte River and teaches writing at Central Community College. She has published in *Many Mountains Moving, Black Bear Review, Poets On, Poetry Motel, Kinesis,* and others. Her writing has appeared in *Leaning into the Wind: Women Write from the Heart of the West* and *Jane's Stories: An Anthology by Midwestern Women.*

Barbara Schmitz (159, 255) holds degrees from Wayne State and University of Nebraska at Omaha and was Allen Ginsberg's apprentice at Naropa Institute. She taught writing and literature in Norfolk, Nebraska, for thirty years and ran the Visiting Writers Series there. Her books of poetry are *How to Get Out of the Body* (Sandhills Press) and chapbooks from Suburban Wilderness Press and Sandhills Press. Her poems are published in *Chiron Review, Kalliope, Kansas Quarterly, Midwest Quarterly, The Prairie Schooner, River Styx, Wind,* and in anthologies including *All My Grandmothers Could Sing, The Plain Sense of Things,* and *The Logan House Anthology of 21st Century American Poetry.*

Rita Shelley (245, 301) writes poetry and non-fiction in Omaha. She has been published in *GreenPrints: The Weeder's Digest* and has worked as a news reporter for the *Topeka Capital-Journal* and also as a corporate writer for an insurance company. She holds degrees in journalism and mass communication from Kansas State University.

Hazel Smith Hutchinson (298, 300) grew up in Maine, but has lived for more than twenty years in Kansas. A member of Prairie Poets & Writers, she has been published in *Mid-America Poetry Review, Snark, The Aurorean, Prairie Poetry, The Penwood Review*, and *The Flint Hills Review.*

Judith Sornberger (105, 164, 250) holds the PhD from the University of Nebraska. She edited an anthology called *All My Grandmothers Could Sing* (Free Rein Press, 1984). Her poetry collections are *Open Heart* (Calyx Books), *Judith Beheading Holofernes*, winner of the Talent House Press chapbook prize 1993, and *Bifocals Barbie: A Midlife Pantheon* (Talent House Press). A new chapbook will be published by Parallel Press in 2003. Her poems and essays have appeared in *Prairie Schooner, Calyx, West Branch, Puerto del Sol*, and *The Jabberwock Review* and in anthologies such as *Claiming the Spirit Within* and *An Intricate Weave: Women Write on Girls and Girlhood*. Sornberger teaches at Mansfield University of Pennsylvania.

Laurel Speer (27) has been publishing poetry since 1963. She is a contributing editor for *Small Press Review*. Her work has appeared in *Indiana Review, Prairie Schooner, Owen Wister Review, Denver Quarterly, West Branch*, and other publications. She currently lives in Tucson, Arizona.

Jane St. Clair (227) grew up in Chicago but went home to Nebraska most summers. She graduated from Northwestern University, became a social worker and later worked on the television show, "Sesame Street." She lives in Arizona.

Mary K. Stillwell (57, 90, 180), a native of Nebraska, has studied writing in both New York and on the plains. She has published in a variety of journals, including *The Paris Review, Prairie Schooner, The Massachusetts Review, Confrontation, The Little Magazine*, and others. Her book of poems, *Moving to Malibu*, was published by Sandhills Press.

Linda Stringham (112) is a Norfolk, Nebraska, native, Hastings College (Nebraska) graduate, former Seward (Nebraska) High teacher and current Lincoln (Nebraska) Chaparral poet. She has been published in *Plainsong*.

Amy Stuber (327) received her PhD from the University of Kansas and has taught creative writing and literature at Haskell Indian Nations University in Lawrence, Kansas, and at Roger Williams University in Bristol, Rhode Island. Her short fiction has been published in a variety of journals, including *The Antioch Review, The Santa Monica Review*, and *CutBank.*

Gail Sudman (174) grew up in a family of three girls on a Western South Dakota ranch during the Dirty Thirties. After earning a degree in a field that no longer exists, she became a wife, a homemaker/volunteer and a mother and grandmother. Her publication credits include the *USD Long Neck, Rapid City Journal* and *Reflections: Poems, Essays and Stories*, published in collaboration with two friends.

Gladys Swan (14) has published five collections of short fiction and two novels, *Carnival of the Gods* (Vintage Contemporary Series, 1986) and *Ghost Dance: A Play of Voices* (nominated for the 1993 Pen/Faulkner Award by LSU Press). Her most recent book, a novella and stories under the title *News from the Volcano* was nominated for the 2001 PEN/Faulkner Award, the National Book Critics Circle Award and the American Book Award. She was writer-in-residence on a Fulbright Fellowship in Yugoslavia and held a fellowship from the Lilly Endowment. She has been awarded residencies at Yaddo, the Fundacion Valparaiso in Spain and the Chateau de Lavigny in Switzerland. In 1997, she received a fellowship in painting at the Vermont Studio Center. She teaches workshops exploring the creative process through writing and drawing.

Kim Tedrow (312, 313) is originally from southern Minnesota, and after nine years on the East Coast, returned to the Midwest to live in Lincoln, Nebraska. Her work has appeared in *Cyphers* (Dublin), in numerous online literary venues, and is forthcoming in *Prairie Schooner*.

Maureen Tolman Flannery (29, 71) lives in Chicago, works for a surgeon, and teaches English as a Foreign Language. She received AB and MA degrees in English Literature from Creighton University. Her poems have appeared in over a hundred anthologies and publications, including *Atlanta Review, Blue Mesa Review*, and *Mid-America Poetry Review*. She is the author of *Remembered into Life* and *Secret of the Rising Up: Poems of Mexico*. She recently edited *Knowing Stones: Poems of Exotic Places*.

Beth Torgerson (266) is a native of Montana. She recently graduated from the University of Nebraska-Lincoln with her PhD in English. She has published in *The New Review, The Texas Review*, and *Disability Studies Quarterly*.

Wyatt Townley's (104) latest book of poems is *The Breathing Field* (Little, Brown & Company, 2002). Her first book, *Perfectly Normal* (The Smith), was a finalist for the Yale Series of Younger Poets. Poems and essays have appeared in magazines ranging from *The Paris Review* to *Newsweek*, and she recently won a Hackney National Literary Award and the Kansas Voices Prize in Poetry.

Tammy Trucks (102, 142, 237) received a BS and MA from Central Michigan University and is currently in the University of Nebraska PhD program. She is a mixed-blood American Indian and much of her writing focuses in that particular area. Her writing has appeared in The South Dakota Review, The Haight Asbury Literary Journal, The Rockford Review, The Midwest Poetry Review, Manna, and The Shattered Wig Review. She is a winner of the Academy of American Poets Award and the Vreeland Award.

Sondra Upham (87, 162, 296, 297) graduated from the University of Nebraska and received her Master of Arts from the University of Massachusetts, Boston, where she won the Academy of American Poets competition in 1992. In 2000, her chapbook *Freight* won the Slapering Hol Press Chapbook Contest. Her poems have appeared in *Field, Prairie Schooner*, and others. She has been a high school English teacher and is currently a poet-in-the-schools.

Sarah Voss (72) is a Unitarian Universalist minister, author, and lecturer. Among her published works are *What Number Is God?; Voice to Voice, Heart to Heart; Zero: Reflections about Nothing*; as well as many poems and articles in various journals. Some of her poems are drawn from her work as an Omaha police chaplain.

Gail Waldstein (294) is a physician, having practiced Pediatric Pathology for almost thirty years in Denver. She has been nominated for a Pushcart Prize and has won various awards for her fiction, essays, and poems, publishing in *New Letters, High Plains Literary Review, Negative Capability*, and several anthologies.

Drucilla Wall's (92, 259, 275) poetry appears in *Kalliope, Pearl, Plainsong, Indefinite Space*, and Missing Spoke Press. She has won an Academy of American Poets award, Kansas Flint Hills Poetry Society award, and Mari Sandoz Prairie Schooner Short Story Award. Selected short fiction and essays appear in *Eighteenth Century Life* and are anthologized in *American Jones Building & Maintenance* and *True West: Authenticity in the American West*. Sometimes her work explores her Muscogee (Creek) American Indian heritage.

Deb Walz (82) attended University of Nebraska — Lincoln and has written poetry since her teens. Her work has been published in *The Plain Song Review*.

Connie Wasem (106) teaches at Spokane Falls Community College. Her poems have appeared most recently in *Sycamore Review, 5 AM., Slipstream, The Oval*, and the anthology *Essential Love: Poems about Mothers and Fathers, Daughters and Sons*.

Rebecca West (303) attended Grinnell College, graduating with a B.A. in American Studies and Education, and doing post-graduate work in curriculum development and literature. She is a winner of the Minnesota AAUW poetry contest, working now on a screenplay and a collection of essays.

Anne Whitney (64) has continued teaching writing and literature at the University of Nebraska-Lincoln since receiving her PhD there in 1994. A native of Aurora, Nebraska, who spent 15 years outside the Plains, Anne returned in 1984 to Nebraska where her family has resided continuously since the mid-19th century. Her poems and essays have appeared in regional and NCTE publications.

Terry Wiechman (238) was born and raised on a farm in north central Kansas. She graduated from Kansas State University with a degree in Elementary Education. Her poem "Hailstorm" was published in Washburn University's 2000 edition of *Inscape*. Wiechman lives in the Flint Hills outside Topeka, Kansas.

S.L. Wisenberg (191) spent her first eighteen years in Houston, and the last twenty-seven in the Chicago area, with the exception of sojourns in Paris, Iowa City, Miami and Provincetown. She is the author of a fiction collection, *The Sweetheart Is In* (TriQuarterly Books/Northwestern University Press), and an essay collection, *Holocaust Girls* (University of Nebraska Press, 2002).

Mary Yadon (26, 41) was born in New York City and has lived in Lawrence, Kansas, since 1994. She received a B.A. Ed. in Spanish and MA in English/Creative Writing from Wichita State University. She has taught English and reading at the secondary level for twenty years.

Dianne Yeahquo-Reyner (219) was born in Lawton, Oklahoma. She received a Bachelor of Arts in American Indian Studies from Haskell Indian Nations University in Lawrence, Kansas. Currently she is working on the Master's degree in Indigenous Nations Studies at the University of Kansas. She is writing a play titled *Weaving the Rain*.

Rosemary Zumpfe (98) is a poet and artist in Lincoln, NE. She has worked as an illustrator and graphic designer, a college instructor, and writer. She has an MA in drawing/printmaking from the University of Missouri and has done post graduate work in print-making at the University of Illinois. She is presently in the graduate English program of the University of Nebraska.

Publication Acknowledgements

The Editors would like to thank the following presses, magazines, and anthologies for allowing these pieces to be reprinted here.

Lucy Adkins: "Grandma Ellen Tells it Like it Was" *Plainsongs*, Fall 2001

Jonis Agee: "Size" from her short story collection *A .38 Special and a Broken Heart*, Coffee House Press, 1995.

Kaye Bache-Snyder: "Gathering Morning Fire" *I Am Becoming The Woman I Wanted*, Papier Mache Press, 1994, "Driving my Glass House" *Slant*, Summer 2002, and Pudding House Anthology, *Fresh Water: Poems of the Rivers, Lakes, and Streams*.

Grace Bauer: "Geography Lessons" *Nebraska Life*, Spring 1997, "Latter Day Saints" *Doubletake*, summer 1998, number 13.

Melissa F. Beery: "Mattress" *Plains Song Review* Vol. iii, 2001

Miriam Ben-Yaacov: "Laying the Snakes to Rest" *Rock Falls Review* Vol. 6, #3 Fall 1995, and "Yom Kippur 5750" *Many Voices, One Song*

Imogene Bolls: "The Black Velvet Horse" Mississippi Valley Review, Vol. XX, #2, 1991

Kathleen Cain: "What This Means, Being Cottonwood" *City Kite on a Wire/38 Denver Poets*, 1986

Chauna Craig: "Big Sky Blue" *Phoebe*

Kathleen Davis: "Arthur County Sunday" *Buffalo Bones*, 1997

Marilyn Dorf: "Owl Sound" from her book, *Of Hoopoes and Hummingbirds*, Cricket-Ink Press, 1998

Martha Elizabeth: "Sunday Lunch in Ponder, Texas" *Midwest Quarterly*, 1999

TigerLily Ernst: "Buffalo Dreams" *Plains Song Review*, Vol. ii

Sarah Fairchild: "Her Old Songs" *Whole Notes*, Vol. vii, Spring 1991

Kate Flaherty: "Leaving" *Briar Cliff Review*

Karen Fields: "Tulips for Michael" Permission granted by her family

Karen Gettert Shoemaker: "Charley and Evelyn's Party" in *Foliage*, 2000, and also in her book, *Night Sounds and Other Stories*, Dufour Editions, 2002

Irene Rose Gray: "Drillbits" *Nebraska Poets' Calendar*, Black Star Press

Anne Haehl: "Changing" in Chiron Review and "Traveling Directions" in *Coal City Review* and *Studio*

Twyla Hansen: "Spring: the Second Night" from her book *How To Live in the Heartland*, Flatwater Editions, 1992, "Sumac Scattering like Bones" in *Any Key Review* and again in her book *Sanctuary Near Salt Creek*, Lone Willow Press, 2001, "Monday, Snow" *Sanctuary Near Salt Creek*, Lone Willow Press, 2001

Mary Jackson Krauter: "Camp Clarke Days Celebration" from her book *Clippings*, Pudding House Publications, 1995

Josephine Jones: "Two Small Sundaes" in *Cabin*, 1996, "Tradition" in *The Idaho Statesman*, 1996, and also in *Cold-Drill*, 1994

Monica Kershner: "Man at the DMV" *The Rockford Review*, Autumn 2001

Amy Knox Brown: "Sex" *Witness*, Vol. X, no. 1, 1996

Mel Krutz: "And So — October 2000 — Breast Cancer Month in America", *A Journey Not Chosen: Stories of Breast Cancer Survivors*, Bryan/Lincoln General Medical Center, October 2001

Marilyn Krysl: "Dirt" *High Plains Literary Review*

Sam Lines: "Craft" *Cold Mountain Review*

Karen List Wingett: "Children in the Earth" *Nebraska Poets' Calendar 2001*, Black Star Press

Roseann Lloyd, "Too Much Give", and "County Mental Health, 1976" from her book, *War Baby Express*, Holy Cow! Press, 1996

Kelly Madigan Erlandson: "How We Met" in *Iowa Woman*, Vol. 14, 1994

Carol MacDaniels: "For My Daughter" *Nebraska English Journal*

Nancy McCleery: "My Daughter Brings Me Garbage Flowers" in *Blown Roses*, bradypress, 2001, "Sunday Afternoon My Son Bakes Bread," "Girl Talk (coffee/china)," and "Girl Talk (high/bird) in *Girl Talk*, The Backwaters Press, 2002

Jazmyn McDonald: "Fists of Honey" in *The Owen Wister Review*

Judith Minty: "Snowgeese Over Lincoln, Nebraska" in *Bloomsbury Review* as well as in *Walking With The Bear: Selected and New*, Michigan State University Press,

2000. "Hawk," Recognizing," and "Deer at the Door" in *Walking With The Bear: Selected and New*.

Sheryl L. Nelms: "City Life" *Capper's, Wherever Home Begins, The Aurorean, Iowa Woman, The Beebe News, Horizon, A Galaxy Of Verse, Strings Anthology, "Depression" The Oval, Expressive Spirals, Literally Horses, The Pittsburgh Quarterly, The Unforgettable Fire, The Plastic Tower, Rock Falls Review, Anything That Moves,* and *Heeltap*

Biljana D. Obradovic: "Advice," "Awaiting the Bombing of Serb Forces in Bosnia and Herzegovina," and "Yin-Yang" from her book, *Frozen Embraces*, Belgrade, Center for Emigrants from Serbia, 1997, and *Cross-Cultural Communications*, Merrick, NY, 2000

Ginny Odenbach: "Belonging" *Wyoming's Prairies, Peaks, And Skies*

Hilda Raz: "September, Getting Married Again" and "My Dream, Your Dream" from her book *The Bone Dish*, State Street Press, 1989; "Sarah's Response" from her book *Divine Honors*, Wesleyan University Press, 1997; "Said To Sarah, Ten" from her book *Trans*, Wesleyan University Press, 2001.

Susan Richardson: "A Pantheist Comes Upon A Church Five Miles From Manhattan, Kansas" *Hodge Podge*

CarolAnn Russel: "Heirloom" and "Her Story" from her book, *Feast*, Loonfeather Press, 1993, "Abandoned Farm" and "Photo of Women Plowing" from her book, *The Red Envelope*, University of Florida Press, 1985

Marjorie Saiser: "Keeping My Mother Warm" and "Pulling Up Beside My Husband at the Stoplight" from her book, *Bones Of A Very Fine Hand*, The Backwaters Press, 1999

Barbara Sanders: "Strong Onion Lullabye" and "Watering Tank" *Crazyhorse*

Barbara Schmitz: "My Mother Never Knew" from her book *How To Get Out Of The Body*, Sandhills Press, 1999

Hazel Smith Hutchinson: "When the Four O'Clock Whistle Blows" *PlainSpoken: Chosen Lives, Chosen Words*, Weary Woman Press, 2000

Laurel Speer: "Buffalo Stones" from her book, *The Book That Couldn't Be Saved*, 1995, also in *The Scandal of Her Bath*, and *Sweet Jesus in the Afternoon*

Mary K. Stillwell: "After Zeit und Sein: Marilyn Monroe in Omaha" Vol 3, Number 2, Fall 2000, http://www.janushead.org/3-2/stillwell.cfm

Amy Stuber: "Stop, Then Go" *Primavera*

Gladys Swan: "News from the Volcano" reprinted from her book *News from the Volcano* by permission of the University of Missouri Press. Copyright © 2000 by the Curators of the University of Missouri

Maureen Tolman Flannery: "Litany for a Rancher" *Chachalaca Poetry Review*, Vol iii, Number 1, 2000

Beth Torgerson: "The Garden" *The Texas Review*, Spring/Summer 2002

Sondra Upham: "Mother Believes" *Skylark*, "The Sixties" from her book *Freight*, Slapering Hol Press, 2000

Gail Waldstein: "ER Euphemism" *Explorations '99*

Dru Wall: "Closet Cleaning" *Plainsong*, May 1977

Connie Wasem: "The Whiskers On His Face" *5 A.M.* Number 12, 2000

Terry Wiechman: "Hailstorm" *Inscape*, Vol. 25, 199-2000, Washburn University

S.L. Wisenberg: "Plain Scared, or: There is No Such Thing as Negative Space, The Art Teacher Said" Crab Orchard Review, reprinted by permission from *Holocaust Girls:History, Memory, and Other Obsessions*, Copyright, © 2002 The University of Nebraska Press

Every reasonable effort was made to gather previous publication credits. The editors apologize to any press which was inadvertently omitted.